Mozart's piano sonatas form a richly diverse and significant part of his instrumental output, and span much of his mature composing career, thereby representing a microcosm of the composer's changing style. Part I examines the contexts in which the sonatas were composed and in which they were performed, and reviews likely sources of influence. Part II concentrates on the genesis of the sonatas and the surviving autographs, which reveal important information about Mozart's compositional process. In part III the music is studied from the standpoint of rhetoric – a discipline featured in numerous contemporary aesthetic and theoretical textbooks on music – and proceeds through an investigation of the nature of the musical ideas (the *inventio*), followed by a discussion of formal design (the *dispositio*) and finally a consideration of the *elocutio* (style, or expression), which attempts a detailed rhetorical analysis of several extracts – ranging from the construction of themes to whole movements. The resulting picture affords a cross-section of Mozart's compositional strategies.

MOZART'S PIANO SONATAS

MOZART'S PIANO SONATAS

CONTEXTS, SOURCES, STYLE

JOHN IRVING

LECTURER IN MUSIC,

UNIVERSITY OF BRISTOL

CAMBRIDGE
UNIVERSITY PRESS

Published by the Press Syndicate of the University of Cambridge
The Pitt Building, Trumpington Street, Cambridge CB2 1RP
40 West 20th Street, New York, NY 10011-4211, USA
10 Stamford Road, Oakleigh, Melbourne 3166, Australia

© Cambridge University Press 1997

First published 1997

Printed in Great Britain at the University Press, Cambridge

A catalogue record for this book is available from the British Library

Library of Congress cataloguing in publication data

Irving, John.
    Mozart's piano sonatas: contexts, sources, style / John Irving.
        p.   cm.
    Includes bibliographical references and index.
    ISBN 0 521 49631 4 (hardback)
        1. Mozart, Wolfgang Amadeus, 1756–1791.   Sonatas, piano.
    2. Sonatas (Piano) – History and criticism.   I. Title.
    ML410.M9174   1997
    786.2′183′092 – dc20   97-14259
                                                                        CIP
                                                                        MN

ISBN 0 521 49631 4 hardback

Contents

To my parents

Preface

Mozart's sonatas have won a place in the affections of generations of musicians and music-lovers: indeed, one of Mozart's most famous pieces, the Rondo 'Alla Turca', is a movement of a sonata (K.331 in A major). Ever since the early nineteenth century, these sonatas have been a staple of the pianist's repertoire. Their accessibility, combining agile passagework with a charming melodic gift, has made them favourites with players and listeners alike. They are still regularly performed, broadcast and recorded, on 'period' instruments now, as well as modern replacements. The 'home pianist', the examination candidate, the competition hopeful: all share a familiarity with this body of works. To the less experienced player they offer scope not only for practice in the shaping of a melodic phrase, but in the proper control of an accompaniment, and in acquiring the mental and physical stamina required to sustain, in performance, a musical argument over several pages. The sonatas are not 'easy' works, however. To the knowing professional, indeed, they pose difficulties of interpretation that few would claim to have solved to their complete satisfaction. To the listener, however, they seem, in a good performance, to possess an elegant simplicity of utterance, perfectly poised and yet possessing a certain detachment, a coolness of expression that sets them somewhat apart from the turbulent emotional upheavals of Beethoven's more famous thirty-two sonatas.

Mozart's sonatas are without doubt less challenging technically than those of Beethoven. Pedagogically, they often serve, either in whole or in part, as a kind of 'preparation' for those more 'advanced' icons of emerging romanticism. In the evolution of the piano literature Mozart's sonatas have been regarded more than once as works which lay the foundations for Beethoven – a historical concept which assigns Mozart's pieces little or no independent value. 'Laying the foundations for Beethoven' is a historical nonsense that, happily, is scarcely prevalent nowadays. Mozart's sonatas were not written expressly for Beethoven's benefit any more than were those of Haydn, Mysliveček, Kozeluch, Clementi and a host of other late eighteenth-century composers whose work has been marginalised for want of a more enlightened cultural critique.

Mozart's sonatas, while arguably less innovatory than his concertos, quartets and quintets, nonetheless comprise a significant quantity of his instrumental output and are deserving of an in-depth study. Together, they form a coherent body of eighteen pieces, written between late-1774 and mid-1790 in a variety of situations and for a variety of reasons. Some were composed for teaching purposes. Others served Mozart himself as vehicles for the demonstration of his peculiar piano virtuosity. He evidently intended some as 'dedication' pieces, in the hope of short-term financial reward; others he prepared for publication (half of his solo sonatas are known to have been published during his lifetime). It is unlikely that he made much money from such ventures, though. The D major Sonata, K.284, written for Baron Thaddeus von Dürnitz in Munich in early 1775, was raised in correspondence by Mozart's father, who urgently enquired if Dürnitz had paid Mozart for it (so far as is known, he did not). While Mozart may have profited from the publication (by Artaria) of the C minor Fantasia and Sonata, K.475 and 457, in 1785, the earlier set of three sonatas, K.309–11, presents a less happy story. The first two (K.309 and K.311) were composed in Augsburg and Mannheim in November–December 1777, while the third (K.310) was written in Paris during the summer of 1778, perhaps expressly in order to make up a set of three sonatas for publication in the French capital. At any rate, Mozart evidently left the sonatas with the Parisian publisher, Heina, on his departure for Salzburg in September of that year, though they were not actually printed by that firm until about 1782, and then in an abysmal engraving riddled with errors and inconsistencies.

Despite their continuing popularity, there is currently no English-language study of the Mozart piano sonatas. Obviously, there are references to the sonatas in the course of more general Mozartean studies, principally *The Mozart Companion*[1] and *The Mozart Compendium*[2] and in studies of the piano literature.[3] In a different context, necessarily brief accounts of the sonatas appear in the introductory matter to editions such as the *Neue Mozart-Ausgabe* (by Wolfgang Plath and Wolfgang Rehm) and the Associated Board edition of the sonatas (by Stanley Sadie and Denis Matthews). As may be seen from the bibliography to the present volume, there are specialised treatments of issues such as instruments, autograph manuscripts, editions, style and analysis and performance practice which are either devoted to or impinge on Mozart's piano sonatas. Many of these studies are in German, and occur in specialist periodicals such as the *Mozart-Jahrbuch* that are primarily the territory of the professional musicologist. There is a need for an up-to-date study of Mozart's sonatas that attempts broad coverage of the repertoire including issues such as aesthetic contexts, stylistic influences, source-materials and compositional process, as well as an extended consideration of musical style. Such is the aim of the present study.

I have deliberately avoided the issue of performance practice in the following pages. This seems to me to be an area so fluid at present (involving principles as diverse as instrumentation, ornamentation, fingering, pedalling, articulation and

[1] Donald Mitchell and H. C. Robbins Landon (eds.), *The Mozart Companion* (London, 1956).

[2] H. C. Robbins Landon (ed.), *The Mozart Compendium* (London, 1990).

[3] For instance, the chapter 'Haydn, Mozart and their contemporaries' by Eva Badura-Skoda in Denis Matthews (ed.), *Keyboard Music* (Harmondsworth, 1972); especially pp. 143–65.

many more) as to be more appropriate to detailed discussion in relevant journals than in a monograph on the sonatas.[4] Full consideration of this vast and important topic would have extended the present study well beyond its intended scope.[5] In an attempt to compensate for its side-stepping I include brief mention of some relevant performance issues here.

Clearly, a fortepiano commensurate with those known to, or owned by, Mozart will be the most appropriate choice for the faithful realisation of his own expectations. Some of these instruments survive and good quality modern copies are available. In addition, a reasonable amount of documentary evidence survives in the family correspondence and in the reports and reviews of other musicians who heard Mozart playing upon which an informed decision might be made.[6] A modern concert grand piano falsifies Mozart's sound-world to a considerable extent. Its heavy action, combined with a percussive attack to each note, and a shrill resonance enhanced by its metallic frame, enable such an instrument to attain a degree of volume sufficient to counterbalance a symphony orchestra, and while it is capable of a range of colour that far outstrips that of any fortepiano by Stein or Walther (the makers that Mozart preferred) it is incapable of capturing the *cantabile* tone that Mozart had in mind when he wrote. 'More' is not necessarily 'better', as anyone who has tried to play the opening solo entry in the slow movement of Mozart's A major Concerto, K.414, knows only too well. The left-hand octaves here have to be thinned out to the remotest degree in order that they do not overbalance the right-hand theme above. This problem of balance between the hands is a persistent one in Mozart's piano sonatas, too, and one to which he was acutely sensitive himself. In his autograph manuscripts he frequently appended dynamic markings separately to a theme and its accompaniment, for instance at the beginning of K.311's Andante con espressione, alternating *piano*, *forte* and *piano*. But he did not have to distinguish between *piano* in the right hand and an 'editorial' *pianissimo* (or less) in the left, in order to achieve a satisfactory balance: the construction of the fortepiano, its action, attack and resonance provided this anyway. Sometimes the overpowering resonance of the modern instrument clouds Mozart's textures. Bars 30–2 of the slow movement of K.309 (a movement which, according to one of Mozart's letters, must be played with the utmost sensitivity to the notated dynamics) are near-impossible to balance satisfactorily on a modern pianoforte: on a

---

[4] A number of significant articles of this kind are included in the bibliography.

[5] Fortunately, there is already an excellent study of piano performance practice: Eva and Paul Badura-Skoda, *Interpreting Mozart on the Piano* (London, 1962); originally published as *Mozart-Interpretation* (Vienna, 1957). Among other, more recent, studies, see Malcolm Bilson, 'Interpreting Mozart', *Early Music*, 12 (1984), 519–22; Bilson, 'Execution and expression in the Sonata in E flat, K.282', *Early Music*, 20 (1992), 237–43; Robert D. Levin, 'Improvised embellishments in Mozart's piano music', *Early Music*, 20 (1992), 221–33.

[6] Among recent published studies, see David Rowland, *A History of Pianoforte Pedalling* (Oxford, 1993), especially pp. 82–94; Katalin Komlós, *Fortepianos and their Music: Germany, Austria and England, 1760–1800* (Oxford, 1995), and the review of this book by Dorothy DeVal in *Music and Letters*, 77 (1996), 122–4; Richard Maunder and David Rowland, 'Mozart's Pedal Piano', *Early Music*, 23 (1995), 287–96. Some discussion of appropriate choices of instrument for specific pieces occurs in chapter 1.

fortepiano such as Mozart would have played, the thinner tone allows all of this passage to be heard in clear focus, highlighting an element (the correct contrapuntal resolution of the chord-tones over the pedal F) that is obscure on the pianoforte.[7] On a modern pianoforte, the sensitive player has to intervene as 'silent editor' in bar after bar, adapting Mozart's notated instructions to the capabilities of that instrument. In a sense, the pianoforte is insufficient to the task of playing Mozart. That is not to deny that beautiful interpretations of Mozart's sonatas can be obtained on a modern instrument, of course. In the hands of someone who has carefully thought through the implications of Mozart's texts, and interprets these with a combination of musical intelligence and technical aplomb, anything is possible. But it needs to be remembered that, in adapting the fortepiano, successive generations of piano manufacturers were striving towards a sound quality far removed from the late eighteenth century. Expansions of the range and power of the piano clearly held many advantages for later ninteenth- and twentieth-century composers, but these factors detract from, rather than enhance, the clarity of Mozart's lines and textures. In the end it is, perhaps, a matter of personal preference. Mozart is still Mozart, whether played on a Steinway or a Stein.

Some performance issues involve the interpretation of the text. Mozart's published sonata texts frequently differ from the autographs in their range of dynamic markings, ornamentation and marks of articulation, as in variation 11 of the finale of the D major Sonata, K.284. Sometimes, the printed versions contain much more elaborate melodic lines than the original manuscript, as in the slow movement of the F major Sonata, K.332, in which the reprise of the opening theme is substantially embellished, compared to the autograph text. In each case, it seems that Mozart made revisions expressly for publication. His textual amendments can give us valuable insights into his own playing habits. In the case of K.284, the print appeared nearly a decade after the composition of the work itself, and the additional dynamics and articulations might have been added in recognition of the increasing availability of the touch-sensitive fortepiano in the intervening years.[8] Other evidence is of a 'negative' kind. Dynamics and tempo indications are frequently lacking in the sonatas, and are presumably to be inferred from the changing character of the material, as in the first movement of K.330.[9] Mozart appended no tempo markings in the autograph of K.333, though some were added to his manuscript by a second scribe, and were taken over in the published edition. In some cases (the first movement of K.333, the slow movement of K.533 and the finale of K.545, for example) the early manuscript or printed sources have no dynamic indications at all. The slurring of important motives in the first movement of K.570 and in the finale of K.576

---

[7] Two other 'muddy' passages clarified by performance on the fortepiano occur at bars 124–8 and 245–52 in the finale of K.309; in this case, the lack of focus in the low register is compounded by a plethora of percussive semiquaver 'attacks'.   [8] This issue is addressed in chapter 3.

[9] There is no dynamic mark at the opening (it is probably *forte*); neither is there any dynamic at the beginning of the recapitulation (bar 88), though a *forte* is marked two bars later (but there is no separate dynamic marking in the analogous bar of the exposition).

is inconsistent in early prints. Whether this is Mozart's fault or the engraver's is impossible to tell, since in K.570 only a fragment of the autograph survives (and provides no help at all in resolving this particular issue), while in K.576 the autograph is altogether lost. In neither case will a 'definitive' reading ever emerge. Issues such as these require intelligent and tasteful input by the player. Those arising from textual problems may only be satisfactorily attempted with a full range of source material to hand.[10] Assuming a text can be agreed upon, the player must then decide what the symbols are intended to convey. The interpretation of Mozart's staccato dots or wedges is a case in point, and one that is by no means specific to the sonatas. It occurs in other instrumental contexts, particularly string-writing, some of which evidence should probably be applied also at the piano. Mozart's intended meaning in this respect is often unclear, since he was inconsistent in the use of each symbol. The choice of staccato dot or wedge in a particular passage seems to indicate a distinction of some sort in the length of the notes,[11] though it might also have some implications for the precise quality of attack.[12] Some fascinating problems of interpretation occur in the performance of his chamber music for piano and strings and in the piano concertos, in which the dialogue between the 'soloist' and the 'ensemble' necessarily involves consideration of the possible ways of realising a staccato dot or wedge consistently with the finger and with the bow. Probably there is much for the fortepianist to learn from string players in this respect.

Manuscript studies have, in recent times, become an important facet of Mozart scholarship. Where autographs of the sonatas survive, they reveal information on Mozart's working methods in relation to a specific compositional situation. Fortunately the autographs of some of the sonatas have become more easily accessible of late, allowing new judgements to be made on their significance. The six early sonatas, K.279–84, considered lost at the end of the Second World War,[13] were in fact secretly transferred, along with many other treasures of the former Prussian State Library in Berlin, to the Bibliotheka Jagiellonska in Kraków, Poland, where they may now be inspected at first hand. Mozart's autographs of two other sonatas, K.311 and 330, are also in the Jagiellonian collection. Without doubt the most sensational 'find' in recent Mozart scholarship, though, has been the rediscovery of

---

[10] In this respect, at least, the publication of the *Kritische Berichte* to the *Neue Mozart-Ausgabe* (*NMA*) of the sonatas is an urgent priority!

[11] See, for instance, Frederick Neumann, 'Dots and Strokes in Mozart', *Early Music*, 21 (1993), 429–35; Clive Brown, 'Dots and Strokes in late 18th- and 19th-century Music', *Early Music*, 21 (1993), 593–609.

[12] For example, in the Andante of the G major Sonata, K.283, the opening bar has a staccato wedge on its fourth-beat crotchet F in the right hand. This occurs in the context of a cantabile theme whose periodicity is clearly in balanced successions of two- and four-bar groups, the integrity of which would be seriously compromised by a jerky staccato on the crotchet F. Perhaps in this context the wedge indicates some kind of (light?) accent, reinforced by the change of chord position beneath. The same wedge symbol occurs over a quaver value but in a different context of phrase interruption at bars 19 and 27, this time coinciding with a prominent change of harmony. Clearly Mozart's intention is different; precisely how these quavers are to be articulated, though, remains in question.

[13] And so recorded in the sixth edition of *Köchel*.

the autograph of the Fantasia and Sonata in C minor, K.475 and 457, in an American Baptist College in 1990. This manuscript, unheard of for many years, is now in the collection of the Internationale Stiftung Mozarteum, Salzburg.[14] It is examined in chapter 6.

Among the most significant developments in Mozart studies over the last two decades has been the exhaustive and penetrating palaeographical work of Alan Tyson, whose encyclopaedic knowledge of Mozart's paper has led to major reevaluations of the genesis and chronology of a wide range of Mozart's music, including the sonatas. Fortunately, Tyson's watermark catalogue is at last available, allowing the interested scholar to reconstruct the interrelationships between different works that has been its author's painstaking task over many years; a collection of his writings on the autographs is also available.[15] So far as the sonatas are concerned, some radical redating has been necessitated by Tyson's paper-studies. The B flat Sonata, K.333, long thought to have been composed in Paris in 1778,[16] has been conclusively assigned instead to November 1783.[17] The three sonatas in C (K.330), A (K.331) and F (K.332), formerly presumed also to date from 1778, were almost certainly written at about the same time as K.333. Such an exodus of pieces from one decade to the next undoubtedly has implications for our evaluation of Mozart's sonata style.

EDITIONS

Comparatively little is known about the dissemination of Mozart's sonatas during his lifetime and in the years immediately following his death. He performed the early set of six sonatas, K.279–84, quite frequently on tour during the late 1770s (see chapter 3) but they were never published as a set in his lifetime (K.284 was published – with K.333 and the Violin Sonata, K.454 – in 1784). Publication (or else circulation in authorised manuscript copies) was the most usual aspiration of a composer intent on establishing a reputation in the late eighteenth century. Mozart was relatively successful in this respect.[18] So far as his solo sonatas are concerned

---

[14] A superb colour facsimile edition of the autograph has now been published: *Wolfgang Amadeus Mozart: Fantasie und Sonate c-Moll für Klavier, KV 475 + 457. Faksimile nach dem Autograph in der Bibliotheca Mozartiana Salzburg*, with an introduction by Wolfgang Plath and Wolfgang Rehm (Internationale Stiftung Mozarteum Salzburg, 1991).

[15] Alan Tyson (ed.), *Dokumentation der Autographen Überlieferung: Wasserzeichen-Katalog*, 2 vols. (Kassel, Basel, Tours, London, 1992); Tyson, *Mozart: Studies of the Autograph Scores* (Harvard and London, 1987).   [16] And so recorded in the sixth edition of *Köchel*.

[17] Tyson, *Mozart: Studies of the Autograph Scores*, especially chapter 6, 'The date of Mozart's piano sonata in B flat K.333/315c: the "Linz" Sonata?'; the latter was originally published in M. Bente (ed.), *Musik – Edition – Interpretation: Gedenkschrift Günther Henle* (Munich, 1980), pp. 447–54.

[18] A useful review of the dissemination of printed copies of Mozart's music is Cliff Eisen, 'Sources for Mozart's Life and Works' in *The Mozart Compendium*, ed. H. C. Robbins Landon (London, 1990; reprinted 1991), pp. 160–204, especially pp. 185–6. A general pattern seems to be that publishers issued the orchestral, piano and chamber music before venturing into the realm of opera. This is not to say that the operas were necessarily slow to gain acceptance: *Die Entführung*, for instance, was not printed (in a vocal score) until 1785, though it had been performed frequently prior to this (Eisen,

K.309–11 were published in Paris around 1781–2; K.330–2, 333, 457, 533 and 494
in Vienna between 1784 and 1788; and K.545, 570 and 576 were published posthumously, again in Vienna, between 1796 and 1805. Their texts are not unprob-
lematic. Those of K.309–11 are especially poor, for instance, and in several cases
there are discrepancies in detail between the autographs and the first editions, some
of which may be explicable by Mozart's own revisions for publication. This much
is hypothetical, however. While the varied reprise of the main theme in the slow
movement of the F major Sonata, K.332, in Artaria's edition of 1784 arguably represents Mozart's own practice in performing such a movement, it might just as easily
have been added by another hand. At any rate, there is no surviving document from
Mozart's pen suggesting that he was unhappy with the engraving, issued as 'Opus
VI'.

The first attempt at a complete edition of Mozart's works was the so-called
Oeuvres Complettes begun by Breitkopf & Härtel in 1798. This bold enterprise contained three projected series: *Klaviersachen*; *Partituren größerer Werke als Opern,
Cantaten, Kirchenstücke*; and *Musik für mehrere Instrumente in Stimmen als Sinfonien,
Concerten, Quintetten, Quartetten*. All of the first series was accomplished by 1806,[19]
along with some other works from the remaining series, including the Requiem,
some masses and the piano concertos. By this time, Breitkopf had been joined in
the race to produce an edition of Mozart's music by Johann Anton André who, in
1799, concluded an agreement with Constanze Mozart to purchase, with a view to
'authentic' publication, the bulk of Mozart's autograph manuscripts.[20] No original
solo sonatas are identified in this agreement however. Evidently Breitkopf already
had these, since he had published them all by 1800. They are referred to in a notice
that appeared in the *Grätzer Zeitung* on 28 August that year.[21] That Breitkopf possessed at least two of the sonata autographs is confirmed by a statement of 13 March
in which Constanze explained some of her dealings with Breitkopf and, subsequently, André.[22]

Other early editions of Mozart's sonatas (mostly from the first three decades of
the nineteenth century) survive in considerable quantity. A listing can be found in

'Sources', p. 188). Operas, being long and complex works, were relatively difficult to engrave (far
more so than piano sonatas, for instance), and were issued on demand in manuscript by copyists such
as Traeg, Lausch and Sukowaty. Mozart sometimes refers to his published works – or works he
intended to publish – in his letters. He seems to have been especially proud of the violin and piano
sonatas, K.296 and 376–80, K.301–6; the three piano concertos, K.413–15, and the 'Haydn
Quartets', mentioned in a letter to the Parisian publisher, Sieber, on 26 April 1783 (*Anderson*, no.
487). Reference to the publication history of his sonatas is made in chapters 3–7, as appropriate. Some
130 of Mozart's works were published during his lifetime. The standard reference work to first editions of Mozart's works is Gertraut Haberkamp, *Die Erstdrucke der Werke von Wolfgang Amadeus Mozart*,
2 vols. (Tutzing, 1986).

[19] The autographs of K.279–84 contain a handwritten comment by an unknown annotator to the effect
that they were to be found in vol. VI of the Breitkopf edition.

[20] The contract is transcribed in Otto Erich Deutsch, *Mozart: a Documentary Biography* trans. Eric Blom,
Peter Branscombe and Jeremy Noble (London, 1965; repr. 1990), pp. 490–2.

[21] Deutsch, *Doc.Biog.*, p. 496.   [22] Deutsch, *Doc.Biog.*, p. 495.

RISM Series A/I.[23] New or reprinted editions of sonatas appeared in Berlin, Brunswick, Frankfurt am Main, Hamburg, Leipzig, London, Mainz, Paris, Stuttgart, and Vienna. Some of these are arrangements including string accompaniments, such as the trio version of K.331 published as *A Favourite/ Sonata/ for the/ Piano Forte/ with an Accompaniment for/ Violin & Violoncello,/ ad libitum,/ Composed by/ W.A. Mozart./. . ./Opera 19/ Price* [added in ink by hand] *3/- / London, Printed for/ The Regent's Harmonic Institution* [1819][24] or the different version printed in *Storace's/ Collection/ Of/ Original/ Harpsichord Music/. . ./ Printed for S. Storace, No. 23, Howland Street, Rathbone Place;/ and Sold by Messrs. Birchall & Andrews, No. 129, New Bond Street* [London] (vol. I, 1788),[25] which also contains the F major Sonata, K.533 and 494. Storace's text of K.331 derives from the Artaria print of 1784, as does his text of K.330 published in *Storace's/ Collection/ Of/ Original/ Harpsichord Music/ Vol. II/ Price 8/- / Printed for S. Storace, No. 23, Howland Street, Rathbone Place;/ and Sold by Messrs. Birchall & Andrews, No. 129, New Bond Street* [London].[26] That of K.533 and 494 derives from the first edition issued in 1788 by Bossler in Speyer. K.331 was especially popular in England (perhaps because of its 'Alla Turca' finale) to judge from the numerous editions that survive. One of these (printed from the same plates as Storace's version, but without violin or cello parts) was *Mozart's/ Favourite Sonata,/ for the/ PianoForte or Harpsichord:/ From Op.19/ Price 3^s/- / London. Printed for R. Birchall and his Musical Circulating Library No. 133 New Bond Street./ Where may be had all the above Author's Works.*[27]

Among more recent editions may be cited the 'new' Associated Board edition by Stanley Sadie and Denis Matthews[28] and the *Neue Mozart-Ausgabe* (*NMA*), edited by Wolfgang Plath and Wolfgang Rehm.[29] The former was intended as a replacement of the earlier Associated Board edition, by York Bowen and Aubyn Raymar.[30] The 'new' Associated Board edition and the *NMA* present the most reliable texts available to date. A new edition of the recently-rediscovered autograph text of the C minor Fantasia and Sonata, K.475 and 457 is in preparation for future publication in the *NMA*.

And so to the present study. Part I investigates the broader contexts within which we ought to evaluate Mozart's sonatas. Chapter 1 examines mid-century percep-

[23] Karlheinz Schlager (ed.), *Répertoire Internationale des Sources Musicales* (Kassel, Basel, Tours, London, 1976). The relevant portion of this volume was issued separately as an offprint: *Wolfgang Amadeus Mozart:Verzeichnis von Erst- und Frühdrucken bis etwa 1800,* ed. Karlheinz Schlager (Kassel, Basel, Tours, London 1978). The sonatas are listed on pp. 174–84 (M.6738–6934).

[24] Copy consulted Oxford, Bodleian Library, Mus. I.173 (3).

[25] Copy consulted Oxford, Bodleian Library, Mus. I.222 (3).

[26] Copy consulted Oxford, Bodleian Library, Mus. I.222 (4).

[27] Copy consulted Oxford, Bodleian Library, Mus. I. c.303.

[28] *Mozart: Sonatas for Pianoforte,* ed. Stanley Sadie and Denis Matthews, 2 vols. (London, 1970–81).

[29] (Kassel, 1986). The sonatas appear in Series IX, *Klaviermusik*; Werkgruppe 25. It is reprinted as vol. XX of the *NMA Taschenpartitur-Ausgabe* and in a two-volume edition, *Mozart: Piano Sonatas* (henceforth *Mozart Sonatas I* (or *II*)).

[30] *Mozart Pianoforte Sonatas,* ed. York Bowen and Aubyn Raymar (London, 1931).

tions of a solo sonata, what its functions were, the social milieu within which they were played and discussed, the expectations of the audience, along with some aesthetic issues. Chapter 2 reviews the likely sources of influence on Mozart's sonatas, including the work of Salzburg composers (whose work Mozart knew from an early age), French, English, Italian and German traditions. The sonatas of specific composers are related to those of Mozart, including those of his father, Leopold, J.C. Bach and, of course, Haydn. Part II concentrates on the sources (manuscript and printed) of Mozart's sonatas. Chapters 3–7 each treat a specific group of sonatas, where possible retaining the integrity of a manuscript or published 'set'.[31] In these chapters, information is given, where possible, on the genesis of the sonatas and on the autograph manuscripts, with particular emphasis on what these reveal about Mozart's composing strategies. Chapter 8 deals with the sonata fragments. Part III, which considers the sonatas from the viewpoint of their musical style, approaches the sonatas as musical 'orations'. This presupposes, of course, that Mozart's music (or, for that matter, *any* music) can be conceptualised as 'language'. Such a conception was by no means uncommon in the eighteenth century. Rhetorical explanations of musical form were common to several traditions of European musical theory, extending back at least as far as the renaissance and attaining renewed prominence following the publication of Joachim Burmeister's *Musica Poetica* in 1606. Eighteenth-century music theorists therefore inherited a mature tradition of applying rhetorical models to music, described by Quantz in 1752 as 'an artificial language by which one makes one's musical thoughts known to the listener'.[32] Johann Mattheson, in his *Kern melodischer Wissenschaft* (Hamburg, 1737) and *Der vollkommene Capellmeister* (Hamburg, 1739) and Johann Nikolaus Forkel, in his *Allgemeine Geschichte der Musik* (Leipzig, 1778), attempted to relate musical form (and specifically, sonata form) to the subdivisions of an oration. Added to this is the central position held by grammar and rhetoric within the Latin choir-school education of the time (rhetoric being introduced at a fairly advanced stage in the course of study, once grammar had been mastered). Haydn, for instance, received instruction in Latin at St Stephen's, Vienna, following his admission as a chorister there, and recent musicological research has shown quite convincingly that he evidently had at least a working knowledge of rhetoric.[33] Leopold Mozart would have made an extensive study of the classical texts on forensic rhetoric by Cicero (specifically the treatises *De Oratore* and *De Inventione*), Quintilian (specifically, the *Institutio Oratoria*) and the anonymous author of *Ad Herennium* during his philosophical and legal studies at the University of Salzburg, from which he graduated in 1738. His

---

[31] Several of the sonatas from the later 1780s have been grouped together in chapter 7 purely for convenience. They were not composed as a set, nor were they all published together; three (K.545, 570 and 576) were published posthumously.

[32] Johann Joachim Quantz, *Versuch einer Anweisung die Flöte traversière zu spielen* (Berlin, 1752), p. 102. Translation from Marc Evan Bonds, *Wordless Rhetoric: Musical Form and the Metaphor of the Oration* (Cambridge, Mass., 1991), p. 63. Bonds's study is the most detailed yet attempted of rhetorical readings of music in the eighteenth and nineteenth centuries.

[33] See, for instance, Elaine Sisman, *Haydn and the Classical Variation* (Cambridge, Mass., 1993), pp. 22–5.

attitudes towards language (and, by extension, *musical* language) were formed by such rhetorical concepts as are found in these works and in the many musico-theoretical textbooks (including Mattheson's *Der vollkommene Capellmeister*) that he owned and to which he referred in some of his letters. It provides ample justification for a rhetorical approach to Mozart's sonatas. In taking Mozart's sonatas as case-studies for the application of eighteenth-century understandings of rhetoric to music, I realise that I am in danger of using these works as 'vehicles' for the pursuit of a particular methodology. I hope not to debase them thereby, but rather to reveal layers of meaning or significance that could otherwise pass unnoticed. Rhetorical 'figure-hunting' has, of course, been applied to baroque musical repertoires with varying degrees of success and credibility over the years, attracting both praise and blame in reviews. It is my view that rhetoric can open up many new paths to musicologists provided that it is not too narrowly or too literally applied. One problem with equating particular rhetorical 'figures of speech' to musical 'figures' such as the turn or a chain of falling suspensions, is the lack of a context for the comparison. 'Figures', such as have become the stock-in-trade of some historians of baroque music, were part of that division of rhetoric known as *elocutio* (style or expression); they were a means by which a speaker adorned his speech, and not ends in themselves. Higher divisions, or levels, of rhetoric included *inventio* (the 'invention' of a subject to be discussed) and *dispositio* (the arrangement of the speech into sections). In tracing the possible rhetorical motivation for any unit of musical expression, be it a movement, a section, phrase or motive, it is essential to keep these divisions in mind, otherwise rhetoric quickly becomes a labyrinth that, far from clarifying its subject, results in obscurity. The progression from *inventio* through *dispositio* to *elocutio* is reflected in the organisation of chapters throughout part III, which, having introduced the subject of rhetoric in a discussion of eighteenth-century approaches to the comprehension of form, proceeds through an investigation of the nature of the musical ideas in Mozart's sonatas (the *inventio*), followed by a discussion of formal design (the *dispositio*) and finally a consideration of the *elocutio*, which attempts a detailed rhetorical analysis of several extracts – ranging from the construction of themes to whole movements. The resulting picture affords a cross-section of Mozart's compositional strategies within the sonatas, rather than a blow-by-blow account of each sonata in turn. This perspective is balanced by the fairly full discussion of the slow movement of K.533 at the end of chapter 12.

Wherever possible, references to (and quotations from) Mozart's letters have been taken from Emily Anderson's English translation, since this will be the most easily accessible source for the majority of readers, although recourse to the German-language edition, *Mozart: Briefe und Aufzeichnungen*,[34] has been unavoidable. All other English translations of foreign-language texts are taken from sources acknowledged in the relevent notes. A fairly full bibliography is given in an attempt to bring

[34] *Mozart: Briefe und Aufzeichnungen, Gesamtausgabe*, ed. Wilhelm A. Bauer, Otto Erich Deutsch and Joseph Hans Eibl, 7 vols. (Kassel, Basel, Tours, London, 1962–75).

together in one place a broad overview of relevant scholarly writing on the sonatas and related matters. Most of the theoretical works owned by Leopold Mozart, and referred to in chapter 9, have been excluded from the bibliography, though, since their contents do not have a direct bearing on the classical style in general or Mozart's sonatas in particular. Full details of these, including citations of modern facsimiles, are given in appropriate notes.

Texts of musical examples by Mozart are from the *Neue Mozart-Ausgabe*; those by Haydn are from the Henle *Urtext* edition; others have been transcribed from eighteenth-century editions identified in the main text.

Access to a copy of the Mozart Sonatas (preferably the *NMA* text, or the 'new' Associated Board edition by Denis Matthews and Stanley Sadie) has been assumed throughout this study, in order to keep the number of musical examples within reasonable limits. Eighteen solo sonatas are included in this study. I have deliberately omitted reference to two sonatas that are occasionally found in older editions of Mozart's works, namely, those in B flat, K.498a, and in F, K.547a. Both first editions were published posthumously in Leipzig, the former by J. P. von Thonus in 1798, and the latter by Breitkopf & Härtel (in the sixth volume of Mozart's complete works).[35] A number of early editions also included them alongside the 'canonical' sonatas.[36] Their direct association with the composer is uncertain. The former (B flat) has four movements, of which the second bears a strong affinity to the slow movement of the B flat Concerto, K.450, while the 6/8 rondo finale is clearly related to those of K.450, 456 and 595. Its opening movement rehearses some of the textural manoeuvres found in the first movement of K.533 (for example, texture-inversion at bars 4–5). In the finale there is a most unusual – and unconvincing – modulation from the tonic, B flat, to B major, in which the main theme is presented. Perhaps the kindest thing that may be said about the piece is that it is 'a reconstruction from memory, with variable exactness, by someone else who had heard Mozart play it, possibly as an improvisation'.[37] The other sonata, in F, was certainly not conceived as a piano sonata. It has just two movements, of which the first is borrowed from the second movement of Mozart's Violin Sonata, K.547, and the second from the finale of the C major Sonata, K.545 (transposed to F). There is no conclusive evidence to suggest that Mozart had anything to do with this compilation, although in *Köchel*[6] it is suggested that, compared to the texts of the originals, that of K.547a exhibits subtle improvements that may derive from the composer.

---

[35] Mozart, *Oeuvres Complettes*, cahier 6, (Breitkopf & Härtel, Leipzig, 1799), p. 13.

[36] They are listed in *Köchel*[6], pp. 894 and 620, respectively. Both are found in the 'old' Associated Board edition, by York Bowen and Aubyn Raymar (vol. II, nos. 19 and 20).

[37] Aubyn Raymar, in the 'old' Associated Board edition, vol.II, p. 175.

Acknowledgements

It is my pleasant duty to record my gratitude to individuals and institutions for advice and assistance of various kinds. My colleagues in the Music Department at Bristol University have willingly discussed particular points of detail, sometimes leading to significant rethinking of issues that ultimately found its way into the finished text. Jonathan Scott provided expert assistance with the preparation of the musical examples. My parents have been unfailingly supportive at every stage of the book's development. Much of the book was written at their home during what was in fact supposed to be an extended family holiday. I cannot adequately express my gratitude for their patience. For access to Mozart autographs and early prints, and for supplying copies of various kinds I am especially grateful to Professor Dr Rudolf Angermüller, Frau Geneviève Geffray and Dr Johanna Senigl (Internationale Stiftung Mozarteum, Salzburg); to Pater Petrus (St Peter's Abbey, Salzburg); to the staff of the Museum Carolino Augusteum, Salzburg; to Professor Zygmunt Szweykowski and Dr Alexandra Patalas of the Department of Musicology, Jagiellonian University of Kraków; and to the staff of the Bodleian Library, Oxford, the British Library, London, the Staatsbibliothek zu Berlin, the Pierpoint Morgan Library, New York, the Princeton University Library (William H. Scheide Collection) and the Hebrew University, Jerusalem. For comments and suggestions of various kinds following a lecture on the sonata autographs at the University of Salzburg in 1995 I wish to thank Professor Gerhard Croll, Dr Faye Ferguson and Dr Sibylle Dahms. Penny Souster and Hazel Brooks at Cambridge University Press have steered the book through its various stages of production with commendable skill and professionalism. I owe a special debt to Cliff Eisen, who read the entire manuscript with admirable thoroughness and saved me from a number of errors or inconsistencies. Any that remain are my responsibility alone. I have received financial support from a variety of sources for travel and for the purchase of materials, specifically the J. K. Rhodes Bursary Trust, the British Council, Austria, the Royal Musical Association, St John's College, Oxford (where I held a Visiting Senior Scholarship during the summer of 1994), and the Research Fund of the Faculty of Arts, Bristol University. I gratefully acknowledge permission to reproduce excerpts from manuscripts in the possession of the Jagiellonian Library, Kraków, the Staatsbibliothek zu Berlin, the Internationale Stiftung Mozarteum, Salzburg, and the British Library, London.

Abbreviations

Anderson *The Letters of Mozart and his Family*, chronologically arranged, translated and edited with an introduction, notes and indexes by Emily Anderson. 3rd edition revised by Stanley Sadie and Fiona Smart (London, 1985)

Briefe *Mozart: Briefe und Aufzeichnungen, Gesamtausgabe*, ed. Wilhelm A. Bauer, Otto Erich Deutsch and Joseph Hans Eibl, 7 vols. Published by the Internationale Stiftung Mozarteum Salzburg. (Kassel, Basel, Tours, 1962–75)

Deutsch, *Doc.Biog.* Otto Erich Deutsch, *Mozart: a Documentary Biography*, translated by Eric Blom, Peter Branscombe and Jeremy Noble (London, 1965; 1990). Original German version, Deutsch, *Mozart; die Dokumente seines Lebens* (Kassel, Basel, Tours, 1961)

JAMS *Journal of the American Musicological Society*

Köchel[6] Ludwig Ritter von Köchel, *Chronologisch-thematisches Verzeichnis sämtlicher Tonwerke Wolfgang Amadé Mozarts*, ed. F. Giegling, A. Weinmann and G. Sievers, 6th edn (Leipzig, 1964)

MJb *Mozart-Jahrbuch* (Internationale Stiftung Mozarteum, Salzburg)

Mozart Sonatas I/II *Wolfgang Amadeus Mozart: Piano Sonatas*, ed. Wolfgang Plath and Wolfgang Rehm. Urtext of the New Mozart Edition (*NMA* – see below), 2 vols. BA 4861b, 4862b (Bärenreiter; Kassel, 1986)

NMA *W.A. Mozart: Neue Ausgabe sämtlicher Werke*, issued by the Internationale Stiftung Mozarteum, Salzburg, series IX *Klaviermusik*; Werkgruppe 25, *Klaviersonaten*. Also available as vol. XX of *W.A. Mozart: Neue Ausgabe sämtlicher Werke Taschenpartitur-Ausgabe*

PRMA   *Proceedings of the Royal Musical Association*

RISM   *Répertoire Internationale des Sources Musicales*, series A/I:
                    Einzeldrücke vor 1800 (Kassel, Basel, Tours, London,
                    1971–92)

The New Grove   *The New Grove Dictionary of Music and Musicians*, ed. Stanley
                    Sadie, 20 vols., 6th edn (London, 1980)

PART ONE

CONTEXTS

CHAPTER ONE

The solo sonata in context

What kind of a composition was the solo sonata inherited by the young Mozart? In what situations would such a sonata have been played? For what sort of audience was it intended? In what ways might the cultural identity of that audience have influenced its expectations of a solo sonata and, consequently, the composer's work? Answers to preliminary questions such as these are required in order to arrive at a proper contextual appreciation of the solo piano sonata of the early classical period, and specifically, Mozart's contribution to this important genre.

J. A. P. Schultz, writing in 1775 put the matter thus:

in no form of instrumental music is there a better opportunity than in the sonata to depict feelings without words . . . [except for symphonies, concertos and dances] there remains only the form of the sonata, which assumes all characters and every expression.[1]

This was in sharp contrast to the views held by the preceding generation of aestheticians, most notably by the rhetorician, Johann Christoph Gottsched, trenchantly expressed in his translation of Batteux's *Les Beaux Arts Réduits à un même Principe*:

Music by itself is soulless and unintelligible when it does not cling to words, which must speak for it, so that one knows what it means . . . [a sonata is] a labyrinth of tones, which sound neither happy nor sad, neither touching nor moving.[2]

Such an observation stems from the philosophical principle that music is an *imitation* (*mimesis*) of nature, intended to impart a kind of secondary effect (such as 'moral improvement') in the perceiver, and that instrumental music is powerless to achieve this task without a clear succession of objects provided by a text.[3] Accordingly, instrumental music is quite literally, meaningless – a random succession of gestures with no connection to the natural world that music was supposed to represent. While the vast quantities of instrumental music written, published and circulated throughout the eighteenth century demonstrate that such philosophical speculation bore little resemblance to compositional reality, the acknowledgement of vocal music's superiority to instrumental music remained a prominent feature of much of the theoretical literature from Mattheson's *Der vollkommene Capellmeister* (1739) to Heinrich Christoph Koch's three-volume *Versuch einer Anleitung zur Composition* (1782–93).[4]

The *mimesis* model outlined above is typical of contemporary French thought on the aesthetics of instrumental music, as expressed in the writings of Batteux, Blainville and Rousseau, all of which became increasingly well known in the German lands during the 1760s through the translated extracts that appeared in Johann Adam Hiller's *Wochentliche Nachrichten*.[5]

Mozart may have encountered something of the prevailing French attitudes during his Parisian visits as a small boy in 1763–4 and 1766, perhaps through Friedrich Melchior Grimm (1723–1807), founder of the journal *Correspondance Littéraire*, to which his father was a subscriber.[6] His views on contemporary aesthetics, at this stage or any other in his life, are unknown, though given his father's evident attraction to the ideals of the Enlightenment,[7] he may well have encountered some of the key issues of the day concerning the nature of expression in music and other arts.[8]

In its full context the extract from Schultz's essay, quoted above, contrasts the domestic, or chamber, genre of the sonata with the public genre of, for example, the symphony. Composers were acutely sensitive to this distinction. It is essential, therefore, to keep in mind the respective roles of the sonata, a relatively small-scale piece best suited to conveying quite sophisticated musical ideas of an intimate nature, either within a purely domestic context (perhaps even for the private satisfaction of the player alone) or else to a semi-private gathering of cultivated music-lovers, and the altogether grander dramatic statements of a symphony or concerto, whose direct mode of expression properly belonged to the theatre or concert hall.[9]

The Allegretto of C. P. E. Bach's Sonata in F major, printed as an appendix to his textbook, *Versuch über die wahre Art das Clavier zu spielen* (1753),[10] demonstrates something of the intimacy attainable in a solo piano sonata: flexibility in the shaping of motives; their subtle rhythmic and intervallic variation; a feeling for appropriate phrase succession, balance and cadential emphasis (feminine cadences, resolving onto a weak beat, are especially prominent); and judicious harmonic intensification, all of which is absolutely at one with the nature of an erudite conversation in a domestic setting (example 1.1). The idiom is utterly at variance with the grandiose sweeps of sound and energy in, for instance, a symphonic passage by Stamitz or Cannabich (and later Haydn), a genre whose realm was public. In 1779 Bach began issuing sonatas *Für Kenner und Liebhaber* ('for connoisseurs and amateurs') whose musical techniques appealed specifically to a cultivated, rather refined, audience – not necessarily aristocratic – whose literary upbringing (perhaps including familiarity with several European languages) and musical training enabled them to appreciate a musical work as a kind of discourse, a logical unfolding, even progression, of ideas. Numerous musical theorists of the classic period actually expressed the formal organisation of musical themes, phrases, sections and movements in explicitly rhetorical terms. A logic in the progression of musical ideas was thought to exist

Example 1.1   C. P. E. Bach, Allegretto from Sonata in F, Wq. 63/5; H.74

in a manner analogous to a formal oration, and, in fact, technical vocabulary from the art of rhetoric (*exordium*, *propositio*, *tractatio*, *peroratio*, etc.) was routinely appropriated by musical theorists such as Mattheson, Kirnberger, Quantz, Forkel and Koch in their descriptions of musical form.[11] Perhaps the most influential of the German rhetoricians was Johann Christoph Gottsched, whose *Ausführliche Redekunst* (Augsburg, 1736) was many times reprinted during the rest of the eighteenth century. Leopold Mozart was aware of his work, and in letters to the Augsburg publisher, Johann Jakob Lotter, of 9 June and 28 August 1755, he sought out copies of each of Gottsched's major works, including the *Ausführliche Redekunst*.[12]

In his *Kern melodischer Wissenschaft* (1737), Mattheson likened music to oratory as follows:

[In music] *disposition* differs from the rhetorical arrangement of an ordinary speech only in the subject, the matter at hand, the *objecto*. Hence it must observe the same six parts that are normally prescribed for the orator, namely: the introduction, the narration, the proposition, the proof, the refutation, and the closing, otherwise known as: *Exordium, Narratio, Propositio, Confirmatio, Confutatio*, [and] *Peroratio*.[13]

A similar approach to large-scale formal organisation was advocated by Forkel, in the *Allgemeine Geschichte der Musik* (1788):

As musical works of any substantial length are nothing other than speeches for the sentiments, by which through a certain kind of empathy one seeks to move the listener, the rules for the ordering and arrangement of ideas are the same as in an actual oration. And so one has, in both, a main idea, supporting secondary ideas, dissections of the main idea [probably what we would term the 'development section' in a sonata form], refutations, doubts, proofs and reiterations . . . This order and sequence of the individual sections is called the aesthetic ordering of the ideas . . . A musical work in which this ordering is so arranged that all thoughts mutually support and reinforce one another . . . is well ordered.[14]

In the eighteenth century such rhetorical models were typically applied to symphonic and other concert works rather than solo sonatas. Within the intimate domain of the solo sonata, however, rhetoric still had a part to play in the sense that the oration required logical organisation and inter-relation of its components, as described above by Forkel. This matter is taken up at length in part III.

SOME AESTHETIC MATTERS

Consideration of the aesthetics of instrumental music is common to all the major strands of Enlightenment thought, though few commentators address their attention specifically to the sonata (Schultz's view, quoted at the beginning of this chapter, being one exception). French, German and English writers on music all tended to agree that instrumental music was inferior to vocal, normally supporting their view by recourse to a theory of 'Imitation'. This is well put by Blainville in his *L'esprit de l'art musicale*[15] according to whom music may move the soul of the listener by means of the voice or else by instruments, but whereas melody ('la melodie', meaning *vocal* music) possesses *natural* beauties, instrumental music ('la symphonie') possesses them only indirectly. Only if music is joined to words does it have the power to convey true emotional significance. Instrumental music, in other words, conveys its meaning at second hand. According to the theory of Imitation espoused by Jean-Jacques Rousseau in his *Dictionnaire de Musique*[16] the composer may

stir up the sea, fan the blaze, make rivulets flow, rains fall and torrents rage . . . calm the tempest . . . [however, he] will not literally imitate things, *but he will excite in the soul feelings similar to those that it experiences when it sees them* [my italics][17]

Elsewhere in his writings Rousseau's technical justification for music's expressive power (even at second hand) was melody, which alone was possible of rendering instrumental music sensible. In his *Essai sur l'origine des langues* (Paris, 1764) he had noted that 'Melody is the musical equivalent of design in painting; it is melody that delineates the features and forms, harmonies and timbres being only the colours'.[18] Later, in the *Dictionnaire*[19] Rousseau explains this overtly: 'c'est toujours du chant que se doit tirer la principale Expression, tant dans la Musique Instrumentale que dans la Vocale'. Though Rousseau does not mention any specific categories of instrumental music (such as the sonata) here, French musical writings of the previous decade do. Cahusac's article on 'Expression' noted that concertos or sonatas could paint a variety of moods but would be lifeless (because they lacked words),[20] a view repeated in Lacombe's *Le Spectacle des beaux-arts*.[21] As has already been implied, melody does not necessarily hold the principal position in the organisation of a sonata movement, in the way that, say, the solo voice ('chant') would in a French opera aria. A range of technical procedures to do with harmony, texture, rhythm and phraseology, all vie for attention from one bar to the next. Perhaps this was one reason why Rousseau regarded counterpoint as a meaningless babble, like several people talking at once.

In the *Allgemeine Theorie*, Sulzer touches on some specific ways in which emotion could be expressed, irrespective of vocal or instrumental genre. Among the technical means that Sulzer lists for suitable portrayal of a narrative in instrumental music are metre, dynamic variation, melody, rhythm and accompanimental style. Foremost though (and here he is at odds with Rousseau), is harmony, which:

must move easily and naturally, without great complexity or ponderous suspensions, if the mood is gentle or pleasant. If the mood is violent or recalcitrant, however, the progressions should move haltingly, and there should be fairly frequent modulations into remote keys; the progressions should also be more complex, with frequent and unexpected dissonances, and suspensions which are rapidly resolved.[22]

The concept of an instrumental movement as a narrative was advocated by the Scottish philosopher and economist, Adam Smith (1723–1790). For Smith, instrumental music was a discourse, resembling in the sequence of its figures a conversation.[23] His *Essays on Philosophical Subjects*, published posthumously in 1795, and probably written and revised between about 1777 and his death in 1790, is little-known to musicians. Smith, a Fellow of the Royal Societies of Edinburgh and London, Professor of Logic (1751) and subsequently Moral Philosophy (1752) at Glasgow University until 1764, and one of the group of Scottish Enlightenment philosophers whose most famous other member was David Hume (1711–76), is best known for his treatise *The Wealth of Nations* (1776), though his interests ranged far wider than economic theory; he was well read, passionately interested in continental 'Enlightenment' ideas, a keen lover of the arts and sciences. He owned a copy of Charles Avison's *An Essay on Musical Expression* (1752) as well as works by Rameau and Burney; he was familiar with some of Rousseau's ideas from his study of the *Encyclopédie*, to which he was a subscriber. Part II of Smith's essay, 'Of the Nature of the Imitation which takes place in what are called the Imitative Arts', contains a more spirited justification of music independent of words than any other authors examined here:

Music seldom means to tell any particular story, or to imitate any particular event, or in general to suggest any particular object, distinct from that combination of sounds of which itself is composed. Its meaning, therefore, may be said to be complete in itself . . . What is called the subject of such Music is . . . a certain leading combination of notes, to which it frequently returns, and to which all its digressions bear a certain affinity.[24]

Smith seems here to be acknowledging the existence of an 'ordering' among the tones of a composition similar to that advocated by Forkel, in the *Allgemeine Geschichte der Musik*.

Though elsewhere in his essay Smith acknowledges the 'superiority' of vocal music over instrumental he nevertheless regards the latter as a 'system' from which the listener might derive intellectual pleasure.[25] The passage from which the following quotation is drawn specifically considers instrumental music (though not specifically the sonata) as he felt it to be *perceived*; by 'concert', Smith probably means simply 'performance', rather than a public concert:

In a concert of instrumental music the attention is engaged, with pleasure and delight, to listen to a combination of the most agreeable and melodious sounds . . . *The mind being thus successively occupied by a train of thoughts* [my italics] of which the nature, succession, and connection correspond [to varying moods] is itself successively led into each of those moods or dispositions; and is thus brought into a sort of harmony or concord with the music which so greatly engages its attention.[26]

Naturally it is impossible to know to what extent, if any, these various aesthetic appraisals of instrumental music may have been held by salon audiences when listening to solo sonatas, though we may be sure that such matters, which were distributed widely in published form on the continent, were vigorously debated among those who had any pretence to 'Enlightened' conduct during the mid to late eighteenth century. We must remain sensitive, however, to the likelihood that, for an eighteenth-century audience, certain compositional techniques were genre-specific and that a change of genre may have radically altered the parameters of musical understanding. In his recent penetrating study of the reception of Haydn's late symphonies, David Schroeder has likened the use of syncopation as a specific means of creating tension in Haydn's symphonic transition sections to 'its use as a device in eighteenth-century opera to emphasize points of intense conflict and confusion' (citing examples from the Introduzione (bars 87–8) and Act I (bars 477–8) of *Don Giovanni*).[27] Schroeder argues that dramatic confrontation between different types of material in Haydn's symphonies – specifically the first movement transitions of nos. 82 and 86 – may therefore have been heard in an 'operatic' way by a concert audience. While the intended meaning of such effects probably survived transplantation from an opera to a symphony (that is, between two 'public' genres), it is debatable whether or not such effects retained their status within the 'domestic' environment of the solo sonata. In the first movement of Mozart's F major Sonata, K.332, the meaning of the syncopations at bars 56–66 is not 'dramatic' in the same way as an opera. Mozart's figure syncopates both at the level of the beat (bars 56–63) and at the metrical level (bars 64–5), producing a temporary accentual shift from 3/4 to 3/2. Within the same bars there is an analogous shift of harmonic rhythm, from a single chord per bar (bars 56–63) to chord changes every minim (bars 64–5) and at the end of the phrase, every crotchet, resulting in a carefully measured rhythmic accelerando (example 1.2). Such sophisticated interlocking of surface rhythm

Example 1.2 Mozart, Sonata in F, K.332, 1st movement, bars 56–67

and harmonic rhythm is a technical device perhaps better appreciated in a small room than in a concert hall, always supposing, of course, that Mozart's intended listeners were sufficiently aware of, and attentive to, the niceties of his musical language. Can we assume that they were? In order to satisfy ourselves that they might have we must investigate further the didactic role of the solo piano sonata and the most usual environment in which it was performed, the salon.

SONATAS AS TEACHING MATERIAL

Among the primary functions of the solo piano sonata was its usefulness for teaching purposes. In part, this was a reflection of the appointments held by composers such as Georg Christoph Wagenseil (piano tutor to Archduchess Maria Anna of Austria) and Johann Christian Bach, one of whose appointments, advertised on the title-page of his Op.17 *Six Sonatas for the Harpsichord or Piano-Forte* (Paris, *c*.1774; London, 1779), was 'Music Master to her Majesty and the Royal Family'. While at times both Op.17 and its precursor, the *Six Sonates pour le Clavecin ou le Piano Forte*, Op.5,[28] are technically very demanding the general level of difficulty is quite modest, restricted to uncomplicated hand positions based on tonic and dominant triads in the opening movement of Op.5 no.1, for instance. Rather more dexterity is required in the G major Sonata, Op.5 no.3, which, while principally constructed from tonic and dominant scales and arpeggios, contains a greater number of passages

involving smooth transitions between adjacent hand positions and calling for secur-
ity across a wider range of the piano; the ensuing theme and variations move in a
deliberately graded way through right-hand semiquavers (variation 1), transferred
to the left hand in variation 2, to triplet semiquavers for right and left hand respectively in variations 3 and 4. Wagenseil's various sets of published sonatas (entitled
'Divertimentos') work on similar principles. The first movement of his Op.1, no.1
(1753) is clearly for neatness of execution and reliability of fingering, while the third
movement of Op.1, no.2 is for execution of ornaments.[29] Many of Haydn's solo
sonatas up to about 1770 must also have originated as teaching pieces. The G minor,
Hob. XVI:44 (c.1768) requires no great virtuosity of the player but proceeds, in its
exposition at least, in a 'patchwork' of textures, each typically just a bar or two in
length, that require of the player a high degree of rhythmic accuracy (bars 12–16)
and clarity of part playing in the contrapuntal sections (bars 14–17 and 21–4).

Occasionally, Mozart refers to his use of his own piano sonatas in lessons. During
his visit to Mannheim at the end of 1777 he became friendly with the family of
Christian Cannabich (1731–98), director of instrumental music at the court of
Elector Karl Theodore at Mannheim, and taught his daughter, Rosa, the piano.
Mozart's C major Sonata, K.309, was written for her, the slow movement suppos-
edly being her 'musical portrait'.[30] We are fortunate indeed to possess the following description, in a letter to his father of 14 November 1777, of Mozart's thoughts
on the slow movement of this sonata, and how he proposed to teach Rosa the piece:

We finished the opening Allegro today. The Andante will give us the most trouble, for it is
full of expression and must be played accurately and with the exact shades of forte and piano,
precisely as they are marked. She is smart and learns very easily. Her right hand is very good,
but her left, unfortunately, is completely ruined . . . I have told her too that if I were her
regular teacher, I would lock up all her music, cover the keys with a handkerchief and make
her practise, first with the right hand and then with the left, nothing but passages, trills, mor-
dants and so forth, very slowly at first, until each hand should be thoroughly trained.[31]

The slow movement is indeed highly expressive, calling for considerable sensitivity
from the player. While the autograph is lost, a copy made by Leopold in December
1777 (now in private ownership in Switzerland, upon which the text of *NMA* is
based) confirms Mozart's comments about the precision of the dynamic markings:
in addition to *pp*, *p*, *f* and *fp* there is a profusion of slurs and other articulation signs.
Good control of *cantabile* and a smooth *legato* is needed at bars 33 and 53, along with
reliable part-playing (beginning at bar 40, for instance).[32] While the first movement
of K.309 is not especially difficult, its rondo finale contains taxing passagework
(triplet semiquavers in awkwardly linked hand positions at bars 40 ff. and 143 ff.,
and intermittent tremolando demisemiquavers (bars 58, 111, 162 and 221)). To
achieve fluency in this rondo is not easy; both Rosa and Nannerl must have been
accomplished technicians.

Talented female keyboard players were, in fact, relatively plentiful in the second
half of the eighteenth century.[33] Indeed, the social etiquette of the age virtually dic-

tated a certain degree of keyboard proficiency: among aristocratic families, for instance, ability in this direction could be important in attracting an acceptable husband. During the 1780s several of Mozart's Viennese pupils were ladies from the higher echelons of society: Countess Thun, Countess Rumbecke; somewhat lower down the the scale were Maria Therèse von Trattern[34] (wife of the important book-seller and publisher), Barbara von Ployer and Josepha Auernhammer, the latter two of whom carved out successful careers as performers.[35]

Against this background we may speculate on some of the subtler aspects of sonata writing as they may have been appreciated by eighteenth-century listeners (particularly ladies) who had themselves been taught to play (in however rudi-mentary a fashion) similar pieces as a part of their musical education. Practically, this includes the precise technical coordination of mind, ears, eyes and hands. In addi-tion, there are musical qualities such as: distinction between the characters of suc-cessive themes (sometimes of a 'singing' quality, sometimes rather more pithy and motivic in character) and 'patterns' (passagework); phrasing, including not just a feeling for melodic shape but also a sense of closure provided by the cadential network; correct accentuation; uniformity of pulse (against which syncopation might be measured, for instance); contrasts of texture; and points of particular har-monic interest, bound up (for more advanced players) with an overall sense of tonal continuity in the piece as a whole. Such was (and is) the intimacy of musical contact involved in learning to play a classical sonata movement. For a connoisseur listen-ing to a fine performance of a sonata in a household salon in the second half of the eighteenth century, memories of their own previous experience of playing such music would perhaps have embraced some of the above. Arguably their critical framework was in part bound up with their own prior physical and mental engage-ment with the notes of a sonata as much as, if not more than, the abstract princi-ples of rhetoric that they took along to a concert or theatre performance of a symphony. Both solo piano sonatas and concert symphonies shared similar designs (sonata form); but the listener's understanding of the two genres was probably quite different.

SALON PERFORMANCES OF SOLO SONATAS

Vienna

At the centre of Viennese cultural life in the reigns of Maria Theresia and Joseph II was the aristocratic salon. Our knowledge of salons comes partly from entries in the diaries, journals and memoirs of those who attended, such as Count Johann Karl Zinzendorf, Georg Förster, Charles Burney and Karoline Pichler.[36] At such salons the participants, consisting of Princes, Counts, Barons; the lesser Viennese nobility (the von Greiners, von Trattners etc.); and wealthy court officials or middle-class businessmen, would exchange ideas, gossip, play cards, discuss their latest reading matter (foreign-language textbooks and novels were popular with the Viennese:

Countess Thun – whose salons will be discussed presently – was quite fluent in English), entertain foreign guests, eat, drink, and listen to music.[37] Such documentation as we possess has survived by accident as much as design and provides a tantalisingly incomplete picture of what was clearly a major slice of musical activity in the Austrian capital and elsewhere.[38] It is seldom possible to recover any programme details of such private gatherings, though we do know that Mozart performed his sonatas in B flat, K.281 and D, K.284 at Hohen-Altheim, the country residence of Count Kraft Ernst von Oettingen-Wallerstein (1748–1802) on 26 October 1777.[39]

We glean something of the character of a Viennese salon of 1772 from the following reminiscence of Charles Burney:[40]

I went to Mr L'Augier's[41] concert, which was begun by the child of eight or nine years old, whom he had mentioned to me before, and who played two difficult lessons of Scarlatti, with three or four by M. Becke[42] upon a small, and not good Piano Forte. All the *pianos* and *fortes* were so judiciously attended to; and there was such shading off [*sic*] some passages, and force given to others, as nothing but the best teaching, or greatest natural feeling and sensibility could produce . . . The company was very numerous, and composed of persons of great rank; there was the Princess Piccolomini, . . . the duke of Braganza, Prince Poniatowsky, lord Stormont, general Valmoden and his lady, Count Brühl, the duke of Bresciano, &c.&c. It was one of the finest assemblies I ever saw. When the child had done playing, M. Mut, a good performer, played a piece on the single harp, without pedals . . .

The room was too much crowded for full pieces: some trios only were played by Signor Giorgi,[43] a scholar of Tartini, Conforte,[44] a scholar of Pugnani, and by Count Brühl, who is an excellent performer on many instruments, particularly the violin, violoncello, and mandoline. The pieces they executed were composed by Huber,[45] a poor man, who plays the tenor at the playhouse; but it was excellent music, simple, clear, rich in good harmony, and frequently abounding with fancy and contrivance.

As Burney notes in detail the names of the performers, the great sensitivity with which the young boy played on a second-rate fortepiano and the musical characteristics of the works played, we may safely assume that these were among the topics he had discussed with L'Augier's visitors. It was clearly a musical occasion that met with Burney's approval.

Burney was also impressed with the salon of Countess Wilhelmine Thun, which he visited on several occasions. He described her harpsichord playing in favourable terms, noting also that '[she] possesses as great skill in music as any person of distinction I ever knew.'[46] This assessment was praise indeed, for her distinguished visitors included Emperor Joseph II, of whom Burney noted:

the Emperor [is] perhaps just [musical] enough for a sovereign prince, that is with sufficient hand, both on the violoncello and harpsichord, to amuse himself; and sufficient judgement to hear, understand and receive delight from others.[47]

Not quite a decade later, Mozart actively sought Joseph's patronage, with mixed success. He complained bitterly to Leopold[48] that a last-minute summons from Archbishop Colloredo had prevented him from meeting the Emperor at Countess

Thun's salon, at which the composer had become a regular visitor. The Countess, for her part, was a staunch patron of Mozart during his early years in the capital, even loaning him her fortepiano for the famous contest between himself and Clementi before the Emperor on 24 December 1781.[49]

Countess Thun's salons were perhaps the most famed in Josephine Vienna and were attended by the principal aristocrats, freemasons, intellectuals, writers and musicians of the day. Competing salons were held by (among others) Franz Sales von Greiner, Count Johann Baptist Esterházy, Prince Dmitri Golitzin and Baron Gottfried van Swieten.[50] In such an enlightened and sympathetic environment piano sonatas were evidently played (and no doubt eloquently discussed), including, perhaps, Mozart's two published collections, K.330–332 (issued by Artaria as 'Op.VI' in 1784)[51] and K.333, 284 and 454 (issued by Torricella as 'Op.VII' in the same year).[52] Many points of detail in these pieces benefit from the intimacy of performance in a small room. The opening movement of K.330 in C contains several formal subtleties which depend for their effect on the listener's close concentration. For example, the recapitulation restates the main secondary idea still in the dominant (bar 106), veering back to the tonic only on its repetition at bar 110; perhaps the most musically literate members of Countess Thun's salon would have spotted such an unusual tonal strategy. More difficult to spot is the role of the sequential phrase that opens the development section (bars 59–66), thematically unrelated to anything in the preceding exposition (or, indeed, the ensuing development). It returns only at the end of the movement (bars 145–50), and functions in a manner analogous to the design of many of Mozart's piano concertos from this time, in which the brief passage closing the 'tutti exposition' is only brought back at the end of the movement, following the cadenza.[53]

Paris

The Parisian nobility also maintained a busy calendar of salons at which many of the foremost literary and intellectual ideas of the age were discussed and at which there was regular informal music making. As in Vienna during the 1780s, accomplishment on a keyboard instrument was recognised as a desirable attribute for a young lady. Diderot's daughter played: Burney described her in 1770 as 'a great performer on the harpsichord, and has a prodigious collection of the best German authors for that instrument.'[54] Earlier that same year Burney had met and dined with the famous claveciniste, M^{dme} Brillon:

After dinner we went into the music room where I found an English [square] pianoforte [by Zumpe] which Mr Bach had sent her. She played a great deal and I found she had not acquired her reputation in music without meriting it. She plays with great ease, taste and feeling.[55]

Doubtless many impromptu and unrecorded piano performances took place in the various salons. Mozart himself had taken part in a private performance at the summer palace of Louis François de Bourbon as a child.[56] On his subsequent return to Paris in 1778, Wolfgang was instructed by his father to seek out as many as possible of their acquaintances made on that earlier visit, including the Duchesse de Bourbon and the Comtesse de Tessé, to whom the sonatas for piano and violin, K.8 and K.9, had been dedicated.[57]

Mozart's experience of Parisian salons in 1778 was decidedly mixed, to judge from his long letter of 1 May,[58] detailing a (presumably introductory) encounter with the Duchesse de Chabot:

I had to wait for half an hour in a large ice-cold unheated room . . . At last the Duchesse de Chabot appeared. She was very polite and asked me to make the best of the clavier in the room . . . I said that I would be delighted to play something, but that it was impossible . . . as my fingers were numb with cold . . . She then sat down and began to draw and continued to do so for a whole hour, having as company some gentlemen . . . while I had the honour to wait . . . At last . . . I played on that miserable, wretched pianoforte. But what vexed me most of all was that Madame and all her gentlemen never interrupted their drawing for a moment . . . Give me the best clavier in Europe with an audience who understand nothing, or don't want to understand and who do not feel with me in what I am playing, and I shall cease to feel any pleasure . . .

On 18 July Wolfgang related to Leopold a happier occasion, among more astute musical company at which he 'played off [i.e. improvised] a galanterie sonata in the style and with the fine spirit and precision of [probably Michael] Haydn[59] and then played fugues . . . My fugal playing has won me everywhere the greatest reputation!'[60] Possibly Mozart's most satisfying musical encounters in Paris were with Count Karl Heinrich Joseph Sickingen (1737–91):

a passionate lover and a true connoisseur of music. I spent eight hours quite alone with him. We were at the clavier morning, afternoon and evening until 10 o'clock, playing, analysing, discussing and criticising all kinds of music.[61]

Possibly among the works Mozart discussed with Count Sickingen were his recent sonatas, K.309, 311 and especially K.310, written about this time in Paris, which Mozart was attempting (unsuccessfully as it turned out) to have published, along with the six sonatas for piano and violin, K.301–6.

Despite such musically rewarding contacts as Sickingen it appears that Mozart's music was not hugely popular with the Parisians. Deutsch quotes a criticism (possibly relating to the 'Paris' symphony, K.297) of Mozart's contrapuntal idiom through which 'the Author obtained the suffrages of Lovers of that kind of music that may interest the mind, without ever touching the heart.'[62]

The A minor sonata, K.310, was written in Paris during the early summer of 1778 and it is not difficult to imagine how its frequently contrapuntal textures would likewise have failed to please this Parisian critic (though he acknowledged that there evidently were 'Lovers of that kind of [contrapuntal] music'. Melodic beauties 'touching the heart' are undeniably present in the slow movement (marked 'Andante cantabile con espressione') and in the episode beginning at bar 143 of the finale, but on the whole, Mozart is making a serious statement on an expansive scale, in which rigorous thematic organisation plays a major part, extending over quite lengthy time-spans. The development section of the opening movement contains a close-knit contrapuntal treatment of one of the exposition themes (bars 58 ff.; see bars 16–20); the finale indulges in an invertible counterpoint texture at bars 203 ff., while melodic reinterpretations of its opening theme's accompaniment rhythm give rise to a polyphonic flowering at bars 87–99. Even within the lyrical Andante Mozart generates much of the forward momentum from the interplay of complementary strands of counterpoint (from bar 15 to the end of the exposition, for example). This 'intellectual' approach to musical organisation and continuity clearly did not have any appeal for a section of the Parisian public which favoured lighter textures and simplicity of melody and phrase patterning. Certainly K.310 is far removed from the galant idiom of Schobert, Eckard, Hüllmandel and J. C. Bach, then in vogue.

Having discussed the broader questions of musical, social and intellectual context posed at the start of this chapter, we must now turn to a consideration of the closer compositional environment within which Mozart's solo sonatas came to being. What did he learn from the piano sonatas of his contemporaries?

CHAPTER TWO

Stylistic models for Mozart's sonatas

SOME PRELIMINARIES

Determining likely influences on Mozart's piano sonatas is no easy task. Any study that attempted a comprehensive survey of such influences would inevitably be frustrated by all or some of the following problems:

(1) Given the wide range of musical styles and genres to which Mozart's acutely receptive mind had been exposed during his formative years, it is unlikely that his sonatas were influenced solely by other sonatas, his trios only by trios, his quartets only by other quartets, and so on. Rather, features of all these various types, and others, were absorbed and reformulated over time. The field of enquiry is potentially endless. Nevertheless, we have to start somewhere, and restricting the repertoire to be studied purely to the piano sonatas of Mozart's contemporaries will at least prove manageable.

(2) During the 1760s and 1770s the 'keyboard' sonata was most often 'avec accompagnement de violon ad libitum', so that, in assessing the sonatas of composers such as Schobert, Honauer, Raupach, Eckard and Hüllmandel (composers whose music Mozart came to know in Paris) it is mainly to their *accompanied* piano sonatas that we have to turn.

(3) We simply do not know (nor are we ever likely to) the full extent of the music Mozart was aware of, and at what stage in his development. His letters, and those of his immediate family, provide many valuable clues and yet are frequently unhelpful (as in the case of Haydn's sonatas, none of which is specifically mentioned – nor is there any reference to any work of his at all before 18 August 1771),[1] or else downright confusing (as in the case of C. P. E. Bach, discussed below). Precise publication dates for the works of a number of relevant composers whose music is discussed in this chapter are often difficult to determine. Rarely, dates appear on title-pages (usually on pirated reprints, rather than first editions); mostly we have to rely on pre-publication announcements in newspapers or else on publishers' catalogues. The latter prove to be a mixed blessing. In the case of Parisian publishing houses, in which music from the pens of many of the foremost composers was engraved (Stamitz, Wagenseil, J. C. Bach, Haydn), we have very good documentation,[2] and yet the catalogues are

annoyingly unspecific at times, noting simply the genre ('Pièces de Clavecin', 'Trios' etc.) and a composer's name ('Bach': J. C. (?), C. P. E. (?), W. F. (?) – even J. S. (?)). Opus numbers are regularly given, but can be confusing. Three examples will suffice to illustrate this minefield:

Johann Schobert's *Six Sonates pour le clavecin . . . oeuvre XIV . . . les parties d'accompagnements sonts [sic] ad libitum* (Paris, auteur; gravée par Mlle Vendôme et Sr Moria), appeared again in Amsterdam, published by Johann Julius Hummel, as *Six Sonates pour le clavecin, avec accompagnement d'un violon . . . oeuvre quatrième*. In this latter form they were advertised in the 1770 supplement V to Breitkopf's thematic catalogue ('Trii di Schobert a Cemb[alo] e Viol op. IV Amsterd[am]').[3]

J. C. Bach's two sets of piano sonatas, Op.5 and Op.17 were each published in a number of separate editions by London and Parisian houses. His Op.17 *Six sonatas for the harpsichord or piano forte, opera XVII* (John Welker; London, 1779)[4] had previously been published in 1774 by Sieber of Paris as *Six sonates pour le clavecin ou le piano forte . . . oeuvre XII*.

Thirdly, Mozart's own 'accompanied' piano sonatas, K.6 and 7, K.8 and 9, K.10–15 and K.26–31, were published respectively as Opp.1 and 2 (Paris, 1764), Op.3 (London, 1765), and Op.4 (The Hague and Amsterdam, 1766). They were available in various pirated editions over the years, including the version of K.26–31 offered as *Six sonates pour le clavecin avec l'accompagnement d'un violon . . . oeuvre IV* by the Parisian firm of Le Menu et Boyer in 1771, and advertised in their catalogue that year under the heading 'Pièces de Clavecin', as 'Mozart IVe' at the price of 7 livres, 4 sols. Neither of these 'Op.IV' sets is to be confused with the *Trois sonates pour le clavecin ou le forte piano . . . œuvre IVe. Mises au jour par M^d Heina* (Paris, 1782), consisting of the solo sonatas, K.309, 311 and 310.[5]

(4) Finally, the sonatas of the foremost piano composers as we now regard them (Haydn and Clementi in particular) appear, for one reason or another, to have had little influence on Mozart's own sonatas. Haydn will be dealt with in detail at the end of this chapter, but Clementi's work may be touched on briefly here. Mozart was clearly aware of Clementi, both as composer and as executant. The two appeared together in a piano contest before Emperor Joseph II on Christmas Eve, 1781.[6] Possibly because Mozart saw Clementi as an unwelcome rival for the affections (and the purses) of the Viennese nobility, his correspondence of this time loses no opportunity to rubbish the Italian.[7] He includes specific mention of Clementi's sonatas in a letter to Leopold of 7 June 1783,[8] which reveals that he had studied Clementi's works in detail but that they had no bearing on his own piano writing:

as compositions they are worthless. They contain no remarkable or striking passages except those in sixths and octaves . . . [producing] an atrocious chopping effect and nothing else whatsoever. Clementi is a *ciarlatano* like all Italians . . . he has not the slightest expression [in his playing, and by implication, in his piano compositions] or taste, still less, feeling.

In the light of all this we clearly have to proceed with caution in pursuing likely sources of influence on Mozart's own solo piano sonatas, most especially, perhaps, the earliest surviving ones, K.279–84, composed during the winter of 1774–5. This early set and the three sonatas, K.309, 311, and 310, were written at a stage in Mozart's development when he still had something to learn from other composers (many of whom are mentioned in his correspondence) and when he was trying to make his mark within the established genres, each of which – including the piano sonata – carried its own patterns of expectation and required from a young composer adaptability above all else. That Mozart was sensitive to the need to cater for a variety of stylistic preferences is confirmed by correspondence between himself and his father from Mannheim towards the end of 1777, in particular regarding the C major Sonata, K.309, written for Rosa Cannabich, which Leopold described as 'having something of the rather artificial Mannheim style, but so very little that your own good style is not spoilt thereby.'[9] Whether Leopold had in mind the opening of the first movement, whose bare octave figure approximates in piano terms to the opening manner of numerous Mannheim symphonies,[10] or some other feature (the unusually decorative Andante, perhaps) is uncertain; this matter is pursued further in chapter 4. The main point here is that by 1777 Mozart was able to adapt the style of his music to the requirements of the particular environment (Mannheim, in this case) with ease.[11]

Exploring the myriad of likely influences on Mozart's piano sonatas is the purpose of this chapter, and for reasons of space it has been necessary to restrict the discussion only to those composers whose piano works were certainly or probably known to Mozart. While it would be quite easy to point to thematic parallels between Mozart's pieces and those of his contemporaries, resemblances of this sort probably amount to no more than standard classical figures: certain turns of phrase, such as a preference for triadically based themes, Alberti bass figures, and so on.[12] Because Mozart absorbed enormous quantities of music in a wide range of styles so early on in his career it is important, when selecting possible stylistic models, to be rigorous with regard to geographical traditions and (especially) chronology. As will be seen in due course, the influence of Haydn's sonatas on those of Mozart has long been accepted as a fact (by Einstein and Wyzewa and Saint-Foix, for instance) but under close scrutiny it becomes quite problematic to establish with certainty. The following account is restricted to those solo (or sometimes accompanied) sonatas by composers known to have been associated with Mozart, or else to whose work there is reference in his, or his family's, correspondence.

WAGENSEIL

Mozart learnt at least two scherzos by the Viennese composer and piano virtuoso, Georg Christoph Wagenseil (1715–77) during 1761, as noted by Leopold in the 'Nannerl-Notenbuch'.[13] Wolfgang met Wagenseil on 13 October 1762 at

Example 2.1   Georg Christoph Wagenseil, *Divertimento* in D, Op.1 no.1 (WV 21), 1st movement, bars 1–6

Schönbrunn palace.[14] Some five years later, during Mozart's second visit to the capital, Wagenseil was ill but still well-disposed towards the young prodigy according to a letter from Leopold to Lorenz Hagenauer in Salzburg of 30 January – 3 February 1768.[15] Wolfgang probably had an opportunity to purchase some of Wagenseil's recent piano sonatas (entitled *Divertimenti*) during one or other of these stays in Vienna.[16] Wagenseil's *divertimenti* were published in Vienna in sets of six: Op.1 (1753); Op.2 (*c*.1755); Op.3 (*c*.1761); Op.4 (1763); a further set of just three was also printed in 1761.

Wagenseil's major contribution to the development of the solo sonata was to make the decisive break from the standard sequence of dance movements typical of the late baroque suites of his teacher, Fux. The number of movements ranges between two and four, though most of Wagenseil's *divertimenti* contain three. Contrasts of texture from phrase to phrase also signal a departure from the baroque. Possibly for Mozart the most attractive features of Wagenseil's *divertimenti* were their piano textures, which, in a passage such as that shown in example 2.1, from the first movement of Op.1 no.1 (WV 21), look towards the emerging classical idiom in their elegant juxtaposition of melodic contrasts and balanced phrases. Strangely, the published works hardly betray the apparent virtuosity of their composer. Wagenseil had been a famous player and a piano tutor to members of the Imperial family and Burney, who met him in 1772, notes that:

[Wagenseil's] left hand had been so ill-treated by the gout, that he was hardly able to move two of his fingers. However, at my urgent request, he had a harpsichord wheeled to him, and he played me several *capriccios*, and pieces of his own composition in a very spirited and masterly manner . . . I can easily believe that he once played better.[17]

THE PIANO SONATA IN SALZBURG

Among solo piano sonatas in Salzburg, Mozart's most immediate models were surely those of his father, Leopold. These must have influenced his early perception of the genre. Three examples survive; all were published in Johann Ulrich Haffner's important anthology, *Oeuvres melées*, which appeared in twelve instalments between 1755 and 1766, copies of which Leopold owned.[18] Leopold shows himself to be somewhat conservative in these pieces in F, B flat and C, each in three movements (fast-slow-fast or minuet). As in a number of examples to be examined presently, the opening allegro movements tend towards 'developed' binary form, in which there is no full tonic recapitulation, a feature which, if not sacrosanct in later examples of fully developed sonata form, was to become one of its most significant manifestations.[19] His F major and C major sonatas contain no tonic return of the opening theme or figure from the beginning of their first-movement expositions; instead, this theme opens the development (commencing straight after the central double-bar), transposed to the dominant, and is thereafter abandoned. The B flat sonata, on the other hand, is built on a more expansive scale altogether, containing a full tonic recapitulation of all significant exposition material (heralded by a reworked transition). In matters of structure, Leopold's works were clearly influential upon Wolfgang's early symphonies and sonatas, for instance in important features of tonal planning such as excursions into the minor mode.[20] Similar techniques are also to be found in analogous places in the piano *Divertimenti*, Op.1 nos. 1 (in C) and 4 (in A) of Josef Antonín Štěpán (Steffan), while the development of no.3 (in F) treats the opening subject extensively in the minor. Steffan's Opp. 1, 2 and 3, published in Vienna between *c.* 1759 and 1763, were known in Salzburg in manuscript copies soon afterwards.[21] In other respects too, Steffan's work, which demonstrates a far surer feeling for the role of tonal proportion in the building of sonata structures than that of Wagenseil, displays some similarities to Mozart's later K.279–84. Full tonic recapitulations are quite common. At times the lyrical quality of Steffan's piano writing comes remarkably close to Mozart's (example 2.2).[22]

Two further Salzburg composers whose piano sonatas require brief mention are Anton Cajetan Adlgasser (1729–77), from 1760 organist at Salzburg Cathedral and at the Dreifältigkirche,[23] and his father-in-law and possible teacher, Johann Ernst Eberlin (1702–62), the court *Kapellmeister*. Like Leopold Mozart, both composers published sonatas in Haffner's anthology, *Oeuvres melées*.[24] Their work must have seemed a touch old-fashioned to Wolfgang Mozart and resemblances between his sonatas and theirs are superficial. While Eberlin's A major Sonata (*Oeuvres melées*, vol.VI, no.3) begins with a sonata-form movement whose exposition is polythematic and whose development incorporates an interesting digression into related minor keys, the sonata as a whole has four movements, of which the third is a minuet and trio and the finale is a fugue. Adlgasser's Sonata in the same key (*Oeuvres melées*, vol.V, no.1), is a 'hybrid' piece, mixing keyboard patterns that would be at

Example 2.2   Josef Antonín Štěpán (Steffan), Sonata no. 57 in E flat, 2nd movement, bars 1–11

home in a baroque suite with an emerging feeling for periodicity. The first movement's opening theme (of which there is subsequently no tonic recapitulation)[25] is
seven bars long. It is repeated in its entirety – producing a symmetrical paragraph
of fourteen bars – and is followed by a number of two- or four-bar balancing
phrases. Mozart pursues a similar strategy at the opening of the C major Sonata,
K.309 (1777), though the resemblance is surely coincidence. The extent of
Adlgasser's influence on the young composer was probably restricted to certain
melodic turns of phrase such as those found at the beginning of the slow movement
of the same sonata, quoted in example 2.3.

GERMAN EXPATRIATES IN PARIS: SCHOBERT, ECKARD, HONAUER, RAUPACH

Mozart discovered the works of these German composers and piano virtuosi
during his first visit to Paris. In 1767, he arranged several movements from their
accompanied or solo sonatas as piano concertos, K.37, 39, 40 and 41.[26] Mozart's
main task in these parody compositions was to slot sonata sections effectively into
a concerto framework, presupposing judicious choice of material (and equally judicious omissions). He may have been helped by his father, judging from the appearance of Leopold's hand alongside Wolfgang's in the autographs. The resulting

Example 2.3   Anton Cajetan Adlgasser, Sonata in A (*Oeuvres melées*, vol. V, no.1), 2nd movement, opening

expansion of sonatas into concertos is analogous to the principle considered theoretically by Heinrich Christoph Koch in the third part of his composition treatise (1793),[27] in which an eight-bar phrase is extended into a fully fledged sonata exposition.

All of these sonata collections of Schobert, Eckard, Honauer and Raupach presumably originated in Paris during the 1760s, though none of the title-pages bears a date. Their frequent reprinting attests to their contemporary popularity. All subsequently appeared in London (perhaps due to J. C. Bach's links with Paris) in editions by Welker, Bremner, and Preston, whose new title-pages betray a growing interest in the fortepiano as an alternative to the harpsichord ('clavecin'). While the Parisian first editions mention only the latter instrument the English reprints routinely specify fortepiano.[28]

Quite how influential the works of these composers were upon the young Mozart is uncertain. Wyzewa and Saint-Foix perhaps overestimate the importance of Schobert.[29] Only a single movement of his Op.17 no.2 was adapted by Mozart as the slow movement of the B flat concerto, K.39, during June 1767, that is, three years after their meeting in Paris noted by Leopold in a letter of 1 February to Frau Hagenauer in Salzburg, in which he describes Schobert as 'mean', 'jealous', 'envious' and a 'laughing-stock' who 'flatters to one's face and is utterly false.'[30] The immediate influence of these four composers as a group is perhaps strongest in Mozart's early accompanied sonatas for piano and violin;[31] nevertheless, their handling of the style and design of individual movements and whole sonatas approaches that of Mozart in his early set of six sonatas, K.279–84, and it is appropriate to examine some of the patterns and procedures developed in their works here.

The number and order of movements tend towards a three-movement plan: fast-slow-fast (or minuet). Schobert favours the polonaise in second place (Op.1 no.2; Op.4 no.2; Op.14 no.1), while the minuet (sometimes with variations) and 'developed' binary forms appear as finales in roughly equal numbers. In Eckard's sonatas the number of movements is variable: half of his Op.1 and Op.2 sonatas are in three movements; of the remainder, two are single-movement sonatas and the others have two movements.

While there are many thematic features in these composers' sonatas that bear passing resemblance to the idiom of Mozart they are less interesting as points of possible influence than are the details of their structure, in particular, the design of first movement expositions; the conclusion of a movement by full tonic recapitulations of both first and second theme-groups; and the emerging use of full sonata form in the finales. Mozart chose sonata form for the finales of K.279, 280, 281 and 282, in which respect he may perhaps have been influenced by sonatas such as Schobert's Op.3 no.2, in G, and Op.14 no.2, in B flat; and Honauer's Op.1 no.5, in D, and Op.2 no.6, in G minor.

In both of Schobert's Op.3 sonatas the expositions unfold according to the pattern that would later become normal for Mozart. Op.3 no.2, in G, for instance, has all the standard ingredients: clearly defined first and second subject groups (each with two or more distinct ideas); a transition modulating to the dominant of the dominant, in preparation for the entry of the second subject in D, and a separate, distinctive, closing theme, stated then repeated.[32] The clear definition of tonal and thematic function within the exposition is perhaps most strongly marked in Honauer's sonatas, particularly as regards the careful preparation of the tonality of the secondary material.[33] In K.279–284, Mozart lays out each of his first-movement sonata form expositions on precisely these lines, though with some variants. He only extends his transitions tonally as far as the dominant, and prefers to bring them back either literally (or nearly so), as in K.281, 283 and 284, or else modified, as in K.279 (curtailed) and 280 (extended), whereas Schobert and Honauer routinely shorten theirs upon recapitulation. Otherwise, the only major difference is of scale (Mozart includes a greater number of themes within each of the tonic and dominant key areas).

Full tonic recapitulations of all important exposition themes occur in Schobert's Op.3 no. 2; Op.4 nos. 1 and 2; Op.14 nos. 1 and 2; Honauer's Op.1 nos. 2, 3 and 5; Op.2 nos. 4 and 5; and Eckard's Op.1 nos. 1 and 3, and Op.2 no.1, which begins its restatement of the opening theme in the tonic minor. Only two of Raupach's Op.1 sonatas contain full recapitulations, the first movement of no. 5, in F (arranged by Mozart as the first movement of his Concerto, K.37) and the finale of no. 1 in B flat (which Mozart reworked as the finale of K.39). Within these various sets of sonatas the shift from 'developed' binary to full-blown sonata form is not a gradual one, however; frequently, as in Honauer's Op.1 set and Schobert's Op.3, both structural approaches coexist within the same publication. In some sets, though, (Schobert Op.14; Honauer Op.2, for instance), the trend is markedly in favour of full tonic recapitulation of all significant exposition material towards the end of the movement.

ENGLAND: PARADIES AND J. C. BACH

From Paris, where they were resident from November 1763 until April 1764, the Mozart family journeyed to London. We do not have a full picture of the range of native English music to which Wolfgang may have been exposed during his stay; there is no mention of Arne's sonatas[34] in the family correspondence, for instance. According to two of Leopold's letters of December 1774[35] the family did own a copy of the only other important sonata publication from England besides J. C. Bach's Op.5 set (to be discussed presently): Pietro Domenico Paradies's twelve *Sonate di Gravicembalo*, (Johnson; London, 1754).[36] In his letter Leopold exhorts Nannerl to 'practise the clavier most diligently, especially the sonatas of Paradisi and [J. C.] Bach.' Paradies's sonatas are all two-movement works in a hybrid baroque-cum-pre-classic style, and it is debatable how strong an influence they might have had on Mozart's understanding of the sonata. In the first movement of no. 1, in G, for instance, there is a full tonic recapitulation of the exposition material (not just its secondary ideas), preceded by some genuine development of its figures following the double-bar; within the exposition itself, though, there is no clear delineation of first theme – transition – second theme – closing theme functions. The exposition of no. 5, in F, by contrast, has a very striking transition, moving from F to G, approaching the second group from its own dominant in the manner of the Parisian sonatas outlined above;[37] but in this case, Paradies omits to recapitulate the first subject in the tonic.

More significant is the impact of J. C. Bach's music on the young Mozart. The Mozarts met the 'London' Bach during their protracted stay in England between April 1764 and August 1765. Wolfgang evidently hit it off both musically and socially with Bach, whose music is frequently singled-out for praise in Mozart's later letters to his father. In one of these, he writes enthusiastically of a chance meeting with Bach in Paris in August 1778 while the composer was over from England to select singers for his new opera, *Amadis de Gaule* (performed in Paris at the end of the following year).[38] Mozart had a particular fondness for Bach's aria, 'Non so d'onde viene' (which he had first heard in London in November 1764 in a performance of the *pasticcio Ezio*), and he used Bach's piano music for teaching purposes in Mannheim in 1778.[39]

In 1772 Mozart arranged three of Bach's Sonatas, Op.5 (nos. 2, 3, and 4) as concertos, K.107. Bach's sonatas had been published in 1766, in versions with both English and French title-pages (but with music engraved from the same plates).[40] They were dedicated to 'son Altesse Serenissime Monseigneur Le Duc Ernest, Duc de Mecklenbourg', and announced in *The Public Advertiser*, London, on 17 April, 1766 (English title) and 1 May (French).[41] The set was reissued by Johann Julius Hummel in Amsterdam (*c.*1766); again by Le Duc (Paris) with engraving by Mlle Vendôme;[42] and in later English editions, printed by Robert Bremner and Peter Welker as *Six Sonatas for the Piano-Forte or Harpsichord . . . opera 5*. As in the case of reprints of sonatas by Schobert and Eckard, mentioned earlier, these English editions specify the fortepiano and harpsichord as viable alternatives. While many of the dynamic markings in Op.5 could be adequately realised on the harpsichord by a change of manual, the opening of Op.5 no.3, in G, which alternates between *forte* and *piano* over a tied crotchet (bar 1), could not, and the entire sonata is heard to best effect on the fortepiano.[43]

Bach's Op.5 sonatas present a mixture of two- and three-movement pieces in which the opening movements mostly approach full-blown sonata form. The G major movement just mentioned clearly betrays its binary form origins and may have been one of Bach's earliest efforts, perhaps composed in Milan before his removal to London in 1762. Its semiquaver passagework is quite Italianate (bars 48 ff., for instance) and closely resembles the Paradies-Galuppi-Rutini idiom that Bach would have encountered in his studies with Padre Martini. Formally, it is an example of 'developed' binary, with twin themes, A^1 and A^2, as described above. The 'first subject' (transposed to the dominant) is stated immediately after the central double-bar; and is then used to generate a modulation through keys that would not be out of place in one of Bach's late father's allemandes (incidentally, the 'topic' of this movement);[44] while the 'first subject' is not subsequently recapitulated, the 'second subject' material, originally in the dominant (bars 17 ff.), is given full restatement in the tonic (bars 66 to the end). Bach designs his exposition in a rather more forward-looking way: it distinguishes between a first subject; a transitional modulation to the dominant of the dominant (bar 16); a secondary idea in the related key (bars 17 ff., followed by a separate theme at bar 23); and a cadential closing figure (bar 27), typically stated twice, the second time at the lower octave. In this case Bach adds a final cadential gesture (bars 31–2), developed sequentially in the second section of the bipartite form (bars 57 ff.).

Still more modern in outlook is Op.5 no. 4, in E flat. This displays Bach's understanding of sonata form at its most developed. Like its predecessor, it contains a 'segmented' exposition, clearly divided into thematic, transitional, and cadential elements, but here the transition (bars 17–29) plays a much more significant part in the proceedings. It contains several motives of its own (bars 17, 21, 24) and covers a reasonable proportion of the exposition as a whole (twelve bars out of forty-three) while confirming the tonal shift to B flat very firmly.[45] Both first and second subject groups are divided into separate thematic parts, some of which are taken up in the ensuing development. For instance, at bar 60 Bach employs the transition figure from bar 24; this is followed immediately by the subsidiary idea from the first subject group (bar 5). At bar 72 a new theme is introduced, leading to a significant preparation for the tonic-key recapitulation that begins in bar 85.

Such technical devices must have appealed to Mozart, in whose own sonatas similar principles and proportions obtain. Not only the lyrical quality of Bach's melodies but their subtle interrelationships are built upon in Mozart's work. Among these may be noted the rhythmic relationship between the closing tag of Bach's exposition (bar 41) and the consequent part of the second subject at bar 31, and the similarity of profile between the first subject, the initial transition figure and the antecedent portion of the ensuing second subject (bar 29), all of which span six crotchet beats, but with varied rhythmic and harmonic articulation and emphasis.

The most direct connection between J. C. Bach's Op.5 sonatas and those of

Example 2.4
(a) Johann Christian Bach, Sonata in D, Op.5 no.2, 1st movement, bars 19–26

(b) Mozart, Sonata in D, K.284, 1st movement, bars 22–5

Mozart is to be found in the first movement of the D major sonata, K.284, written
in Munich in February–March 1775, and clearly with a copy of Bach's Op.5 no. 2
(in the same key) to hand.[46] There are a number of close resemblances between the
two movements, not only in their use of a full textured 'orchestral' piano idiom, but
in terms of exposition design (both formal and thematic). Indeed, one reason for
Mozart's second thoughts over this movement may have been that he felt the
exposition to have been too closely modelled on Bach's. Is is notable, for instance,
that Mozart's original version repeats the arresting opening gesture; this is sacrificed
in the final text which leads straight into the transition over a tonic pedal.
Immediate repetition of the opening material is characteristic of many of J. C.
Bach's expositions, including that of the D major, Op.5 no. 2. Likewise omitted
from Mozart's later version is the formal closure of the exposition which originally
had ended (like Bach's) with a two-fold statement of a cadential figure; this is
replaced by a cadential trill more familiar in concerto expositions than in the solo
sonata.[47] Nevertheless, a number of features from Bach's exposition remain thinly
disguised in one or other of Mozart's two versions of K.284. The 'orchestral' writing
of bars 9 ff. of Bach's piece returns at bars 13 ff. of Mozart's; the transition in both
works ends virtually identically (though Mozart moves only as far as the dominant),
while Mozart's second subject is quite obviously a reinterpretation of Bach's refined
cantabile (example 2.4a and b). Possibly also Mozart's memorable left-hand arpeggio figure at bar 38 of the final text ultimately derives from Bach's right-hand figure

(c) Mozart, Sonata in D, K.284, 1st movement bars 26–38

at bars 31–2, though Mozart invests it with greater energy. Additionally, there are close connections between Bach, bars 31–3 and Mozart, bars 38–40; Bach, bars 41–2 and Mozart, bars 44–5. Comparison of the two composers' treatment of the second subject group (polythematic in each case) throws some light on Mozart's method of recasting his model (example 2.4b and c).

Beginning in bar 22 of the final text,[48] Mozart introduces his second subject without any chordal underpinning whatsoever (in contrast to Bach's tonic–dominant alternations) and continues without stressing A major at all strongly until bar 38. For sixteen bars the new tonic region is present only by implication;

the chords used are those which suggest, but do not state, A major. For example, the momentum in bars 30–2 (D6–5 E6–4 F sharp 6) is directed towards the F natural 6♯–5 (marked out by melodic syncopation) in the next bar, which itself functions only to highlight the ensuing dominant pedal over E (compare Bach's bars 26–9), finally yielding to strong A major at bar 38. During this section Mozart shows an awareness greater than Bach's of the possibilities of coordinating melodic chromaticism with harmonic, accentual and cadential forces to lend the sharpest possible structural focus to his exposition.[49] Compare, for instance, the treatment of the figure at bar 24 of Bach's exposition (the 'scotch-snap' rhythm, highlighting a rising chromatic step, E sharp – F sharp), which Mozart introduces in a variety of contexts (independent of Bach's original rhythm) between bars 27 and 37 of his own exposition:

(1) melodic decoration (bars 27–8), particularly the syncopated scale-descent on the level of the *beat*;
(2) harmonic preparation (bars 30–33), marking-out a rising scale-progression, – this time on the level of the *bar*), leading up to the pedal-point on E at bar 34;
(3) harmonic articulation (bars 34–6), giving melodic identity to a pedal-point that clinches the arrival of the dominant, A, at the conclusion of this section of the movement. Bach uses the device only as a means of local 'colour' in bar 24 of his piece: Mozart, by contrast, gives this innocuous gesture an unexpected new prominence. In one sense, then, his is a 'parody' exposition, maintaining some of the more obvious gestures of its model while reinterpreting some of its thematic and structural details.

In summary, one may note several senses, both general and specific, in which J. C. Bach's approach to the solo sonata would have impressed itself on Mozart's growing awareness and mastery of the genre:

(1) *Clear sectionalisation*:   First subject (or group)
                                 Transition (often to V of V)
                                 Second subject (or group)
                                 Closing, cadential theme (usually repeated)
(2) Lyrical character of themes, often involving descending stepwise fourth progressions in uniform quavers.
(3) Tendency to use scalic material and non-lyrical rhythmic 'fragment' figures for transitions and closing themes, so that the different elements of the exposition ((1) above) are clearly demarcated not only by tonal grammar but by thematic quality too.

Bach never uses sonata form in the finales of his Op.5 sonatas. Three of his Op.17 sonatas do have full sonata form finales, though: nos. 3, 4, and 5, in E flat, G and A major respectively. Two of Leopold Mozart's letters (16 and 21 December 1774) refer to 'sonatas of [J. C.] Bach' owned by the Mozart family.[50] They give no details but probably refer to Op.5 (which they had known since the London visit);

although Bach's Op.17 had been published in Paris earlier in 1774 it is unlikely that
the Mozarts already had them in Salzburg by December.[51] If Mozart knew Bach's
Op.17 sonatas at all it is most plausible that he bought them in Paris in 1778.[52] In
this case, of course, they could not have had any bearing on the composition of
K.279–84 (of 1774–5), or K.309 and K.311, both written by the end of the previous year,[53] although Bach's tendency to use sonata form finales in his later set is far
closer to Mozart's practice than any of, say, Haydn's sonatas before this time.

C.P.E. BACH

The influence of C. P. E. Bach's piano pieces upon Mozart is highly problematic.
Mozart had included a reworking of Bach's character-piece, *La Boehmer* (Wq.
117/26; H 81), of 1754, as the finale of the concerto arrangement, K.40, in 1767.[54]
Beyond this, though, specific connections between the two composers' piano works
are no more easy to establish with certainty than those popularly thought to exist
between those of C. P. E. Bach and Haydn. A. Peter Brown has attempted, through
a painstaking survey of the chronology of C. P. E. Bach prints available in Vienna,
to pursue substantive links, and has concluded that if Haydn learnt anything from
Bach, it was through a study of his textbook, *Versuch über die wahre Art das Clavier
zu spielen* rather than Bach's music.[55] Many of C. P. E. Bach's solo piano works were
available in Vienna in published editions, including the 'Prussian' Sonatas of 1742,
the *Musikalische Allerley* (1761) and *Sonates à l'usage des Dames* (1769). More significant for Mozart's solo sonatas were the various volumes of Bach's sonatas with
'varied reprises', as will shortly become apparent. Mozart could have become
acquainted with these in Vienna as early as 1767: the original *Sechs Sonaten fürs
Clavier mit veränderten Reprisen* (1760) were available in the Imperial capital from the
Trattner bookshop in 1767, while the 1763 second supplement (*Zweyte Fortsetzung
von sechs Sonaten fürs Clavier*) could be obtained from the same source in 1769.[56]
Though C. P. E. Bach does not feature prominently in Mozart's letters, we nonetheless learn that he particularly sought out Bach's fugues, which he encountered at
the Sunday salons of his patron, Baron Gottfried van Swieten:

I go every Sunday at twelve o'clock to the Baron van Swieten, where nothing is played but
Handel and [J. S.] Bach. I am collecting at the moment the fugues of Bach – not only of
Sebastian, but also of Emmanuel.[57]

There is a puzzling connection between Mozart's solo piano sonatas and those of
Bach 'mit veränderten Reprisen'. On 6 October 1775 Leopold Mozart wrote the
first of several letters to the publisher Johann Gottlieb Immanuel Breitkopf in
Leipzig, offering some of Wolfgang's music. He mentions, without being specific,
symphonies, quartets, trios, sonatas for violin and cello, solo violin sonatas

or clavier sonatas. In regard to the latter perhaps you would like to print clavier sonatas in
the same style as those of Carl Philipp Emanuel Bach 'mit veränderten Reprisen'? These
were printed by Georg Ludwig Winter in Berlin, and this type of sonata is very popular.[58]

The first point to establish is which sonatas Leopold had in mind. Evidently they were *solo* piano sonatas, distinguished clearly in the letter from those for violin (that is, piano sonatas with violin accompaniment, such as K.26–31 of 1766).[59] As to which group of solo piano sonatas was meant, two possible candidates suggest themselves: one is the set of six, K.279–84, all composed within the year preceding Leopold's letter, and possibly written for use in concerts at Munich, the city for which *La Finta Giardiniera* was composed and premièred on 13 January 1775;[60] the other is the lost group of four, K.App. 199–202/ 33[d-g], written apparently, like the violin sonatas, K.26–31, in 1766, and known only from their incipits in a manuscript catalogue compiled by or for Breitkopf in 1770.[61] That Breitkopf had already been in possession of these sonatas since 1770, and that they had remained unpublished, may have prompted Leopold's letter of 6 October 1775, suggesting some new sonatas (K.279–84?), written in a style which he assures Breitkopf was 'very popular'.[62] Sadly, Leopold's repeated requests received no favourable response. In 1781 he was still trying to clinch a deal and by now the tone had become a little ruffled: 'I have been wishing for a long time that you would print some of my son's compositions. Surely you will not judge him by the clavier sonatas which he wrote as a child?'[63]

Given all these circumstances, the probability is that the six sonatas, K.279–84, were those described by Leopold as 'in the same style as those of Carl Philipp Emanuel Bach "mit veränderten Reprisen"'.[64] In which case there is no small dificulty, since Mozart's sonatas are stylistically quite unlike those of Bach's 1760 and 1763 sets, which Mozart may have known. Bach's B flat Sonata, Wq. 50/5; H.126, from the original 1760 set,[65] provides, in its first movement, an elegant demonstration of the principle of varied reprise, which he provided, according to his preface, because such modification was the fashion and because it was his experience that:

Most frequently the modifications [supplied by performers] are out-of-place, and negate the spirit of the composition, its emotional content, and the flow of its ideas: nothing could be more infuriating for the composer. Even when the work is performed by someone with all the abilities to make proper changes in it, will it follow that he will always be in the right mood to do so? . . . .In composing these sonatas, I have kept in mind those beginners and Amateurs, who, because of their age, or because of their occupation, have neither the time nor the patience to tackle difficult exercises . . . I have therefore written down explicitly everything which might make the performance of these pieces most effective, so that beginners and amateurs may play them with freedom, even when they are not so disposed.[66]

Formally, this B flat movement is a sonata design after the 'developed' binary model mentioned in relation to Schobert, Honauer and J. C. Bach earlier in this chapter. Bach's opening material lasts for twenty bars and is given an immediate written-out reprise; the second of the binary sections starts off in bar 41, incorporating a 'recapitulation' at bar 53, concluding at bar 72, after which there is once more a written-out reprise of this whole section. None of Mozart's sonatas follows such a procedure: the expositions (and sometimes the remainder of the movement too, as in K.310) are always given simple repeat-marks, with no written-out indications of the manner in which embellishments, over the same harmonic bass-line, might be added the second time around. Indeed, the character of Mozart's thematic material rarely lends itself to such treatment, so clearly is each element defined within the unfolding polythematic design, both individually and contextually. Bach's figures, on the other hand, are of quite a different cut, purposely built around 'abstract' melodic gestures – demonstration models, in a sense, of thematic etiquette – such as the falling scale-steps which lie behind his opening figure. Added to this are regularity of phrasing, uniformity of harmonic pace and a particular concentration on falling semitones or tones at the ends of phrases, all of which invite the kind of sophisticated variation that Bach provides, and which is utterly at odds with the dynamic quality of Mozart's discourse. Only in the first sonata, Wq. 25/1; H.50 (in E flat), of Bach's *Zweyte Fortsetzung*[67] (in which the repeated sections are merely noted by repeat-marks) does his style come at all close to that of Mozart's later K.279–84. Its first movement is fairly extended with polythematic first- and second-subject areas (E flat to B flat). After the double-bar, the first subject is restated in the dominant (not Mozart's usual practice)[68] and there is some recollection – if not actual development – of exposition material (principally from the second group) in new keys. Bach follows this with a full recapitulation, along with the necessary tonal adjustments. In the slow movement there are some expressive melodic embellishments, while the finale is a full-blown sonata form – also Mozart's preference for the finales of his 1774–5 sonatas, though Bach's brisk 3/8 writing is quite unlike that of, say, K.281 or K.283. The remaining sonatas in Bach's 1763 publication tend towards 'developed' binary in their opening movements – different again from Mozart (and Haydn) in their sonatas of the 1770s.

In the light of this, it is strange that Leopold should have commended his son's sonatas to Breitkopf principally on the grounds that they were similar to Bach's 'Reprise' works. Only in the most general sense of 'embellishment' can Mozart's procedures be said to approach those of Bach, and then only in the slow movement of K.281 in B flat in which, at the recapitulation of the opening idea (the movement is in sonata form, and not like Bach's models, 'developed' binary), Mozart embellishes the theme in triplet semiquavers (bars 59 ff.). The technique of embellishment *per se* is taken to far greater lengths in the slow movement of the 'Cannabich' sonata, K.309 in C (1777) whose form may be expressed thus: A; A Rep: B; B Rep; Coda. Here at each return of the main theme, Mozart adds a new layer of richly expressive *cantilena*. Likewise, in the slow movements of K.332, in F, and K.333, in B flat, (*c.* 1781–3; 1783–4), extensive decoration of the opening melody is applied upon its return (K.332, bars 21 ff.; K.333, bars 51 ff.). Both examples are quite different cases from K.309, however, since their slow movements are sonata structures with clear tonic recapitulations of their main themes. In the case of K.332 only the first edition[69] transmits the embellishments (given in small type in *Mozart Sonatas II*, pp. 37–9). The principle of fully-notated decorated binary reprise (A; A Rep: B; B Rep – as in C.P.E. Bach's designs) is found only in K.309's slow movement among all of Mozart's sonatas.

RUTINI, HÜLLMANDEL, MYSLIVEČEK

On 18 August 1771 Leopold Mozart wrote to his wife asking her to ensure that a selection of sonatas was sent to an unnamed family friend in Milan. These were to include 'some good sonatas by Rutini, for instance in E flat, in D, and so on . . . If Nannerl wants to play them [i.e. after they have been sent], she has other copies, for they are amongst the sonatas by Rutini which were engraved in Nuremberg.'[70] While Leopold's meaning is not wholly clear, it seems evident that the Mozarts owned at least one copy of at least one of the several sets of Rutini's sonatas (Opp.2, 3, 5, and 6) published (by Johann Ulrich Haffner) in Nuremberg before 1771. Among these sets only the last contains sonatas in the keys specified by Leopold: they are Op.6 nos. 6 and 2 respectively.[71] These pieces, published in 1765, must have been among Nannerl Mozart's favourites, and although their textures are far simpler than anything found in Wolfgang's early sonatas, in certain structural matters they accord closely with the work of J. C. Bach, discussed above. The E flat sonata, Op.6 no.6, has a finale in 'developed' binary form that nonetheless incorporates most of the features of a 'segmented' exposition, in particular, a twofold statement of a distinct closing theme, itself recapitulated in the tonic towards the end.[72] Structurally closer to Mozart's own emerging sonata style are the sonatas of Rutini's Op.7 (Bologna, 1770), which coincidentally contains sonatas in E flat and D (nos. 5 and 3).[73] This collection was aimed at beginners ('Ai Signori Dilettanti di Cembalo') and written consequently in a deliberately simple style. Metastasio commented favourably on their 'noble and correct harmony and their uncommon inventive fantasy'.[74] Each begins with a Prelude (to test the instrument, or warm-up the fingers), followed by two movements, the first approximating to sonata form. The expositions of nos. 2 and 4 of this set (in F and G, respectively) contain significant excursions into minor keys (example 2.5a), also a feature of the second subject groups of Mozart's K.279 and 280. The second subject of Rutini's Op.7 no.5 (E flat) defines the new dominant key of B flat by means of a modulating sequence rather than straightforward statement (example 2.5b), a procedure analogous to Mozart's K.279 at bars 16 ff. The development sections of Rutini's Op.7 nos.1, 2 and 6 quote the first subject in the dominant, which Mozart normally avoids,[75] but that of no.4 (G major) begins with a free harmonic passage in triplets unrelated to the preceding exposition, but defining new harmonic space. This technique is also found in some of Mozart's early sonatas, namely K.279, K.280, and the final text of K.284.

Of the various virtuosi and composers active in Paris during Mozart's third visit of 1778, only Nicholas-Joseph Hüllmandel (1756–1823) is mentioned in Mozart's letters. In that of 3 July 1778[76] Mozart describes Hüllmandel's sonatas (examples of which survive for both piano solo and piano with violin accompaniment) as 'very fine' and offers to buy copies for his father. Hüllmandel studied with C. P. E. Bach

Example 2.5
(a) Giovanni Marco Rutini, Sonata in F, Op.7 no.2, 2nd movement, bars 19–25

(b) Giovanni Marco Rutini, Sonata in E flat, Op.7 no.5, 2nd movement, bars 12–18

in Hamburg, settling in Paris in 1776, where he frequented the various salons and published several collections of sonatas. In 1789 he fled the Revolution for London, where he carved out a career as a teacher and performer.[77] Choron and Fayolle noted in 1801 that Hüllmandel was 'un des premiers pianistes de l'Europe. Comme compositeur il jouit aussi d'une grande réputation.'[78] Some years later he was regarded by Grétry as 'The first composer who so united the parts of his sonatas, as to prevent their servile repetition: an intermediate passage in them frequently connects the two parts into one'.[79]

By 1778 Hüllmandel had published three collections of sonatas.[80] Which one(s) Mozart knew is unclear, although one may observe some points of compositional craft that Mozart would have admired in the first movement of the A minor Sonata, Op.3 no.2 (1777), such as the harmonic interest of the polythematic second-subject group, the continuation of which (bars 52 ff.) contains some passagework very similar to Mozart's second subject in the first movement of K.310 (in the same key), written the following year (example 2.6a).[81] Of particular interest is Hüllmandel's brief minor-key preparation (bars 48–9) for the ensuing C major theme, a strategy adopted in K.310's transition (bars 16 ff., preparing for C major at bars 22–3).

Among Hüllmandel's sonatas there are numerous Mozartean turns of phrase, of which the decorous right-hand part of example 2.6b, from the slow movement of Op.1 no.2, in E flat, is a typical illustration. On a deeper technical level some particular compositional principles stand out in the work of both composers. In one of these a short fragment of a phrase (most often from the middle or end) is isolated and separately reworked in varied repetitions and sequential extensions. In bars 45–51 of example 2.6a Hüllmandel's use of the technique is clearly seen; Mozart employs it in, for instance, K.333 in B flat, in which the falling scale-step at the beginning of bar 2 of the first movement initiates much of the right-hand narrative during the next ten bars. Possibly that aspect of Hüllmandel's style that most appealed to Mozart was the way in which he controls the continuity of a passage such as that from the opening of Op.1 no.4, illustrated in example 2.6c, while exhibiting a wide surface variety of theme and rhythm. The sectional structure of this passage is quite clear (bars 1–4; 5–8; 9–12; 12–16; and 16–19, incorporating an elision of the third and fourth phrases at bar 12). The continuity of all this is assured first, by the repetition of bars 5–8, and secondly by the omnipresence of the upbeat rhythm. The corresponding section of Mozart's K.330 (c.1781–4, also in C) proceeds along similar lines. Again there is considerable variety of material, underpinned by a continuity whose basis is repetition (bars 1–2=3–4; 5–8=9–12, elided, as in Hüllmandel, with the start of the next phrase; 12–13=14–15; 16–18). There is a difference, though. Whereas the only *varied* repetition in Hüllmandel's passage occurs at bar 11 (cf. bar 7), in Mozart this becomes almost an article of faith – every reprise except the last is embellished in some way. The exception (bars 12–13, repeated identically in bars 14–15) points to Mozart's firmer grasp of structure. For Hüllmandel, the embellishment of bar 7 at bar 11 is a cue to introduce continuous

Example 2.6
(a) Nicholas-Joseph Hüllmandel, Sonata in A minor, Op.3 no.2, 1st movement, bars
36–53 (violin omitted)

Example 2.6 (*cont.*)
(b) Nicholas-Joseph Hüllmandel, Sonata in E flat, Op.1 no.2, 2nd movement, bars 25–32
(violin omitted)

right-hand semiquavers for a while, and is a creative use of varied melodic repetition (over the same harmonies) to articulate the progress of the texture in a meaningful way. Mozart, however, proceeds a stage further. He isolates the falling scalic cadential approach in the right hand of his bars 7–8, embellishing it in bar 11 (this much being analogous to bars 7 and 11 of Hüllmandel), and then goes on to decorate it still further at bar 13, and to repeat this final stage in its evolution (bar 15). Over the course of these few bars the figure *evolves*, leading the narrative forwards, indeed dictating the continuity of the passage. Whereas Hüllmandel's variant in bar 11 signals only a local textural change, Mozart's is developed in such a way that it ultimately plays a part in defining the phrase structure (bars 1–18: 2+2; 4[2+2]; 4[2+2(elided)]; **2+2** +2, in which boldface indicates the final stage in the evolution of bar 7).

Mozart first encountered the composer, Josef Mysliveček (1737–81) in Bologna in 1770. Like Mozart, Mysliveček was awarded the diploma of the Bolognese Accademia Filarmonica, and during the 1770s he enjoyed considerable success as an opera composer throughout Europe. Strong affinities have been noted between the styles of the two composers.[82] He is affectionately referred to in Mozart's correspondence, especially after his admission to a Munich sanatorium, where Mozart

(c) Nicholas-Joseph Hüllmandel, Sonata in C, Op.1 no.4, 1st movement, bars 1–19 (violin omitted)

visited him in October 1777. Mysliveček was said to enjoy such a high reputation
in Italy that he could hire and fire singers at will; he apparently offered to help secure
an opera commission for Mozart during their meeting in Munich, but without
success.[83] Mozart wrote approvingly of Mysliveček's piano sonatas. He told his
father: 'I know what Mysliveček's sonatas are like, for I played them at Munich.
They are quite easy and pleasing to the ear. I should advise my sister to play them
with plenty of expression, taste and fire . . . they are sonatas which are easy to memorise and very effective when played with the proper precision'.[84]

Mysliveček's instrumental music, though a minor aspect of his output, is by no
means inconsequential. He published orchestral works, chamber music and a small
quantity of solo piano music.[85] Six sonatas remain in manuscript in the
Staatsbibliothek Preußischer Kulturbesitz, Berlin (incomplete), and the Bayerischer
Staatsbibliothek, Munich.[86] In the Munich source, the 'Sei Sonati/ Per il Cembalo/
Del Sig.[r]/ Giuseppe Misliwecek/ Detto il Boemo' are as follows:

1   (C major)   Allegro con spirito – Minuetto (-[Trio] Minore)
2   (G major)   Andantino – Minuetto (-[Trio] Minore)
3   (B flat major) Vivace – Rondo andantino
4   (F major)   Allegro con spirito – Presto
5   (A major)   Allegro – Minuetto (-[Trio] Minore)
6   (D major)   Allegro con Brio – Minuetto with 6 variations

It is not difficult to grasp those features of Mysliveček's sonatas that appealed to
Mozart. Thematically, they have a singable quality, and there is little independent
polyphonic activity in the accompaniment. Their phraseology is predictable. They
make no great technical demands upon the player (frequently the texture consists
of just two polyphonic parts), and while there is passagework to be mastered, this
consists of patterns that require few awkward changes of hand or thumb position.
In the unfolding of larger paragraphs, Mysliveček proceeds effortlessly between
themes of differing melodic character, as one might expect of a skilled master of
opera. No wonder Mozart described his sonatas as 'pleasing to the ear' and 'easy to
memorise'.

In terms of external design, Mysliveček's sonatas bear no resemblance to those of
Mozart: all are in two movements, of which the second is usually a minuet – a design
previously noted as typical of the Viennese divertimento of Wagenseil and Steffan,
but which never became part of Mozart's thinking. What Mozart's sonatas share
with those of Mysliveček's is a variety of thematic, harmonic, rhythmic and textural
activity to be found within a passage such as example 2.7. Probably both composers mastered such techniques through their experience of Italian opera. The
continuity of Mysliveček's D major Allegro (of which the portion shown begins
with the secondary theme)[87] relies in part upon the subtlety of its motivic evolution, in which each successive phrase seems to reinterpret the material of its predecessor, producing that quality of irresistible forward momentum so characteristic of
Mozart's own work.

Example 2.7
Josef Mysliveček, Sonata in D (D-Mbs, Ms.1712), 1st movement, bars 18ff

Example 2.8   Haydn, Sonata in F, Hob. XVI: 23, 2nd movement, bars 21–4

HAYDN

It has long been supposed that Mozart's early sonatas were influenced by those of Haydn. Einstein specifically points to Haydn's set of six sonatas Hob. XVI: 21–6, written for Prince Nicklaus Esterházy during 1773 and published by Kurzbock in Vienna the following year, as models for Mozart's K.279–84.[88] He regards the F major Sonata, Hob. XVI: 23, as a model for Mozart's K.280 in the same key, citing in particular the similarity in character of their 'siciliana' slow movements. There are, at first sight, some compelling factors suggestive of a direct link: for example, the dotted quaver-semiquaver-quaver melody, C–D flat–C, and the abrupt move from F minor to A flat. On the other hand, there are significant differences too. While both movements are in binary form, Mozart's second section contains a full-blown tonic reprise of the movement's opening theme preceded by a 'false recapitulation' in the dominant (bar 33). Neither feature is found in Haydn's second section, which begins with a reference to the opening idea and then turns its attention to development of a secondary idea originally introduced in bar 5. The structural plans of these two movements are quite different. If Mozart's siciliana was, as Einstein believed, influenced by Haydn's then influence here takes a 'negative' form in which Mozart borrows a couple of ideas (the opening theme and initial tonal shift to A flat) as a starting point (a stimulus to his imagination, as it were) and works the remainder of the movement out along outwardly different lines. Recent work on 'influence' suggests that this type of 'negative' relationship – in which distinctive features of the 'model' are radically reinterpreted in the 'parody' – exists in the six quartets Mozart dedicated to Haydn in 1785.[89] On closer inspection, Mozart's siciliana in K.280 begins to look like a reinterpretation of Haydn's, particularly in the harmonic and tonal planning of its second half (example 2.8). Beginning immedi-

ately after the barline, Haydn introduces the following prominent harmonic progression:

(1) a diminished-seventh chord (A–C–E flat–G flat)
(2) a chord of B flat minor
(3) a 'chromatic dominant minor ninth' (G–B–D–F–A flat), in which the minor
    ninth, G–A flat is quite pronounced
(4) a protracted C minor/major region (bars 24–32³), the later part of which is a
    pedal-point preparing for the reintroduction of the tonic, F minor, at bar 32³,
    where the main secondary idea is reprised.

Mozart begins his second section with a harmonic progression likewise moving
from a diminished-seventh chord (A–C–E flat–G flat) through B flat minor, but
replaces the next step (3) in Haydn's chord sequence with a descending chromatic
pattern (bars 29–32) ending with a fermata on a G in bar 32 that reinterprets
Haydn's chromatic minor ninth, G–A flat (3), as a melodic line in the left hand.
While the broad outline of Haydn's scheme is retained up to and beyond this point,
its proportions are significantly reordered, Mozart's main revision being the
strengthening in tonal articulation (G – C minor/major – F minor): Haydn's stage
(4), the C minor/major region, is reinterpreted by Mozart as a 'false reprise' of the
opening theme (bar 33), a strategy that further enhances the full tonic return of
F minor in bar 37. Towards the end of the movement both Haydn and Mozart recast
an originally diatonic close (in the first section) in more extended chromatic terms
(Haydn, bars 34–7; cf. bars 17–18: Mozart bars 54–6; cf. bars 19–20), Mozart's
rising chromatic semiquavers in bar 56 perhaps being inspired by Haydn's falling
chromatic triplets at bar 37. 'Influence' of this sort is not immediately obvious and
suggests that, for Mozart, meaningful compositional connections operated on a
deeper level of structure. Are there other instances of such connections?

Example 2.9a and b shows the beginning of the development sections of the C
major piano sonatas, Hob. XVI: 21 (1773) and K.279 (1774–5), respectively. Both
composers commence their developments with a tonal shift from the dominant
region (G) to a fermata on a chord of E (Haydn, bar 67; Mozart, bar 76), after which
they each introduce a 'false reprise' of the first subject. At first sight, this seems quite
a plausible illustration of 'model' (Haydn) and 'imitation' (Mozart).

Among the critical vocabulary for defining the quality of influence, that is, the
degree of relatedness, one technique that has recently found favour with musicologists is that termed the 'Revisionary Ratio', a concept originally introduced
some twenty years ago in the study of poetry by the distinguished literary theorist,
Harold Bloom.[90] Might Mozart have reacted in K.279 to Haydn's finale according
to one of Harold Bloom's 'revisionary ratios', specifically the first ratio, 'clinamen'?[91] According to this theory, Mozart would have been so seized by Haydn's
scheme and yet compelled to recreate it *in his own terms*, that in the finale of K.279
he would have deliberately 'misread' Haydn (suppressing certain elements of the
model, while highlighting instead others that better serve his new purpose). In

Example 2.9
(a) Haydn, Sonata in C, Hob. XVI: 21, finale, bars 49–67

Haydn's development the phraseology is notable for its dislocation, beginning with a three-bar phrase (bars 49–51, based on the transitional figure from bar 22 of the preceding exposition) and continuing with a succession of two-bar phrases lasting up to the fermata in bar 67. The initial three-bar phrase features a pedal G, whereas the two-bar phrases which follow wind around a circle-of-fifths. Mozart – assuming, for the moment, that he knew Haydn's piece – recasts this material as follows:

— He converts Haydn's opening three-bar phrase-groups into successive three–fold statements of a (two-bar) imitative figure, (the main finale theme, not a transitional figure): (1) bars 56^4–62; (2) bars 62^4–8. Thereafter, the development continues in two-bar groups to the fermata in bar 76.

(b) Mozart, Sonata in C, K.279, finale, bars 57–76

— He reverses the order of Haydn's functional elements: the pedal-point is now associated with a later stage in Mozart's approach to the fermata (bars 72–4, on E), while Haydn's circle-of-fifths is reinterpreted as a falling sequential pattern in Mozart's scheme and placed *first* (associated with the three–fold imitative statements).

— As can be seen in example 2.9b, Mozart's passage involves some subtle overlapping of two- and three-bar phrase elements at bars 72–4. It is perhaps not without significance that the implied three-bar phrase (formed by pattern-repetition), exactly marks the boundaries of the pedal-point, as if a reminiscence of the 'model'.

Haydn's influence on Mozart is, of course, supported by Mozart's acknowledgement of a stylistic debt in the preface to the 'Op.10' Artaria edition of his six string quartets, K.387, 421, 428, 458, 464 and 465 (1785). Mozart's earlier attempts at quartet writing, K.168–73, composed in Vienna during August and September 1773, seem to betray the influence of Haydn's recent Op.20 quartets (composed the previous year), notably in the positioning of the minuet in third place and in the choice of fugal finales in K.168 and 173. The Andante of K.168 actually takes up the same subject as the fugal finale of Haydn's Op.20 no.5 (and in the same key, F minor).[92] Unfortunately, the matter is not so straightforward: Haydn's Op.20 *Divertimenti* (as they were entitled) were not published until 1774, and then not in Vienna, where Mozart might have known about them, but in Paris, by La Chevardière; they were published in a different edition by André in Offenbach in 1775. If Mozart knew Haydn's Op.20 quartets, he must have known them in manuscript.

In the case of Mozart's piano sonatas the evidence for Haydn's influence is by no means clear-cut. Generally speaking, the two composers' sonatas inhabit different domains, most especially as regards the nature of their piano writing. While it would certainly be going too far to describe Haydn's as 'disjointed' it is not especially idiomatic, tending instead to proceed in a succession of fragmentary gestures, each one sharply characterised in some way (particularly in diversity of rhythm). In such a style the motives acquire memorability as much by local contrast as by intrinsic identity. Indeed, the detailed content and continuity of Haydn's expositions only become apparent after careful reflection (one is grateful in performance for the exposition repeat). Haydn's 'Auenbrugger' sonatas of 1780 contain good illustrations of this kind of exposition: Hob. XVI: 36 in C sharp minor, Hob. XVI: 38 in E flat, and Hob. XVI: 20 (composed some nine years previously), whose diversity is particularly remarkable. Mozart's sonatas are, by comparison, models of fluency, the easy unfolding of their narrative disguising only thinly the virtuosity of the player-composer. Even a cursory glance at any of the Viennese sonatas, K.330–576, will be sufficient to show that their piano idiom is utterly different from Haydn's.

The whole question of Haydn's influence on Mozart's early sonatas is therefore troublesome, and requires some reassessment here. While it cannot be denied that in the case of the slow movements of Haydn's Hob. XVI: 23 and Mozart's K.280 the expressive, even plaintive, use of the classical language is undoubtedly similar, this is not in itself proof of a direct connection; as A. Peter Brown has remarked, sicilianas in the minor mode are by no means unusual at this date.[93] There is in fact no documentary evidence to show that Mozart knew Haydn's 'Esterházy' sonatas when he composed his own set of six, K.279–84. Haydn's sonatas were advertised in the *Wienerisches Diarium* on 26 February 1774, and published later that year. They were not therefore available in print during Mozart's 1773 visit to the capital, though the possibility that these sonatas were circulating in manuscript cannot be ruled out. No work of any sort by Haydn is referred to in the Mozart family correspondence, save for a trio in F major,[94] which Leopold mentions in a letter to his wife from Verona, dated 18 August 1771.[95] No record survives of any personal contact between the two composers prior to 15 January 1785.[96] No early copies of any of Haydn's sonatas survive in the library of St Peter's Abbey in Salzburg (which contains sonatas by Steffan and others, mentioned above). In the light of all this, the assumption that Mozart's K.279–84 derive stylistically from Haydn's 'Esterházy' set appears far from secure.

Haydn's 'Esterházy' sonatas remained popular and were reprinted after 1774. There is no reason why they may not have been known to Mozart in later years (especially after he had settled permanently in Vienna) and so had some bearing on Mozart's more mature sonatas, starting with K.330–333. These were written during the early 1780s in Vienna, where Haydn's sonatas Hob. XVI: 27–32 (1776) were available in authorised manuscript copies; where the 'Auenbrugger' set (Hob. XVI: 35–9,20) was published by Artaria in 1780; where the three sonatas Hob. XVI: 40–2 were available from 1784; and where the late Hob. XVI: 48 and 49 were just possibly on sale through Breitkopf's Viennese agents before July 1790, when Mozart's D major Sonata, K.576, was composed (though it is equally possible that by this date, when Mozart and Haydn were in frequent contact, Haydn had introduced Mozart to his latest piano works in pre-publication manuscript copies). Clearly Haydn's work needs to be borne in mind when assessing Mozart's developing sonata style, but the subject must be approached with caution, especially from the chronological point of view. In addition, the two composers' conceptions of the overall shape of piano sonatas should be considered carefully. From his earliest efforts, Mozart's was a three-movement plan (most frequently fast-slow-fast);[97] such a succession was never so sacred to Haydn: the fifth of the 'Esterházy' sonatas, in E flat, is in two movements; Hob. XVI: 30 (1776) has no clearly separated slow movement, merely a link between the Allegro and the concluding Minuet; Hob. XVI: 40–2 (1784) are all two-movement designs, among which only Hob. XVI: 41 has a first movement in sonata form; Hob. XVI: 48 (1789/90) begins with a set of double-variations, alternating major and minor modes, and marked 'Andante con espressione', followed by one of the composer's most familiar Presto rondos. Likewise of continuing significance throughout Haydn's piano sonatas is the presence of the minuet, either as a middle or final movement: this is seldom found in Mozart's sonatas (K.282 is one example, K.331[98] is another).

Turning next to the specifics of their sonata form first movements, we find that the links between the 'Esterházy' sonatas and Mozart's set, K.279–84, prove equally tenuous. Beyond such obvious features as the clear separation of first subject, transition, second subject and closing ideas within a tonal frame moving from tonic to dominant (or relative major) there is little of specific technical substance that unites the two sets of sonatas. In both pre-compositional decisions and subsequent execution the two composers' paths rarely cross. All of Mozart's six expositions are richly polythematic (particularly in the second subject group); Haydn's first and last (Hob. XVI: 21 and 26) are, by contrast, 'monothematic' in the sense that the first and second subjects begin identically, although his second subject groups always introduce additional melodic material during their course.[99] Hob. XVI: 25 in E flat is an exception. Its exposition contains at least nine distinct themes, most of which are subsequently used in a freely ordered development, mixing first and second subject ideas. For example, the second subject themes of bars 15 and 22 are developed in reverse order (bars 33 and 36), followed (bar 39) by what had originally served as the preceding transitional figure (bar 8).[100]

A distinctive feature of Haydn's 'Esterházy' sonatas is the increasing significance of transitions within the first-movement expositions. This is equally true of Mozart's in K.279–84. Even here, though, the differences are more marked than the affinities. Whereas Mozart prefers to modulate only one degree sharp of the tonic (or else to an imperfect cadence still within the tonic, as in K.279) Haydn normally establishes the dominant of the dominant.[101] All except one of the 'Esterházy' set (Hob. XVI: 22) incorporate important minor-key passages into their exposition structures. While minor-key insertions are found in the expositions of K.279 and 280, these are purely 'diatonic' and generally restricted to contributing elements of a harmonic progression (K.279, bars 27–9, for instance); Mozart prefers to reserve minor-key excursions for development sections. Occasionally, as in the first movement of K.283, bars 33–5 and 38–40, Mozart introduces a brief chromatic progression (untypical of Haydn, though bar 17 of Hob. XVI: 22 comes close).

Both composers' expositions are rounded off by distinctive closing material in the new key (transposed back into the tonic at the end of the movement as a whole); frequently the figure is repeated, sometimes with a change of octave register: Haydn, Hob. XVI: 23, bars 40 ff.; Hob. XVI: 21, bars 45 ff. – with upward octave displacement of the repeat; Mozart, K.279, bar 31 – with embellishment of the repeat; K.280, bars 34 ff.; K.283, bars 43 ff. – with embellishment of the repeat; K.284, bars 38 ff. While this is the closest structural parallel between Haydn's 'Esterházy' sonatas and Mozart's K.279–84 it is not in itself proof of a direct link: the procedure is also found in the Op.5 sonatas of J. C. Bach (no. 2, bars 34 ff., no. 4, bars 36 ff., for instance), a set Mozart had known at first hand since the 1760s.

Haydn's developments routinely commence with a reference to the first subject in the new key, a procedure met with previously in this chapter. Sometimes this takes the form of a straightforward quotation, sometimes the theme is reworked in new combinations, as in Hob. XVI: 26. Subsequently there is always reference to other exposition material, and there is always a full tonic recapitulation, beginning with the first subject. Mozart's developments proceed along quite other lines, according to one of the following plans: either they are non-thematic, that is based on new material (those of K.279, 283 and 284 have nothing obviously to do with

the exposition)[102] or they pick out just one exposition motive (K.280 and 281).[103]
A typical illustration of the first plan is found in K.284, which proceeds through
two stanzas of 'patterned' harmonic sequence (bars 52–60 and 60–6) before leading
back to D major for the recapitulation. A similarly non-thematic development is
that of K.279, again sequentially based but in this case subtly linked to the exposition, for the rhythms of bars 39 ff. and bar 48 derive from bar 1 and bars 5 ff.

The foregoing survey of Mozart's stylistic inheritance in the realm of the solo piano
sonata has necessarily been selective. Some composers' work has been omitted altogether. František Xaver Dušek (1731–99), Mozart's friend, at whose house in
Prague he finished *Don Giovanni*, wrote piano sonatas containing many stylistic
properties similar to Mozart's, though in an altogether simpler idiom.[104] The sonatas
of Leopold Kozeluch (1747–1818) probably all appeared too late to have affected
those of Mozart.[105] At the other extreme, the sonatas of J. C. Bach were clearly of
the greatest significance. From Bach, Mozart learnt something of the elegant,
cantabile style of melody, effective piano textures and use of contrasting registers and
the skilful pacing of harmonic events, but above all, perhaps, a sense of proportion,
enabling him to build upon the work of Schobert, Honauer and their contemporaries, in which the 'segmented' sonata exposition, so central to the classical language, at last became standardised. The influence of Haydn's sonatas remains
something of a problem. It is by no means as conclusive as has previously been supposed: in fact, the relationship of Haydn's sonatas to those of Mozart's is as enig-
matic as that of C. P. E. Bach's sonatas to Haydn's own, and is a question to which
the answer remains elusive.

PART TWO

SOURCES

CHAPTER THREE

Six sonatas, K.279–84

On 21 December 1774, Leopold Mozart wrote to his wife from Munich specify-
ing various preparations which would need to be made before their daughter
Nannerl set out to join her father and brother for the first performance of *La finta
giardiniera*, which ultimately took place on 13 January 1775 to great acclaim.[1]
Leopold refers in his letter to some of Wolfgang's sonatas which he wishes Nannerl
to bring with her, along with some variations – K.179 and K.180 – and sonatas by
[J. C.] Bach, Paradisi and others. Perhaps these were the five sonatas, K.279–83, to
which a sixth, K.284 (written for Baron Thaddeus von Dürnitz at Munich in
February or March 1775),[2] was subsequently added. The 'Dürnitz' Sonata is stylistically quite different from its companion pieces: it is rather longer; includes a
Polonaise en Rondeau as its central movement; has an extended variation finale; is
of a much higher order of technical difficulty than anything in K.279–83; and, most
important, has a first movement conceived on an orchestral scale, probably reflecting the preferences of Baron von Dürnitz for a big sound comparable to the orchestral music with which he would have been familiar at the court of Karl Theodore,
Elector Palatine, whose famous 'Mannheim' orchestra only relocated to that city
from Munich in 1778.

Against this hypothesis must be set the appearance of the autograph manuscript[3]
which gives the impression of having been written in a single sweep, without the
slight differences in handwriting that might be expected if it had been compiled,
say, in two sittings a few months apart.[4] Regrettably, Mozart's paper gives us no help
in assigning a precise date to the sonatas; while it is also found in parts of acts II and
III of *La finta giardiniera*[5] (suggesting that all six sonatas might have been written in
Munich around the same time as the opera, say, February or March 1775), it is of
a type readily available in Salzburg since at least as early as 1772.[6] So the sonatas may
either have been begun in Salzburg towards the end of 1774 (in which case they
may indeed be the sonatas referred to in *Anderson* (no. 192)), or they may all date
from spring 1775 (in which case the sonatas mentioned in that letter cannot be
these, and remain a mystery).

Whatever its true date may be, there is a significant quantity of evidence for
regarding the autograph of K.279–84 as Mozart's *composing* score. The most dramatic case concerns the first movement of K.284 in D, in which Mozart continued

Example 3.1   Mozart, Sonata in E flat, K.282, Menuetto I, original (cancelled) beginning
of second section

for a page and a half with a version of the first movement with which he evidently
became unhappy, since he cancelled it and began afresh with the now familiar
version.[7] Further evidence that the autograph of K.284 was – at least in part –
Mozart's composing score is not hard to find. The variation finale as we know it
prepares for the close with a kind of structural expansion in the penultimate variation 11 (Adagio cantabile) which is a 'double variation', fully written-out in the
form A-A'-B-B', followed by the concluding variation 12 ([Allegro], 3/4). This was
not Mozart's original intention, however, as is revealed by the last two pages of his
autograph. The initial sequence of these sections was as follows: variation 11,
phrases A and B; variation 12, bars 1–2 (cancelled); variation 11, phrases A' and B';
variation 12 (headed as such in Mozart's hand). In heavy inking Mozart then recast
this sequence into the now familiar double variation by appending roman numer-
als I, II, III and IV at appropriate points (corresponding to A A' B and B' above).
So Mozart's original variation 11 consisted of bars $1–8^2$ followed by bars $16^3–25^2$,
the two parts being separated by repeat-marks (which he subsequently forgot to
cancel); and his original variation '12' of the remaining portions of what we know
as variation 11 of the final text (bars $8^3–16^2$, and bars 25^3 to the end). Such large-
scale rethinking of design is not found in Mozart's autographs of K.279–83,[8]
although in these sonatas too there are a number of 'second thoughts', mostly of
local significance. For instance, at bar 14 of the second movement of K.282, in E
flat, Mozart originally wrote the version shown in example 3.1. He decided to
replace the chromatically descending line in the left hand with a contrary-motion
pattern that actually fits better with the continuation, e flat-e natural-f in bars
15–16. Presumably he had already fixed this phrase-ending in general terms (and
how it would fit, proportionally and cadentially, into its surroundings) and so sacrificed the continuing chromaticism (in itself, quite acceptable) in the interests of a
smoother whole. A subtler type of revision is found in bar 11 of the first movement
of K.280, in F, in which Mozart altered the third beat from (semiquavers) a-e'-c'-f'
to (semiquavers) a-f'-c'-f'. The original implies the temporary introduction of an
inner contrapuntal part movement from e' to f' (highlighted above) on a syncopated
quaver value; Mozart evidently found this too fussy and impractical within the
tempo marking 'Allegro assai'.

Mozart's choice of key (C, F, B flat, E flat, G and D) for these six sonatas is in line with the typical patterns found in published sets during the classic era, including those of J. C. Bach and Haydn, as well as those by Schobert, Eckard and others whose works Mozart discovered during the 1760s. J. C. Bach's Op.5 set of sonatas (which Mozart certainly knew) contains works in B flat, D, G, E flat, E and C minor; his later Op.17 (1774/ 1779) has sonatas in G, C minor, E flat, G, A and B flat. Rutini's Op.6 (*c*.1760) offers examples in A, D, F, G, G minor and E flat; his Op.7 (in which each sonata commences with a simple Prelude (marking out the tonal area)) has the sequence C, F, D, G, E flat, A. Haydn's six 'Esterházy' sonatas, Hob. XVI: 21–6, are in the keys of C, E, F, D, E flat and A; the next two sets, Hob. XVI: 27–32, 35–9 and 20, are in G, E flat, F, A, E, B minor and C, C sharp minor, D, E flat, G, C minor, respectively.[9] The predominance of keys such as C, G, D and F major may perhaps be ascribed in part to the origin of the piano sonata as a work for piano with violin accompaniment: the most popular keys lie quite comfortably on the violin. Coincidentally, these same keys were among those most acceptable to the ear before the widespread adoption of systems of equal piano temperament during the eighteenth century. It will not have escaped notice, though, that E flat major is prominent in those sets selected above.[10] Composers who aimed their sonatas at the market-place evidently took care to mix together works well within the capabilities of the amateur (and involving relatively few of the black notes on the piano) and those which gave rise to more complicated and demanding changes of hand position, imposing more substantial technical challenges. E flat was considered to be one of these more 'difficult' keys, as were E major and B flat, and it is immediately obvious that in J. C. Bach's Op.5 set the two most demanding sonatas are nos. 4 and 5 in E flat and E, respectively. Op.5 no.3, in G, is by contrast rather easy to play: indeed, its variation movement seems deliberately designed as a teaching piece, introducing piano figurations in graded order of difficulty. Mozart included sonatas in E flat among K.279–84, and while they have their particular challenges resulting from the flat keys it should not be assumed that K.279, 280, 283 and 284 (in the more straightforward keys) are of the 'easy' variety. On the contrary, these works include many tricky moments, such as the development section of K.279's first movement (particularly bars 39–57), or the whole of K.283's finale. The D major Sonata, K.284, while in an 'easy' key, is actually the most demanding of the six (and, incidentally, is far more difficult than J. C. Bach's Op.5 no.2, on which its first movement was probably modelled in part). In the Mozart family correspondence these sonatas are referred to as 'difficult'. Leopold assured his wife and son on 17 November 1777 that Wolfgang's sonatas were regularly played and carefully practised by Nannerl back home in Salzburg: 'we always choose the most difficult ones and especially your works in C major [K.279] and F major [K.280] with the minor movements, which we often pick out to practise.'[11] This letter confirms, incidentally, that more than one copy of these sonatas existed at this time, for Wolfgang was himself playing them in Mannheim during late 1777 and early 1778.[12] Various reports survive of his performances:[13]

16–10–77	Augsburg	K.283
19–10–77	Heiligenkreuz Monastery	K.283
22–10–77	Augsburg	K.284 and possibly K.279
27–10–77	Hohen-Altheim	K.281; K.284
2–11–77	Mannheim	K.279–84 complete
6–11–77	Mannheim	one of K.279–84

On 4 February 1778 Wolfgang explained to his father that Mlle Weber 'played my difficult sonatas at sight, *slowly*, but without missing a single note!'[14] Given the date, it is just possible that he meant not K.279–84 but the newly-composed C and D major sonatas, K.309 and K.311, although circumstantial evidence suggests that K.279–84 were meant. Although he had sent his father a manuscript of K.309 for copying in November–December 1777[15] no mention in the surviving correspondence of this time is made of K.311, and it is unlikely that Mozart would subsequently have mentioned in passing a work which his father did not know.[16]

It is somewhat surprising that these sonatas, which Mozart played so frequently on his tours, were never published as a set during his lifetime. Some correspondence survives between Mozart's father and the publisher Breitkopf, offering these works (among others) for publication,[17] but only the D major Sonata, K.284, subsequently appeared in print along with K.333 and the violin and piano sonata, K.454, in 1784 as 'Op.VII'[18] – and then in a much revised version suggesting that, in preparing this public version of his work, Mozart was eager to display a more sophisticated awareness of the possibilities of the fortepiano than was evident in the 1775 autograph. At their most radical, these revisions amount to wholesale recasting of the right-hand part of variation 11 of the finale. The differences in detail may be seen in *Mozart Sonatas I*[19] in which the readings of the autograph and the 1784 edition are aligned together. They may well reflect an advance in Mozart's handling of the instrument, particularly after his discovery of Stein's fortepianos in 1777,[20] and his removal to Vienna in 1781, after which he quickly found favour among the aristocracy as a piano (meaning fortepiano) performer. The 1775 autograph and the 1784 print diverge in two significant respects: dynamics and articulation. While the autograph contains only a *piano* indication at the beginning of this variation the print introduces them at every opportunity (even individual semiquavers at bars 7 and 24 now have alternate *forte* and *piano* signs). The reason for such a profusion of dynamics in this later text is far from clear. One explanation might be that Mozart intended it as a teaching aid, providing precise guidance on the shaping of a phrase such as bars 0^3–4 by careful dynamic shadings. It is noteworthy that in the analogous bars 8^3–12 of the theme the original dynamics are altered from *p cresc* | (1) *f* | (2) *p sf cresc* | (3) *f p cresc* | (4) *f calando* | to *p cresc* | (9) *p cresc* | (10) *f* | (11) *p cresc* | (12) *f p* | – tasteful contrasting suggestions for the benefit of an amateur fortepianist, perhaps. As a particular didactic illustration we might take the *sf* right-hand tied crotchet D at the beginning of bar 6, after which it was evidently necessary to drop immediately to *piano* in the accompaniment in order that the decoration on beat 2 could remain audible above the Alberti figures (implying also limited sustaining tone on the instruments of the 1780s). Yet we ought to proceed down this road only with the greatest caution. For one thing this variation is an extreme case within K.284. Elsewhere in the sonata the printed text, while more dynamically 'expressive', diverges from that of the autograph less radically. For another, it should be remembered that this sonata is technically very demanding and not an obvious choice for anything other than *advanced* teaching purposes. In addition, the first item in 'Op.VII' – the first movement of the B flat Sonata, K.333[21] – is very short on dynamics, though not on articulation marks. In this piece, as in K.284, the application of dynamics (and especially contrasting dynamics pointing out the profile of a phrase), seems mainly to have been reserved for expressive sections, as at bars 19 ff. of the slow movement (though, curiously, the moment of greatest harmonic tension, immediately after the central double-bar, has no dynamic indication whatever in either the autograph or the print). There is a noticeable tendency towards increasing sophistication of dynamic range in Mozart's sonata slow movements between K.284 and K.333, the Andante of K.309 being an especially good example, singled out for comment in more than one of the family letters.[22] If such shadings also reflect Mozart's typical performance habits about 1784 then it would seem that he had become a master of dynamic contrast for expressive effect, and that this was of considerable importance in the development of his fortepiano idiom. Returning to the finale of K.284, it should be borne in mind that, within variation 11 as a whole, the application of articulation marks plays just as 'expressive' a role as dynamic gradation. In particular, there are hints here and there that an element of *rubato* was intended at times (such as the last beat of bar 11): the articulation of the last beat of bar 11 includes two staccato dots for each of the descending four-note demisemiquaver groups and in performance, this articulation could perhaps be clarified only by a slight *rallentando* before resuming tempo at the barline (the same principle might be adopted also in bar 15, beats 1–2, which have identical articulations, and even for the alternate *f p* semiquavers in bars 7 and 24, particularly the latter if a smooth finger *legato* in octaves were aimed at).[23]

If the above digression has given the impression that, relatively speaking, Mozart's fortepiano music about 1774–5 made only modest demands on the dynamic sensitivity of that instrument, now is the time to restore the balance. In fact, the autograph of K.279–84 is, at times, quite particular in its application of dynamic and articulation markings. In the slow movement of K.279, for instance, there occur a number of phrases whose markings go further than anything found in J. C. Bach's Op.5 sonatas. While Bach includes detailed performance directions, they are never combined in so sensitive a way as found in the second section of Mozart's Andante (beginning at bar 29). Judging by the autograph, it would seem that K.279–83 (and later, K.284) were all conceived for a touch-sensitive instrument. For the most part they can only be satisfactorily realised on such an instrument: bars 11–13, 51–3 and 71 of K.279's Andante, for instance; while the passage at bars 18 ff. (repeated at bars 58 ff.) clearly makes most sense if the lyrical nature of the counterpoint is given continuity by means of tonal balance and shading on the fortepiano rather than on a two-manual harpsichord, on which the dynamic contrasts have to be effected by ungainly jumping between the manuals. Additionally, the actual mechanics of the harpsichord lend undue prominence to the element of surface *discontinuity* in the Andante because of the uniformity of attack, a problem that becomes especially acute at bars 22–5; such local contrasts of surface rhythmic detail, texture and register are more comfortably resolved into a meaningful whole on a fortepiano – here as elsewhere among these six pieces – by virtue of the greater degree of control the player exercises over the generation of tone (including quality of attack and decay), and over the balancing of voices within the polyphony. Identifying a fortepiano on which K.279–83 might have been composed is, however, problematic. Hardly any evidence of fortepianos in Salzburg exists before late 1780. Just one instrument prior to this date survives ('Zweybrucken 1775'), in the Salzburger Museum Carolino Augusteum, and there is no positive evidence to link this instrument with the Mozarts.[24] Possibly K.279–83, if indeed composed in Salzburg before Wolfgang and Leopold set out for Munich on 6 December 1774, were conceived on the family's five-manual clavichord.[25] Such information on Mozart's playing as survives from this time suggests that he was not altogether familiar with the fortepiano. Schubart's *Deutsche Chronik* of 27 April 1775 reflects on a contest between Mozart and Captain Beecke:[26]

In Munich last winter I heard two of the greatest clavier players, Herr *Mozart* and Captain *von Beecke*; my host, Herr Albert . . . has an excellent fortepiano in his house. It was there that I heard these two giants in contest on the clavier. Mozart's playing had great weight, and he read at sight everything that was put before him. But no more than that; Beecke surpasses him by a long way. Winged agility, grace [and] melting sweetness [characterised his playing].

While there is ambiguity in this passage – clavier (harpsichord) and fortepiano are used interchangeably – the comment 'melting sweetness' suggests a touch-sensitive piano and that the critic (signed simply 'Y') meant fortepiano in this instance. If so, it would seem that by late 1774/early 1775 Mozart's touch sensitivity was not as advanced as his rival's, suggesting, perhaps, that he was relatively unfamiliar with the fortepiano. This would not, of course, have prevented him from writing for the instrument, notating, in the six sonatas, K.279–84, dynamic shadings and articulations which he could imagine, but not, as yet, fully realise in performance. A couple of years later, however, Mozart had first-hand acquaintance of Stein's fortepianos (and previously those of Späth) [27] and was regarded by one Augsburg critic as a skilled player: 'the rendering [of K.284, among other works] on the fortepiano so neat, so clean, so full of expression.'[28] Wolfgang's advancing mastery of the fortepiano during the late 1770s is confirmed by other reports, such as that by his mother in a letter to Leopold Mozart, written in Mannheim at the end of 1777:

Everyone thinks the world of Wolfgang, but indeed he plays quite differently from what he used to do in Salzburg – for there are pianofortes here [there were evidently none back home], on which he plays so extraordinarily well that people say they have never heard the like. . . . Although Beecke has been performing here and Schubart too, yet everyone says that Wolfgang far surpasses them in beauty of tone, quality and execution.[29]

Close investigation of the autograph of K.279–84 affords us some insight into Mozart's composing habits (assuming that this was indeed a 'composing' score – for which more evidence will be advanced presently). The following remarks are based on a detailed examination of the ink shadings in the autograph, often of a subtlety of variation invisible in even quite good-quality reproductions: they can only be accurately detected in the autograph itself. In advance of the conclusions it must be admitted that this type of investigation is a perilous one: at best they are interpretations of the present-day appearance of the ink shades, which, to some degree may have been affected by chemical changes over 200 years; and, of course, they may be (unintentionally) 'selective' – reinforcing a pattern that, on reflection, seems logical but is, in fact, illusory. This much is freely acknowledged. However, repeated scrutiny of the manuscripts convinces me that they have some validity, which I shall have to ask the reader to take on trust. It will be helpful to state the methodology and the conclusions in outline ahead of the evidence. Mozart habitually employed two methods of writing-out (by which I mean composing out of his head – or fingers – onto the page). These are revealed by looking for 'fade' in the strength of ink through a bar or a phrase. The inking is of two 'types': 'type 1' inking involves a pronounced 'fade' of the ink horizontally across the page in one stave (usually the right-hand one) to the end of a phrase. In such a case, Mozart evidently raced ahead with whatever was the leading melodic part, afterwards returning to the beginning of the phrase to fill-in the accompaniment.[30] There are many examples of this type in the autograph of K.279–84, in the first movement of K.283, a movement of pronounced melody-and-accompaniment texture (the opening phrase – bars 1–4, or even 1–8; and the secondary idea in the dominant, beginning at bar 22). 'Type 2' denotes a type of inking relatively uniform in blackness within each bar, and which, on close examination, is seen to be the result of Mozart redipping his pen frequently between writing individual noteheads (which are correspondingly 'blobby'). In such a case, the conclusion is undoubtedly that he wrote slowly, even hesitantly, carefully working-out the precise harmonic or textural details (during which time his quill required reinking). Most occurrences of type 2 inking coincide with passages that involve some particular difficulty (an awkward harmonic progression, for instance), of which we may assume he had a general, but not fully formed aural grasp, and which he conveyed onto paper with some caution.

Several examples will clarify the two procedures, beginning with a 'type 1' horizontal ink fade. In the F major Sonata, K.280, it appears from the inking that in bars 95–108 the right-hand triplet quavers were written in one sweep and the crotchet pairs in another (rather than a whole bar at a time). This suggests that, while he was transmitting the triplets to paper Mozart retained a clear idea of several dimensions simultaneously: the length of this passage and to what cadential degree it was directed – a half cadence on C in bar 108; and also its detailed (sequential) harmonic progressions (which would subsequently be completed by the addition of the crotchet pairs).

Bars 29–32 of the 'Siciliano' slow movement of the same sonata illustrate 'type 2' quite well (illustration 3.1). Here Mozart had quite a difficult harmonic progression

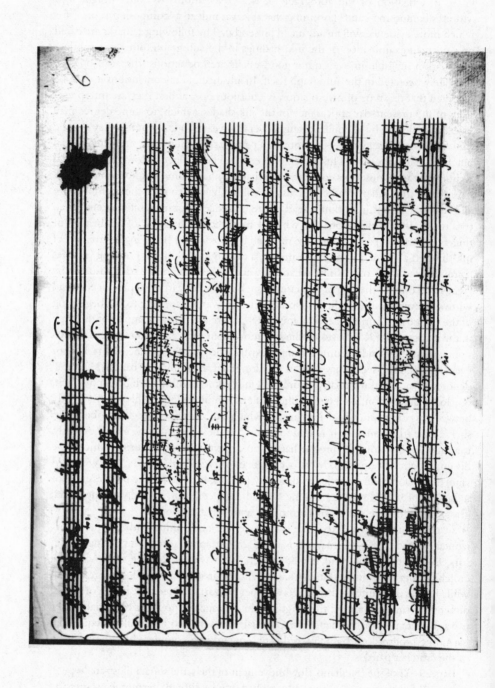

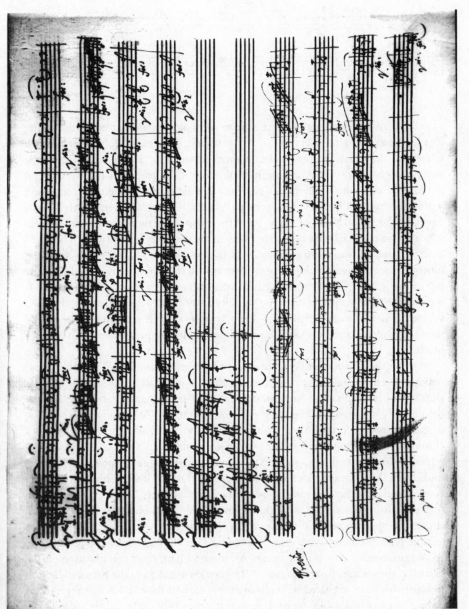

Illustration 3.1 Mozart, Sonata in F, K.280, 2nd movement, autograph (Biblioteka Jagiellonska, Kraków)

Example 3.2   Mozart, Sonata in F, K.280, 2nd movement, hypothetical sketch of bars 29–32

as well as an intricate contrapuntal texture to work out, and the pattern of the inking clearly shows frequent redipping of the pen (and numerous 'blobby' noteheads). Clearly in these bars he proceeded tentatively, a beat at a time, confirming the written notes against his emerging mental grasp of the passage. I believe that, on the basis of variations in the blackness of the noteheads it is possible to reconstruct within the notes of bars 29–32 a working 'sketch' for these bars, in which Mozart first laid the foundations of these bars (the main contrapuntal voice-leading, as shown in example 3.2) and only then filled-in the sextuplet semiquavers of his elaborate texture, leaving insufficient space at the end of bar 31 for the left-hand and inner-part semiquavers, tightly squeezed-in against the dotted quaver (tied) f′ at the top of the texture. (That the semiquaver sextuplets were written after the treble f′ is clearly proved by the fact that they partially cover over Mozart's tie from this note which turns *downwards* – had the f′ been written *after* the semiquavers he would surely have turned this tie *upwards*, so avoiding the already-present semiquaver noteheads.)

At times the autograph offers examples of both type 1 and type 2 inking in close proximity. The Adagio first movement of the E flat Sonata, K.282, begins with a clear type 1 horizontal ink fade through the right-hand theme (extending as far as the quaver g′ in bar 4). When the theme returns (at bar 16) the texture is still that of melody and accompaniment, but with the additional harmonic element of a chromatic descending bass line, d flat′–c′–c flat′–b flat, to the end of bar 18. In this phrase Mozart's inking changes to type 2, with many visible redippings of the pen (indicating that Mozart evidently picked his way through it with some care), and a consequently 'blacker' appearance overall compared to bars 1–4. In the exposition of the G major Sonata, K.283, both types of inking are on show. As mentioned above, the opening melodic phrase and secondary theme (starting at bar 23) each exhibit type 1 inking, with clear horizontal fade through the melody line (the accompaniments being added later). As soon as harmonic complications arise, however, the inking changes to type 2. In bars 33–4 and 38–9 the harmonic idiom suddenly becomes saturated with chromatics – each of the two-chord progressions having been worked-out (and written-out) chordally, rather than melodically through the topmost part. In bars 45–7 (and again in bars 48–51) the inking reverts back to type 1, in which the left hand was evidently written first (exhibiting a detectable ink-fade through to the cadential g-a-A) and the right-hand decorations added later. For the recapitulation of the main theme, beginning at bar 72, Mozart's inking changes from the original type 1 (melody-accompaniment) to type 2, although the texture here remains the same. The explanation for the shift is presumably that this is not a straightforward repetition of the original opening paragraph but incorporates the harmonic interruption and sequential continuation (bars 75–83) which Mozart evidently conceived of in harmonic terms, rather than as a melodically-driven line with accompaniment that could simply be filled-in at a later stage. He worked the passage out a bar at a time on the page, with the result that these bars appear uniformly 'blacker' than their surroundings, with many apparent redips of the pen.

Probably in all the specific cases discussed above Mozart already had a more-or-less clear impression of the passage in question before writing the details on the page. The autograph would seem to have been a composing score, rather than a 'fair copy', a fact supported by the presence of two distinct systems of inking, varying consistently according to the differing 'melodic' and 'harmonic' contexts of the music. If Mozart had been copying these sonatas out from pre-existent draft manuscripts then he would have had no need to vary his system of writing so much (he could simply have written out the music bar by bar, phrase by phrase, or line by line, according to some logical procedure of *copying* something already notated). The autograph of K.279–84, on the contrary, looks like a score into which things were *composed* – a record of the direct process of transmission from his mind onto the page.

CHAPTER FOUR

Three sonatas, K.309–11

ORIGINS

These three sonatas, which belong to the journey Mozart undertook with his mother to Mannheim and Paris (September 1777–January 1779), were eventually published as 'Opus IV' in about 1782 by Franz Joseph Heina in Paris. In fact, Mozart may have offered them to Heina shortly before his departure from the French capital in the autumn of 1778, by which time he certainly had other recent works ready for publication there, including the clavier variations, *Je suis Lindor*, K.354, as well as the clavier and violin sonatas, K.301–6, and the 'Paris' symphony, K.297, published by the rival firm of Sieber.[1] The publication of these solo sonatas is a matter we will return to in due course.

All three were evidently composed within a period of less than a year, K.309 (C major) and K.311 (D major) being complete (probably) by mid-November 1777; the more famous A minor Sonata, K.310, was, according to the autograph,[2] written in Paris in the summer of the following year. Virtually nothing else of substance is known of the origins of K.310 and 311. Mozart made no reference at all to the former in his letters, while in the case of the latter just a couple of brief references to a sonata, apparently promised to M[lle] Josepha Freysinger during Mozart's brief stay in Munich (24 September – 11 October 1777), occur in two letters to his cousin, Maria Anna Thekla Mozart, who lived in Augsburg.[3] In complete contrast, copious reference is made to one other sonata – almost certainly K.309 – in Mozart's correspondence with his father during late 1777 and early 1778 – so much so that we know that its first movement was completed the day after Mozart and his mother had arrived in Mannheim from Augsburg on 30 October 1777 (perhaps it was begun in Augsburg, or else during the journey between the two cities, which took four days);[4] the Andante was complete by 4 November[5] and the Rondo finale was finished on the morning of 8 November.[6] Mozart wrote it for Rosa Cannabich, daughter of the leader of the Elector Karl Theodor's famous Mannheim orchestra, Christian Cannabich (1731–98), with whom Mozart and his mother frequently lunched and dined during their stay. According to Mozart's letter of 6 December the Andante was intended as a musical portrait of this fifteen-year-old girl ('pretty . . . charming . . . intelligent . . . amiable . . . She is exactly like the Andante').

Shortly after it was finished Wolfgang began sending the autograph of the sonata back home to his father for copying.[7] It soon became a favourite of Nannerl's; she apparently played it well, applying to the slow movement 'excellently and with great expression', according to Leopold's letter of 11 December. So did Rosa Cannabich: on 6 December Wolfgang expressed delight at her 'excellent' performance, singling out especially 'The Andante (which must *not be taken too quickly*) she plays with the utmost expression'.[8] Earlier, on 14 November, he had described the Andante as 'full of expression and must be played accurately and with the exact shades of forte and piano, precisely as they are marked'.[9] Frequent alternation between these two dynamics is indeed one of this movement's most striking characteristics, and was no doubt inspired, at least in part, by his recent experience of Stein's sophisticated instruments in Augsburg.[10] Another is the emphasis on the second beat of each 3/4 bar, suggestive of the Sarabande, and notated in at least three ways: by *fp*, *f* and *cresc. f* dynamic marks, but also by precise length and placement of a figure or note, as in bar 7, in which the ascent in demisemiquavers to a high quaver C, followed by a semiquaver rest and change of register, implies that the peak of the phrase is to be emphasised slightly above the prevailing *forte* dynamic indicated in the previous bar. Perhaps this feature, together with the plethora of dynamic shadings, was what led Leopold Mozart to describe the sonata as 'a strange composition' in his letter of 11 December 1777.[11] He goes on to note (perhaps pejoratively) that it 'has something in it of the *rather artificial* Mannheim style, but so very little that your own good style is not spoilt thereby'. Nannerl, too, in her postscript to Leopold's earlier letter of 8 December remarks on the basis of the first two movements that ' . . . I like the sonata very much. One can see from its style that you composed it in Mannheim. I am now looking forward to the Rondo'.[12] Among the stylistic features that link K.309 to Mannheim are the opening unison figure, *forte*, and outlining a triad in the manner of the characteristic Mannheim 'rocket';[13] the 'orchestral' nature of some of its passages, for instance, starting at bar 15 in the first movement (and especially its continuation from bar 21), bars 73–82 of the same movement, and the recurrent *tremolos* of the finale (bars 58, 69, 111, 163, 173, 222);[14] the interspersing of these 'tuttis' (*forte*) with contrasting (*piano*) phrases for reduced forces, which can readily be imagined on strings, or strings with a solo woodwind instrument (bars 3–7 of the first movement, for instance, and bars 77–85 of the finale). Such striking contrasts of texture are frequently found in Cannabich's own symphonies of this time, for example, in the first movement of his E flat major symphony.[15] Another feature apparent from the very opening of K.309 is irregular phrasing: its first paragraph is made up of 2 × (2 + 5) bars, emphasising the 'tutti' / 'solo' contrast; further odd-numbered groups occur at bars 43–9, a seven-bar phrase subdivided (2 + 1) + (2 + 2) bars, and the closing bars (54–8) of the exposition, whose five-bar (= 4 + 1) irregularity is later ironed-out at the end of the recapitulation by elision into a four-bar coda, returning to the opening unison 'rocket'. Such prominent irregularity appeared here for the first time in Mozart's solo sonatas, and was presumably a trait that Leopold found 'strange'.[16] Likewise 'strange' are some of the chord successions in the first movement's development (for which see chapter 11, example 11.3) and in the recapitulation transition (bars 101–8), whose melodic profile may perhaps embody something of what Leopold meant by the '*rather artificial* Mannheim style'.

AUTOGRAPHS AND PUBLICATION

No autograph of the C major Sonata, K.309, is known to survive. The closest we can come, therefore, to Mozart's original text of this sonata is the copy in his father's hand, produced between December 1777 and the beginning of the following February. In the case of the other two sonatas, in D, K.311, and A minor, K.310, we are more fortunate, for both autographs are still available, in the Jagiellonska Library, Kraków, and the Pierpoint Morgan Library, New York, respectively.[17] K.311 is written on small (*c*.20.6 × 16.5 cm) oblong ten-stave paper, the so-called *Klein-Querformat* used by Mozart in Salzburg;[18] K.310 is on a relatively unusual four-teen-stave paper that Mozart obtained in Paris, where he was resident for six months from 23 March 1778. Other contemporary works written on this paper include the clavier and violin sonata, K.306, and one source for the 'Paris' symphony, K.297, in which the composer's hand appears alongside that of two other copyists.[19] Thus in the case of two of these sonatas we can reconstruct their texts exactly as Mozart left them, and we can be pretty sure of the reliability of the copy of the third, made directly from the autograph by Leopold. This is of some importance in addressing the relationship between autographs and Heina's first edition of *c*.1782.

Franz Joseph Heina (1729–90) was a close friend of Mozart during those six months in Paris. Indeed, he accompanied the composer at his mother's death-bed on 3 July 1778, and attended her funeral the next day. Mozart described him as 'a kind friend'.[20] He published the first editions of several of Mozart's compositions: the variations, K.179, 180 and 354 (as 'Trois Airs Variés pour le Clavecin ou le Fortepiano' in 1778);[21] the Divertimento, K.254 (*c*.1782) and the present set of three sonatas. He had established a music publishing business alongside a shop dealing in books and musical instruments with his wife, Gertrude, at the 'rue de Seine, Fauxbourg St. Germain, à l'Hôtel de Lille' sometime before 1764.[22] It is apparent that Mozart had left various (unspecified) works with Heina on his departure from the French capital (probably in return for ready cash for his homeward journey, a ploy he had to use with Sieber also).[23] In a letter of 26 October 1778, from Strasbourg, he tells his father that he has twice written to Heina (presumably requesting a publication date for whatever material he had left with him), but had as yet received no news.[24]

Quite when the three solo sonatas, K.309–311, were published is unknown. The issue consists of [ii] +25 engraved pages; the title-page reads as follows:

Trois/ Sonates/ Pour le Clavecin ou le Forte Piano/ Par/ Wolfgang Amade Mozard/ Oeuvre IVᵉ/ Mises au Jour/ Par Mᴰ Heina/ Gravés par Mˡˡᵉ Fleury./ Prix 6[livres]/ A Paris/ Chez M. Heina Editeur, rue de Seine, Fauxbourg St. Germain, à l'Hôtel de Lille./ Et aux Adresses

Ordinaire[s]./ à Bruxelles; Chez M. Godfroy de la Riviere./ [c.1782]

Regrettably the edition is quite inaccurate. It contains errors too numerous to list here, including inconsistencies of slurring, dynamic placement and staccatos (not that Mozart's autographs are blameless in these respects). Mlle Fleury's engraving is sloppy in detail. For example, in the slow movement of K.310 she frequently positions left-hand passages an octave too low (bars 6^3–9^3, 15–18, 28^2–30^1, 59^3–60^3 and 70^1–72^1; in Mozart's autograph all these passages are written in alto clef); the first movement of K.311 contains different articulations for every subsequent appearance of the right-hand pattern first sounded at bar 29; there are frequent problems over application of accidental sharps (in the same movement, for instance, the left hand in bar 69 is chaotic (the first chord is spelt A$\sharp$/ D$\sharp$), and at the beginning of bar 71 of K.310's slow movement the left-hand chord is E$\flat$/C$\sharp$!); in the finale the engraver wrongly repeats bars 219–20 between bars 228 and 229, with disastrous harmonic consequences; finally, assuming Leopold's copy of K.309 accurately reflects Wolfgang's intentions (and, given the specific reference to the importance of careful dynamic shadings reported above in relation to the Andante, there is no reason to suppose that this should not be so), the Heina text of this sonata is quite lamentable. All this, it should be stressed, is but a brief selection of the first edition's shortcomings and could be multiplied many times over. Its text is so frequently faulty in the application of dynamics as to render a passage such as bars 69–71 of K.311's slow movement (Andante espressione) entirely barren of its carefully calculated contrasts (the phrase is covered by a single *forte* – in effect since the end of bar 66 – that remains in force until the (illogical) *cresc. F[orte]* in bar 73). This can never have been checked or approved by the composer and one wonders what his reaction was (it is nowhere recorded in the Mozart correspondence). In view of the number and nature of the discrepancies between the autographs (or, in the case of K.309, Leopold's copy) and the published text, one is led to suspect either an alarming level of corruption in an intervening manuscript copy or else that the engraver, Mlle Fleury, was hopelessly incompetent. The latter seems the less plausible scenario in view of the much better quality of other surviving examples of her work.[25] Probably she engraved Mozart's sonatas from an intervening manuscript copy (now lost), made by an inexperienced copyist who routinely mistranscribed alto clef passages in the slow movement of K.310 an octave too low and with little regard to the precise placement of dynamics, slurs and articulation marks. It is possible that such a copytext was prepared in some haste before Mozart left Paris with his manuscripts.[26]

CHAPTER FIVE

Four sonatas, K.330–2; K.333

For many years, these four sonatas, composed at some point during the early 1780s and published in 1784,[1] were thought to date from Mozart's stay in Paris between March and September 1778. All editions of *Köchel* assign them to this period, for instance, as does much of the existing writing on the sonatas up to the late 1970s.[2] Wyzewa and Saint-Foix attempted a precise chronology within Mozart's six-month visit to the French capital:

K.331 (A major)   between May and July 1778
K.330 (C major)   between July and September 1778
K.332 (F major)   between July and September 1778
K.333 (B flat major) between July and September 1778[3]

Such a chronology places these sonatas in close proximity to the A minor Sonata, K.310; to the 'Paris' Symphony, K.297, and other works conclusively associated with these months, such as the Concerto for Flute and Harp, K.299, the Violin Sonatas, K.304 and K.306, and the variations *Je suis Lindor*, K.354, and *Lison dormait*, K.264. Such a dating seems, at first sight, quite plausible. Wyzewa and Saint-Foix's stylistic criteria, noted above, are undoubtedly applicable, at times, to these four piano works. The first movements of K.332 and 333, for instance, suggest a broadening of expressive range compared to K.309 and 311. Yet detailed reflection on these criteria reveals more differences than similarities. In what ways are the first-movement development sections of, say, K.309 and 311, less rigorous in terms of thematic control than K.310, K.332 or K.333? Can the expressive range of K.330 be compared to that of K.310? Can the finale of K.332 be said to be less deliberately 'virtuosic' than that of K.311? Many such reservations undermine the validity of Wyzewa and Saint-Foix's reasons for assigning K.330–33 to the Parisian sojourn of 1778.

During the 1970s work on the autograph manuscripts of these four sonatas demonstrated beyond doubt that none of them could have originated in Paris in 1778. Wolfgang Plath's research into the developments in Mozart's handwriting argued strongly that K.330–2 were composed during the very early 1780s, and that K.333 dated from 1783–4.[4] Alan Tyson's work on the watermarks found in Mozart's paper has tended to confirm this. All four sonatas are on paper-types that Mozart used elsewhere only rarely, and none is on French paper (such as was used for K.310 or K.297, for instance). Tyson has plausibly suggested November 1783 as a composition date for K.333, adding that the sonata was possibly written at Linz (and thus contemporaneously with the 'Linz' Symphony, K.425), while Mozart was returning to Vienna from the three–month visit made with his wife, Constanze, to his father in Salzburg during the late summer and autumn of that year.[5] The other three sonatas, K.330–2, may have originated at about the same time.[6] Their pages are each ruled with ten staves, the standard format for Salzburg paper (in Vienna, Mozart normally used twelve-stave paper) and might have been written on paper purchased in Salzburg between July and October 1783.[7] It has been proposed (again by Tyson) that they were intended perhaps for the use of Mozart's Viennese pupils upon his return to the capital, on the grounds that their right-hand parts (and, at times, the left-hand also) employ the soprano clef. Certainly C clefs are unusual in Mozart's piano works and the use of a soprano clef here may signify some special purpose.[8] It is conceivable that the soprano clef, traditionally used in counterpoint manuals, such as Fux's *Gradus ad Parnassum*,[9] was used here by Mozart in order to teach this clef to his students, or, alternatively, that these pieces were actually intended as models in *composition* rather than piano studies, and were categorised symbolically as such by their notation in the C clef. How might such an origin affect our interpretation of these sonatas? In fact, it can go some way towards explaining some of their slightly peculiar features. Viewed in a didactic light, the frequent recourse in the C major Sonata, K.330, to protracted two-part writing, in which simple themes and Alberti-bass accompaniments proceed through straightforward harmonic and tonal areas throughout much of the outer movements, makes good 'educational' sense – setting out 'norms' for the student to follow. Likewise, the phraseology of these two movements is almost *too* regular – even predictable – as if Mozart were manufacturing a 'model' (possibly for a student to copy).[10] This is a credible scenario, and one which would explain something of the 'dryness' of this particular sonata. The opening movement variation-set in K.331, in A major (a strategy employed nowhere else in Mozart's sonatas) might initially have been intended to teach ways of composing (or improvising at the piano) tasteful embellishments on an unchanging harmonic pattern. The first movement exposition of K.332, in F major, contains an unusually wide variety of 'topics' within a short span: 'cantabile' style, bars 1–4; 'learned' counterpoint, bars 5–12; a 'fanfare', bars 12–20; 'Sturm und Drang' bars 22–40, and so on. Perhaps, then, it was calculated specifically to teach the incorporation of a (deliberately large) number of varying 'topics' in a gradually unfolding tonal plan. If, as suggested by their identical watermarks, K.330 and 332 were written as a pair, the gulf in their technical demands and in their harmonic and tonal usage suggests that they were intended for pupils of considerably different abilities. In all fairness, it should be said that the use of soprano clef need not have been didactic. The Ployer and Attwood composition studies are not uniformly in C clefs; in fact, the ordinary treble clef is often used for notating the highest part, in 'fundamental bass' and strict counterpoint exercises, for instance.[11] That K.330–2 originated as teaching material, in either composition or piano technique, is entirely possible, but, in the absence of conclusive documentary evidence at this stage, perhaps the consequences of this should not be taken too far.

The three sonatas, K.330–32 survive in varying states of completeness; K.333 survives entire. K.330 is in the Biblioteka Jagiellonska, Kraków.[12] Only a single leaf of K.331 remains (in the private collection of Antonio de Almeida, Lisbon, Portugal).[13] Most of K.332 survives in the William H. Scheide collection of Princeton University Library, Princeton, New Jersey.[14] K.333 is in the Staatsbibliothek Preußischer Kulturbesitz, Berlin.[15]

For the first edition of K.330–2, published by Artaria in 1784, Mozart seems to have made some quite substantial changes to the texts of K.330 and K.332.[16] In the slow movement of K.330, for instance, Mozart added a major-key coda, bars 60^2–64, mirroring bars 36^2–40) which is not present in the autograph.[17] In the finale of the same sonata Mozart's autograph indicates the reprise of bars 96–123 by a 'Da Capo'; in the print, of course, these twenty-eight bars were engraved in full, allowing him the luxury of a significant number of additional dynamic marks (there are none in the autograph) and such subtle expressive indications as the *sotto voce* marking in bar 96.[18] More substantial revision was applied to the printed text of the slow movement of K.332. Originally the reprise of the opening theme was a plain 'Da Capo'; for the Artaria text, however, Mozart added an embellished version which probably reflects the way in which he would habitually have ornamented such a reprise.[19] Except for the alteration to the first beat of bar 26 and the doubling of the falling thirds at the lower octave in bars 30 and 31, all the changes are to the right-hand part, which, in addition to its melodic embellishment, contains a few additional articulations (such as the staccato wedges in bar 23, second beat, and the telling repositioning of *sforzando* markings in the next bar).

The autograph of the B flat Sonata, K.333, is written on what is, for Mozart, a most unusual paper-type. It is in upright – not oblong – format (378 × 233 mm.) and has twenty-four staves per page. Alan Tyson's watermark investigations indicate that only one other example of the paper is known to survive – a copy Mozart made of Michael Haydn's motet, *Nobis pignus datur*. A close reading of the watermark reveals that the rare paper came from the Austrian village of Steyr, and on this basis, Tyson infers that Mozart purchased it *en route* back to Vienna from Salzburg during November 1783.[20] The sonata was therefore in all probability composed at about this time, perhaps even in Linz at the same time as the 'Linz' Symphony, K.425, which Mozart wrote in great haste for a concert there on 4 November.[21] Perhaps he also played K.333 on that occasion, although, given the pressure on him to compose from scratch a new symphony during the few days following his arrival on 30 October, it is unlikely that he would have found time to write down what is quite an extended sonata (especially its concerto-like rondo finale) as well. The appearance of the autograph tends to confirm this, for it shows some evidence of having been a composing score. During much of the first movement, for example, the right-hand and left-hand staves have separate barlines and are only occasionally joined by a connecting barline drawn through the pair of staves, the implication of which is clearly that Mozart composed a few bars of the leading melody line first (drawing barlines through just this single stave), and then returned to the start of the phrase, adding in the left-hand accompaniment on the blank stave beneath. The connecting barlines, drawn through the pair of staves, appear every few bars (at the end of bars 5, 7, 17, 21 and 28, for instance) and probably mark off the successive stages in which the movement progressed, a phrase at a time, beginning as follows: bars 1–5, right hand, left hand; bars 6, 7; bars 7–17; bars 18–21; bars 22–8; etc.[22] That these divisions do reflect actual *composition* (rather than simply the stages in the writing out of the manuscript) is suggested by the appearance of complementary bars in the recapitulation. Bars 111–26, for instance, which are more or less a straightforward transposition of the corresponding point in the exposition (bars 15–30) have connecting, rather than separated barlines, drawn through the pair of staves, implying that Mozart wrote (i.e. copied) them out a bar at a time. This, of course, would have been the natural thing to do, since at this point in the movement he was no longer working out the detailed continuity, merely transposing an already complete phrase. Conversely, those portions of the recapitulation that had to be *composed* revert to the pattern of separate barlines for each stave. Bars 142–52, for instance, extend the original descending sequence of bars 46–50, and, on the evidence of the autograph, Mozart elaborated the melody first (adapting it at bar 143, so as to keep it within the confines of a piano whose compass ascended to f′) and added the supporting chords once he had arrived at bar 152.

Following the central double-bar in the Andante cantabile is a chromatic development section incorporating a number of unexpected harmonic progressions. Its main tonal route is through F minor, A flat major and B flat major, the latter as a dominant preparation for the return of the main key, E flat, at bar 51. One might suppose, according to the procedures established earlier in relation to the first movement, that much, if not all, of this would exhibit connected, rather than separate, barlines in Mozart's autograph, reflecting its primarily harmonic conception (one complete bar at a time), as opposed to melodic elaboration. In fact, the section is drawn with barlines of both types, implying that both procedures were in use. Bars 32–50 may be seen in illustration 5.1 (in which the subtle variations of inking are not as clear as in the autograph itself). At certain points the vertical separation of barlines for the right-hand and left-hand staves is not immediately apparent, though even in those cases where there seems to be just a single barline drawn through the pair of staves, closer inspection reveals that the top of the left-hand barline was carefully joined to the bottom of the existing right-hand one.[23] These bars are characterised by an elegant flexibility of focus, constantly shifting between primarily melodic or harmonic continuity. Mozart's alternation between these

Illustration 5.1   Mozart, Sonata in B flat, K.333, 2nd movement, autograph
(Staatsbibliothek zu Berlin – Preußischer Kulturbesitz, Musikabteilung mit Mendelssohn-
Archiv)

Example 5.1 Mozart, Sonata in B flat, K.333, 2nd movement, bars 32–5 (simplified progression)

linear and chordal types of composition can be reconstructed to some extent through careful examination of the autograph, and is best explained by approaching the component sections of the development in reverse order.

The section beginning in A flat (bar 43), for instance, proceeds exclusively with separate barlines, suggesting that even within this primarily harmonic territory the main element of continuity in Mozart's thought was linear. How are we to account for this? On reflection, this is not so surprising, given the passage's harmonic context: it is founded on an abstract harmonic process consisting of falling steps in the bass, and the chords move uniformly, 1 bar at a time (Mozart notates beats 2 and 3 in shorthand (//)). Presumably in such cases Mozart had already conceived the harmonic pattern and its length. In these circumstances it would have been a relatively easy matter either to extend the phrase melodically (retaining the ♪ ♫ rhythm), supplying the Alberti bass chords later, or, alternatively, to have notated the left hand part first, superimposing the melody afterwards. The precise sequence does not matter much – what is clear is that melodic and harmonic components of the phrase arose separately.

Bars 32–43 reveal a transition in mid-phrase from linear to chordal thinking. For all their surface chromaticism, bars 32–3 elaborate a quite simple underlying pattern, easily retained in the mind while the precise melodic shape was fixed (example 5.1). Despite the evident harmonic focus the conception was mostly linear, not chordal, since not only are the barlines once again separate but vertical alignment between the hands is mostly lacking, suggesting that right-hand and left-hand staves were not written together. This is true of bars 32–9, but not of bars 40–42, for which there appear to be both connecting barlines (drawn through both staves) and careful vertical alignment. It would seem that in these three bars Mozart was having to 'feel his way' through each stage of the progression to A flat (a significant turning-point in the course of the development) and consequently had to think harmonically – a complete bar at a time. This contrasts with the procedure for the earlier part of the phrase which, like bars 43–50 discussed above, is founded on a process (this time a rising chromatic progression, enlivened by applying the three-quaver upbeat from bar 33), and would not have been difficult to keep in mind while elaborating the right-hand part (assuming this was indeed written first).

Bar 34 contains an example of Mozart revising during the actual act of composition, and confirms that this was his composing score. Originally his first beat consisted of a pair of quavers, F sharp″, G″. He then changed it to crotchet F sharp″, quaver G″. Because this rhythmic change tipped over into beat 2 he cancelled the original quaver G″, replacing it with one a little further to the right (this can be seen in the facsimile). That this is carefully aligned with the left-hand crotchet rest on beat two strongly suggests that, after initial second thoughts regarding the melody line, the rest of bar 34 was worked-out harmonically and completed in all its details before advancing any further with the melodic continuation of bars 35–42.

CHAPTER SIX

Fantasia and Sonata in C minor, K.475 and 457

On 21 November 1990 the newly-rediscovered autograph manuscript of Mozart's Fantasia and Sonata in C minor, K.475 and 457, was auctioned at Sotheby's of London.[1] It was acquired by a consortium of Austrian national and private institutions for £800,000 and is now housed in the library of the International Stiftung Mozarteum, Salzburg. The reemergence of this autograph is the single most significant recent event to affect Mozart scholarship and allows a reappraisal of the genesis of what is perhaps his most important (and certainly his most substantial) solo piano work. For this reason, a separate chapter has been devoted to it alone.

Prior to the rediscovery of the autograph, the Fantasia and Sonata were known from the following sources surviving from Mozart's time:

(1) The so-called 'dedication copy', containing the Sonata only, written by a Viennese scribe with some corrections in Mozart's hand. Mozart also wrote the title-page: *Sonata/ Per il Pianoforte Solo/ Composta/ per la Sig.ra Teresa de Trattnern/ dal suo umilissimo servo/ Wolfgango Amadeo Mozart . . .*, dated 14 October 1784[2]

(2) The first edition of the Fantasia and Sonata together, published by Artaria in Vienna towards the end of 1785: *Fantaisie et Sonate/ Pour le Forte-Piano/ composées pour/ Madame Therese de Trattnern/ par le Maitre de Chapelle/ W.A. Mozart Oeuvre XI*[3]

Although published together during Mozart's lifetime the Fantasia and Sonata were evidently conceived independently: according to Mozart's own thematic catalogue the Fantasia postdated the Sonata by some seven months. The rediscovery of the autograph of the two works confirms this: although bound up together in the early nineteenth century their paper-types and stave spans are quite different.[4] Even the inks are different: the Fantasia was written in a light brown ink, that used for the Sonata was generally rather darker.[5] At some stage during 1785 Mozart decided to bring the two works together for publication, the Fantasia serving to introduce the Sonata. In this coupling they have been familiar ever since, although the various editions printed after Mozart's death followed two main lines of transmission, one emanating from the autograph,[6] the other from the 1785 Artaria print,[7] in which Mozart made some revisions to the Sonata's text, including a wider range of dynamic indications and articulations and significant adjustments to the notes themselves, principally regarding the embellishment of the reprises in the Adagio and the octave placement of bars 92–101 and 290–310 of the finale.[8] These textual matters will be discussed in more detail below.

THE AUTOGRAPH MANUSCRIPT

History

Many of Mozart's manuscripts were sold by his widow, Constanze, to the publisher Johann Anton André (1775–1842). The 'Article of Agreement' between the two parties is signed and dated 8 November 1799. The main substance of the contract is that, in return for 3,150 guilders, the promise of future publication of her late husband's works and a small number of free copies of these after publication, Constanze was to deliver to André those Mozart autographs still in her possession (consisting, apparently, of 'fifteen packets').[9] Although no mention is made of the Fantasia and Sonata in the appendix to the contract itemising Mozart's 'Original Manuscripts', André clearly had these by 1802, when he produced his edition, 'faites d'après le manuscrit original de l'auteur'.[10] So far as can be ascertained the next owner was Johann Andreas Stumpff (1769–1846), a London instrument maker, who was perhaps responsible for having the autographs of the Fantasia and Sonata bound up in a single volume. Stumpff bought a number of Mozart's manuscripts from André in 1811; his signature appears on the first page of the Fantasia and again on the last page of the Sonata. In 1847 Stumpff's manuscript collection was sold; the Fantasia and Sonata fetched £2 at auction (the purchaser is not recorded). The autograph was subsequently owned by Julian Marshall, a London music and art collector, who sold it in 1889 to the American philanthropist, collector and hymn-writer, William Howard Doane (1832–1915) for £55.[11]

Following Doane's death in 1915, most of his collection of manuscripts was donated to the Cincinnati Museum of Art. The autograph of K.475 and 457 was not among these, however, and was considered by the editors of *Köchel*[3–6] to have been lost. However, Doane had entrusted some of his most prized manuscripts (including Mozart's Fantasia and Sonata, and autographs by Haydn, Spohr, Johann Strauss senior and Meyerbeer) to his youngest daughter, Marguerite Doane, who in turn donated them to the Eastern Baptist Theological Seminary in Philadelphia in 1950, where they remained in a safe until being rediscovered by Judith DiBona, accounting manager of Eastern College, St David's, Pennsylvania, on 31 July 1990.

Physical description

The autograph consists of four bifolia and a single detached leaf. It is written on Viennese paper of four types, in oblong format, mechanically ruled with twelve staves; the dimensions are, for the Fantasia, *c.* 32 × 23 cm., and for the Sonata, *c.* 31.5 × 23 cm. When rediscovered in 1990 the structure of the manuscript was as follows:[12]

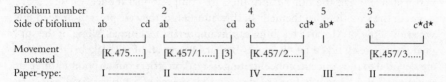

Bifolium number	1		2		4		5	3	
Side of bifolium	ab	cd	ab	cd	ab	cd★	ab★	ab	c★d★
Movement notated	[K.475.....]		[K.457/1.....] [3]		[K.457/2.....]			[K.457/3.....]	
Paper-type:	I ---------		II --------------		IV ----------		III ----	II -----------	

Reconstructed according to the logical sequence of the four distinct paper-types, the original layout of the autograph must have been thus:

Bifolium number	1		2		3		4		5	
Side of bifolium	ab	cd	ab	cd	ab	c★d★	ab	cd★	c★d★	
Movement notated	[K.475.....]		[K.457/1.....] [3.................(blank)]				[K.457/2.....]			
Paper-type:	I ---------		II ------------------------------				IV ----------		III --	

In this form it quickly becomes apparent that there were three distinct phases of composition:

(1) Sonata, movements 1 and 3 (bifolia 2, 3; paper-type II)
(2) Sonata, movement 2 (bifolia 4, 5; paper-types III, IV)
(3) Fantasia (bifolium 1; paper-type I)

From Mozart's thematic catalogue, in which the works are dated, it is clear that phases 1 and 2 account for the Sonata (completed 14 October 1784) and phase 3 for the Fantasia (completed on 20 May 1785). Which portion of the Sonata was completed first? This is impossible to answer with absolute certainty, though the fact that Mozart wrote the first movement and finale of the Sonata straight through bifolia 2 and 3 (the end of the first movement is reached on bifolium 2, side c, followed immediately on bifolium 2, side d by the beginning of the finale, which continues through bifolium 3) hints that the second movement (bifolia 4 and 5) might already have been composed (it is, at any rate, on different paper-types, III and IV). The idea of a sonata comprising two quick movements ('Allegro' and 'Molto Allegro', according to the designations of the autograph) is in any event utterly alien to Mozart's practice. Wolf also suggests that the slow movement may have been composed first, serving as a teaching piece for Thérèse von Trattern[13]. This makes good sense. It is by far the simplest explanation for the unusual running-on of the end of the first movement and the start of the finale on bifolium 2, sides c and d respectively.[14] In fact, given the specific dedication of the Sonata to Mozart's pupil, we are entitled to assume it carried some pedagogical significance for her, and, perhaps, Mozart too. This affects the way we view the distinct stages in the elaboration of the Adagio (which we can now trace in full, having the autograph). On the one hand, the progressive melodic embellishment serves as a useful model for the performer (originally Trattern herself) in those passages which Mozart left notationally bare but which he himself would undoubtedly have ornamented in performance.[15] On the other hand, they are compositional models for successive stages in the variation of a theme.[16] In this latter sense, they are precious indeed, for we know little of Mozart's teaching of this important technique. None of the surviving exercises worked by his pupils Barbara Ployer and Franz Jakob Freystädtler are devoted to the concept, concentrating instead on strict counterpoint in three or more parts and harmonisations of melodies by means of a fundamental bass.[17] In several exercises worked between August 1785 and February 1787 by Mozart's other famous pupil, Thomas Attwood,[18] there are hints that melodic variation may have been discussed, though only in passing during the working-out (or correction) of Attwood's *freie Sätze*.[19] It is worth pausing to examine these before launching into a fuller discussion of the principles lying behind the varied reprises in K.457's Adagio.

Example 6.1a and b presents, respectively, Attwood's version of an eight-bar phrase for string quartet and Mozart's emendation.[20] While Mozart provided no written commentary for this, he must have discussed with Attwood the principles according to which he had substituted certain notes. We can only guess at their nature. For instance, Mozart's revision tightens the connection between melodic and harmonic direction in bars 3 and 4 (in which the descent from d' to c sharp' is better timed) and again in bars 5 and 6 (in which Mozart's treble a' for the first violin (the highest part in the short score) attains its prominent registral position in conjunction with the *sforzando*, while Attwood's arrives just too late). Elsewhere Mozart simply substitutes different pitches within the implied triads. The changes to the overall harmonic effect of the passage are marginal (Attwood's G major triad in bar 5, beat 3 becomes an E minor triad, and his B minor triad in bar 7, beat 1 becomes a G major triad). In example 6.2 a and b we glean something of Mozart's method of elaborating a single pitch into a group of notes while retaining the prevailing harmony. Bars 2–8 of Attwood's viola part (the upper part in the bottom stave of the short score), while satisfactory harmonically, are rather dull, and are enlivened melodically and rhythmically in Mozart's revision. F sharp' in bar 2 is expanded by means of lower and upper neighbour notes and by the substitution of a consonant triadic tone (a'), a technique also applied in the following bars (b in bar 3 is signified by the triadic consonances g' and e', and a passing note, d', for instance, while in bar 4 Mozart substitutes ascending quaver passing notes for Attwood's plain dotted minim, a').

Some similar principles are at work in the embellished reprises in K.457's slow movement, for which Mozart provided two stages of embellishment: stage 1 is found on bifolium 4 side c; stage 2 on bifolium 5 side a. Stage 2 evidently represents his final thoughts (it is this version that was printed by Artaria); stage 1 (unknown before the recovery of the autograph) was a draft, and comparison with stage 2 allows us a valuable insight into Mozart's 'fine-tuning'. Example 6.3 a and

Example 6.1
(a) Thomas Attwood, phrase of a Minuet

(b) Mozart's correction of Attwood's Minuet

Example 6.2
(a) Thomas Attwood, phrase of a Minuet

b shows the draft stage 1 of bars 17–23 and 41–47 of the Adagio.[21] In this version
of bar 17, beats 1 and 2, Mozart retains the falling third, b flat'–g', in outline, but
fills it in by demisemiquaver lower and upper neighbour notes (similar to the
elaboration of Attwood's viola f sharp', noted above); in bar 23[1], the right-hand
scale ascent, b flat'–e flat' is lightly decorated by the addition of *échappées*; bar 43[4],
the original rising semiquaver steps, f'–g'–a flat'–a natural' (b flat' in bar 44), are
represented by demisemiquavers f'–e flat'–d'–e flat'–f'–g'–a flat'–a natural' (b flat' in
bar 44). In addition to techniques of embellishing particular pitches Mozart's stage
1 suggests some redefinition of climax within phrases. For instance, in bar 4[1], the
original line stresses the falling b flat'–g', while passing lightly over the consonant
triadic tone, e flat' above; in stage 1 of bar 20, however, this upper e flat' is more
strongly emphasised by upward scalic motion and repetition, culminating in an
expressive falling sixth to g'.

Stage 2 reveals some fascinating second thoughts on Mozart's part as he prepared
the sonata for publication. These final revisions are of two main types, involving
seemingly casual – but nonetheless telling – alterations of single pitches, such as the

(b) Mozart's correction of Attwood's Minuet

penultimate demisemiquaver a natural' in bar 17[1] (right hand). More significant are those alterations that affect the structure. The most important of these is the wholesale transplantation of bars 20 and 21 of stage 1 (see example 6.3 a), to become bars 41–2 of stage 2 (the Artaria text, reproduced in *NMA* and *Mozart Sonatas II*); bars 20 and 21 of stage 1 revert, in stage 2, substantially to the original text of bars 4 and 5, save for the addition of some highly specialised dynamics in bar 5. Why did Mozart do this? Almost certainly he felt that, in stage 1, his bars 41–7 relied too much on chromatic embellishment of the ascending fourth, b flat'–e flat', which occurs no less than three times in sextuplets. His revision removes this repetition, and allows him to introduce the chromaticism to subtler effect in bar 46, this time in canon at a quaver's distance between the hands, heightening its expressive point in relation to the two earlier appearances of this figure in bars 6 and 22, and throwing into relief the ensuing coda (bars 47[3]–57) with which the Adagio ends.

Example 6.3

(a) Mozart, Sonata in C minor, K.457, 2nd movement, original embellished reprise for
bars 17–23

As was the case in the six sonatas, K.279–84, Mozart's autographs of the Fantasia
and Sonata betray, in their ink patterns, something of the composer's working
methods. Both autographs were clearly composing scores and incorporate the same
two types of inking as were apparent in the earlier sonatas: type 1 (horizontal fade)
and type 2 (uniform). In bars 64–72 of the Fantasia (harmonically quite a complex
passage, involving an enharmonic shift at bar 72) the pattern is a variant of type 2:
the left-hand part within each bar is consistently darker than the right (in other

(b) Mozart, Sonata in C minor, K.457, 2nd movement, original embellished reprise for
bars 41–47

words, there is an upward *vertical* fade), suggesting at first sight that Mozart worked-
out the chordal foundation before adding the fragmentary melodic line above. On
closer inspection, it becomes apparent that the first left-hand note of each bar
exhibits a noticeably blacker note-head than the remainder, perhaps a clue that
Mozart initially sketched the bare bones of the harmonic progression of the entire
phrase up to bar 72 or 73 (that is, the first left-hand note of each bar: f- e flat- d
flat- c- d flat- B flat- c- A flat- G sharp- [F sharp]), then, having fixed these refer-
ence-points, proceeded to add the chords and melody line as described above.
Elsewhere, the inking is clearly of type 1. In the ensuing passage (bars 73–82) there
is a consistent *horizontal* ink fade throughout the right-hand part (triplets, giving
way at bar 78 to duplet quavers), showing that this whole line was written in a single
sweep (evidently Mozart was able to retain in his mind the harmonic aspect – a
descending chromatic line – while advancing the triplet line). Likewise, the
Andantino melody (bars 86–93) exhibits a type 1 horizontal fade: the right-hand

melody was written first, followed by the whole of the left-hand accompaniment. Similar observations may be made of the Sonata (though these are more difficult because of the generally blacker ink). Bars 23–30 of the first movement seem to have been written a bar at a time: the inking is clearly type 2, uniformly dark within each bar, and with numerous redips of the pen visible. By contrast, the right-hand triplets in bars 51–6 of the first movement are of type 1, fading gradually from black to light brown, the accompaniment being added subsequently.

CHAPTER SEVEN

Later Viennese Sonatas, K.533 and 494; K.545; K.570; K.576

Of Mozart's four remaining solo sonatas composed between January 1788 and July 1790, the only surviving autograph material presently known is a portion of the first movement of the B flat Sonata, K.570 (bars 65 to the end).[1] First editions of all these works survive, though in three cases (K.545, K.570 and K.576) they appeared after Mozart's death. The extent to which their texts may be trusted is debatable:

(1) The first edition of K.570[2] is evidently corrupt in that it includes an *obbligato* violin part, of which there is no trace in the surviving pages of the autograph. (In the *Verzeichnüss*, Mozart describes K.570 as a sonata 'auf Clavier allein'.) Perhaps details such as the articulation of the opening theme are not faithfully reproduced in the first edition either: Mozart's notation of this theme in his *Verzeichnüss* joins together bars 1 and 2 under a single slur before continuing with the same one-bar grouping as in found in the edition.[3] On the other hand, Mozart himself may not have been very consistent here, for at bars 41 ff. and several other passages, the autograph has the same one-bar slurring as the print, and at bars 101 ff., where Mozart begins to develop the theme, the autograph notates the entire four-bar figure under a single slur. Unfortunately, we do not know precisely how Mozart notated the first four bars of the piece since, in the autograph, not only are the first sixty-four bars lost, but the first part of the recapitulation (bars 133–64, which may have retained the original phrasing) was indicated merely as a Da Capo.

(2) A small but significant textual difficulty in the first edition of K.545[4] concerns bar 7 of the first movement, the left hand of which gives a crotchet b (and a resulting diminished chord) on the first beat. This may be a printing error, for at the parallel transitional passage in the recapitulation (bar 48) the harmony is different, forming a seventh chord by retaining a crotchet F in the middle of the texture as a suspension resolving at the end of the bar; by analogy therefore, might Mozart have written a crotchet c' in bar 7 of the exposition? If the autograph survived we could determine whether Mozart intended this distinction or not. Some modern editions amend bar 7; others (including *NMA*) do not, arguing that the first edition should take priority.[5] While the point could be

argued either way, it is worth noting that in the ensuing extension of his transition figure (inverting the texture) Mozart repeats the suspended seventh (bar 52).

(3) The first edition of K.576[6] poses an interesting complexity of textual problems at bars 103 ff. of the finale. First, there is the inconsistency in the slurring of this figure (a contrapuntal reworking of the main theme of the movement) with respect to the opening of the movement and other prominent occurrences such as bars 117 ff. During bars 103–11, for instance, the first edition alters the original articulation, slurring together all five notes of the figure's first bar. Might the change to a smoother articulation have been calculated specifically to highlight the temporary shift to a (three-part) contrapuntal idiom? This seems unlikely, given that these bars are part of a larger contrapuntal section (bars 95–131), in which the original (detached) articulation is otherwise consistently retained. All in all, it seems that the slurring in bars 103–7 is a mistake by the engraver. Likewise problematic is the reading of the first left-hand note of bar 107, which appears as E sharp in the first edition. This too is probably a mistake, since, not only does it interfere with the intervallic sequence of successive appearances of the figure in the preceding bars, but it creates actual parallel fifths with the last beat of the previous bar. E natural is surely the correct reading.

So much for textual questions in the posthumously published sonatas. The F major Sonata, K.533 and 494, the first two movements of which were, according to the *Verzeichnüss*, composed by 3 January 1788, is not known to survive in autograph. But it was at least printed before Mozart's death,[7] and one may hope that this publication reflects fairly accurately his intentions, especially regarding the finale, for which he substantially revised the Rondo, K.494, previously composed as an entirely separate piece dated 10 June 1786, and first published in 1788 (again, separately from the sonata).[8] It presents an evidently accurate, attractively engraved text, well-proportioned on the page and easy on the performer's eye.[9] However, in the second and third movements there are no dynamic markings whatever. This cannot have been Mozart's intention, particularly in the expressive Andante. To judge from those sonatas for which both autograph and first edition survive (K.284, 330 and 332, for instance), he tended to add dynamics for publication, so that the omission here is surprising.[10]

The origin of K.533 is not precisely known. No reference is made to it in Mozart's correspondence. However, a clue emerges from the title-page of Hoffmeister's print, on which Mozart is described as 'au Service de sa Majesté'. Mozart had been appointed 'Kammermusicus' to Joseph II in November 1787, in succession to Gluck (at two-fifths of Gluck's salary), and he evidently lost no time in dedicating a new sonata, ideal for chamber performance, to his illustrious royal patron. Moreover, the *Verzeichnüss* date of 3 January 1788 shows that the first two movements were completed within two months of Mozart's new appointment. The opening Allegro, in particular, is notable for the degree of imitative exchange between the hands, along with contrapuntal combinations of various sorts.[11] By striking the 'learned counterpoint' pose, Mozart may well have been exhibiting an aspect of his compositional craft in order to show himself worthy of his position in the emperor's service. At the same time, the music is sufficiently tuneful and periodic in its phrasing to be accessible – a happy blend of the 'learned' and the 'popular'. A projected finale (K.Anh.30 = 590b) survives, but breaks off after just 16 bars. It contains features complementary to the first movement of K.533 (a general triadic conception, a strand of unaccompanied melody at the opening, and texture inversion between the hands at bar 8. It has been convincingly suggested[12] that Mozart was in a hurry to get a sonata ready to present to the emperor and, having composed two movements, got stuck with the finale, and so abandoned his attempt (K.Anh.30 = 590b) in favour of a reworking of a Rondo that was not known in print in the capital (it was published in London, and in Speyer later in 1788). The reworking incorporates a substantial new episode (bars 143–69), including a stretto fugato beginning at bar 152. This texture is reminiscent of the stretto texture found at bars 49, 133 and 176 of the first movement, and it is quite possible that Mozart was deliberately adapting the existing Rondo to the contrapuntal idiom so characteristic of K.533's opening Allegro.

Mozart's own designation of the C major Sonata, K.545, as 'for beginners' ('für Anfänger') invites us to approach this work first and foremost as a teaching piece. In what ways is it suitable for the beginner? The tonality (C) is naturally an important consideration, for it largely avoids the black keys of the instrument and presents few reading difficulties. Added to this are:

the relatively small scale and simple structure of each movement;

the frequent scale and arpeggio passages, affording an acquaintance both digitally and notationally with the most frequently encountered patterns;

the device of sequence which, apart from requiring the application of sequential fingering patterns by the player, incidentally imposes a periodic division upon the music, and therefore an important early introduction to this *sine qua non* of classical style;

the relative simplicity of the textures providing practice in controlling a theme with Alberti-bass accompaniment (especially in the Andante) and semiquaver passagework passing between the hands – in both cases, a pattern which, once learnt, is easily applied elsewhere – added to which, there are hardly any surface rhythmic difficulties;

the regular and relatively slow-moving harmonic rhythm of the first movement, which explores some of the most closely related diatonic keys, especially during the development, moving through G minor, A, D minor and E, and presenting a number of different forms of melodic/harmonic minor scales of G, A and D before recapitulating the main theme in F major – a section that explores new hand shapes because of the prominent B flats (possibly this is why Mozart chose the unusual subdominant recapitulation here);

(following on from the last observation) the fact that bars 33 ff. of the Andante require smooth changes of left hand position in the Alberti-bass accompaniment, moving in and out of the black keys;[13]

the fact that the finale provides practice in controlling thirds, scales, arpeggios and repeated notes.

The complete lack of dynamic indications throughout is puzzling. Mozart became well-known as a fortepianist in Vienna during the last decade of his life, an instrument on which sensitivity to dynamic nuances was *de rigeur*. When teaching his pupils such as Josepha Auernhammer, Thérèse von Trattern and Barbara Ployer he would surely not have omitted instruction in dynamic control. The Andante of K.545 affords ample opportunities for dynamic shading, and its general *cantabile* quality calls for sensitive balancing of volume between the hands, impossible on a harpsichord. If the posthumous printed text accurately reproduces that of Mozart's (lost) autograph then the lack of *fortes*, *pianos*, *fps* etc., can only have been because Mozart intended the piece to serve as a 'clean' text upon which a variety of dynamic shadings could be applied during lessons in order to demonstrate possible differences in interpretation to his pupils.

It is worth considering the further possibility that Mozart's *Verzeichnüss* designation, 'für Anfänger' might apply equally well to compositional as to technical aspects of K.545. It seems that Mozart's pupils in Vienna during the 1780s were taught the rudiments of composition as well as piano playing.[14] In this case, one might draw particular attention to the straightforward tonal and cadential design of each movement (especially, perhaps, the modulation schemes); the melodic embellishment of the right-hand theme of the Andante at bars 9 ff.; the derivation of bars 17–24 and 33 ff. from the main theme, including the device of sequence at bars 21–2 and 37–8; the use of antiphonal dialogue in the finale, incorporating simple invertible counterpoint at bars 28–32 and 40–3. In all three movements a little material is made to go a long way. Perhaps Mozart specifically intended his sonata to demonstrate such economy of means.

Given the incomplete state of the autograph of K.570, it is unsurprising that relatively little can be inferred regarding the compositional process. In particular, almost the whole of the exposition is lost, so that we have no idea whether Mozart elaborated the modulating transitional passage, bars 21–35, melodically or harmonically.[15] However, bars 83–95 of the development (which use this same idea, but within a new harmonic context requiring fresh compositional thought) do appear to reveal that Mozart mapped-out at least part of the section harmonically before filling-in the melodic detail. Bars 81–4 simply transpose bars 23–6 of the exposition from E flat to D flat, requiring nothing more than accurate copying. Beginning in bar 85 though, the music plots a new harmonic course, although still based on the melodic figure of bar 23, moving around a somewhat remote circle-of-fifths before reaching D major at bar 95. The ink pattern of the second and third systems of the first surviving page of the autograph suggests that the bass line of bars 85–95 (in dotted minims throughout) was written at a different stage from the two upper parts. It is in a lighter ink and was evidently either an afterthought, which seems unlikely, since the inner-part quavers do not make satisfactory harmony,[16] or else beforehand.[17] Assuming the latter to be the likelier course of events, it appears that Mozart first sketched out the bass-line of bars 85–95, thus fixing the length of this passage and its cadential goal (D) and retaining in his head both the harmonic implications and the melodic shape, proceeding in two-bar phrases analogous to bars 31–4 of the exposition. Presumably the melody was elaborated next, followed by the inner part.

The Adagio of K.570 contains a near-quotation from the slow movement of the C minor Piano Concerto, K.491[18] – a feature which has led one commentator to propose that it may have started life as a sketch for a concerto movement.[19] It is easy to imagine the repeat of this section (and of bars 17–24) on woodwind after the manner of K.491. Indeed, every section of the Adagio of K.570 could be accommodated to such a profile of solo statement and tutti repeat: its opening comes close to the idiom of several of Mozart's mature Viennese concerto slow movements, not only K.491 but K.466 and K.537. In the concluding Allegretto, too, the capriciousness of the concerto finale is never far away, although there are only occasional flashes of soloistic virtuosity. Once again, one may easily imagine woodwind solos hiding behind passages such as bars 31–4 and the subdominant episode beginning at bar 45.

Likewise concerto-like in some respects is the D major Sonata, K.576. According to Mozart's *Verzeichnüss*, this was completed in July 1789, and would therefore seem to be a strong candidate for consideration as on the projected series of six 'easy' ('leichte') sonatas Mozart mentioned he was writing for Princess Friederika of Prussia in an otherwise embarrassing begging letter to his fellow Freemason, Michael Puchberg on 14 July that year.[20] As noted by Wolfgang Plath and Wolfgang Rehm, however, there are problems with such an assumption.[21] For one thing, the sonata was eventually published not as a set of six by Kozeluch, as Mozart indicated to Puchberg, but (posthumously) as a single work by the *Bureau des Arts et d'Industrie*. For another, K.576 is, by no stretch of the imagination, 'easy': passages such as those at bars 16–41 or 63–82 of the first movement and the whole of the finale are technically as taxing as anything in the concertos, intended as vehicles for Mozart's own virtuosity. It is unlikely that the Princess could have coped with either movement; clearly the piece was written for professional performance.

Perhaps the most obvious concerto-like feature of K.576 is its sheer scale, rivalled only by K.533 and 494, and K.457. Its first movement consists of 160 bars; its finale, 189 and in both the textures are incessantly active, though frequently in only two polyphonic parts. Within the first movement are echoes of a ritornello design: bars 27–41 of the exposition are transplanted wholesale in the recapitulation, occurring after the statement of the lyrical second subject, and dissolving into a coda. The finale is a sonata-rondo, unusual in Mozart's sonatas, but entirely typical of his concertos. While the opening theme recurs between the two episodes any further return is postponed until after the dense contrapuntal elaboration of the second episode (bars 95–116, involving an extended canon at the fifth between the outer parts) has given way to a tonic restatement of the first (bars 117–62). This structural device, in which the thematic embodiment of tonal return is withheld for a significant length of time, is clearly taken over from a procedure met with in Mozart's piano concertos – the finale of the F major Concerto, K.459 is a particularly close relative in that its central episode is rigorously contrapuntal and gives way to the 'exposition' secondary theme group (now transposed to the tonic) before restating the opening theme as a quasi-coda – after the cadenza – with mild subdominant colouring (see bar 175 of K.576).[22]

Substantial portions of K.576's first movement are contrapuntal: the opening unison 'hunting' theme is no sooner finished than it is combined with a similar countersubject; it recurs in stretto at bars 27–8, with further strettos reserved for the development (bars 62–3 – repeated in invertible counterpoint at bars 69–70). Neither the material nor its treatment strikes one as 'easy'. One can only guess at the true circumstances for which the sonata was intended: does its contrapuntal display betoken a purely personal recollection of the hours spent earlier in the 1780s at Baron van Swieten's studying the works of J. S. Bach and Handel? Or was it intended as a more public display of his compositional skill, perhaps for a potential patron (whether Princess Friederika or someone else)? Might it relate, like K.533, to Mozart's position as Joseph II's 'Kammermusicus'? Did Mozart intend to perform this work himself? If so, did he foresee the prospect of engagement at a forthcoming series of concerts? The latter, at least, appears unlikely, for his letters to Puchberg at this time (including the one quoted above in which he refers to the six sonatas for the Prussian princess) bemoan his ill fortune, and suggest that the chances of engagement in Vienna were remote:

Unfortunately Fate is so much against me, *though only here in Vienna*, that even when I want to, I cannot make any money. A fortnight ago I sent round a list for subscribers and so far the only name on it is that of the Baron van Swieten![23]

CHAPTER EIGHT

Fragments

The following fragments of projected sonatas are discussed in this section:

K.Anh.199 (*Köchel*[6] 33d);
　　200 (*Köchel*[6] 33e);
　　201 (*Köchel*[6] 33f);
　　202 (*Köchel*[6] 33g)

Köchel[6] deest: Sonata fragment in C major

K.400 (*Köchel*[6] 372a)

K.Anh.29 (*Köchel*[6] 590a);
　　30 (*Köchel*[6] 590b);
　　37 (*Köchel*[6] 590c);
　　31 (*Köchel*[6] 569a)

K.312 (*Köchel*[6] 590d)

K.ANH.199 (*KÖCHEL*[6] 33d), ALLEGRO IN G MAJOR, 4/4; 200 (*KÖCHEL*[6] 33e),
MOLTO ALLEGRO IN B FLAT MAJOR, 4/4; 201 (*KÖCHEL*[6] 33f), ALLEGRO IN
C MAJOR, 3/4; 202 (*KÖCHEL*[6] 33g), ANDANTE AMOROSO IN F MAJOR, 2/4

These four sonatas, composed in 1766, scarcely warrant even the title 'fragment',
for they are known only from their incipits, which are recorded in a manuscript catalogue of works available at the publishing house of Breitkopf in 1770 (catalogue
S.31.no.1), and reproduced here as example 8.1a, b, c and d respectively. References
to them may appear in the correspondence of Leopold and Nannerl Mozart. They
are perhaps the sonatas referred to in Leopold Mozart's letter to Breitkopf of 12
February 1781, in which he notes 'surely you will not judge [Wolfgang's compositional ability] solely on the basis of these infantile sonatas?'[1] Nannerl Mozart gave
some attention to her brother's early sonatas in her correspondence with Breitkopf
& Härtel, and perhaps K.33d–g are the works concerned. She reckoned them to be
among her late brother's first compositions (originating, it seems, during the tour
to Paris and London of 1764–6), and was quite persistent in her attempts to persuade Breitkopf & Härtel to publish these sonatas. Further correspondence on

Example 8.1   Mozart, incipits of K.Anh. 199–202/ 33d–g

(a)

Allegro

(b)

Molto Allegro

(c)

Allegro

(d)

Andante amoroso

Mozart's sonatas ensued on 30 April 1804, 15 May 1805 and 30 April 1807 – all to no avail.[2] The works were never printed and are now altogether lost (perhaps permanently). Little of the character of these pieces can be gleaned from the remaining incipits (of first movements only, in any case). Perhaps they had an obbligato violin part, like the roughly contemporary sonatas K.6–7, 8–9, 10–15 (probably best understood, in any case, as trios for piano, violin (or transverse flute) and cello, and so printed in *NMA* SerieVIII/ Wg.22/Abt.2) and 26–31. The sonatas in G major, K.11, and A, K.12 (London, 1764) begin, like K.Anh. 202, with an Andante, while that in B flat, K.15, from the same published set, has an Andante maestoso in first place. K.30 in F (The Hague and Amsterdam, 1766) opens with an Adagio. Mozart's somewhat exotic Andante amoroso of K.Anh. 202 is not found elsewhere among his sonatas of these years, although he is occasionally specific about the manner of slow movement required: K.8, second movement, Andante grazioso; K.26, Adagio un poco Andante; K.27, first movement, Andante poco Adagio. Beyond such peripheral observations we may speculate that the form of the first movements of K.Anh. 199–202 would probably have been 'developed binary', in which the second main section, following the central repeat marks, would have

Example 8.2   Mozart, incipit of Sonata fragment in C, *Köchel*[6] deest

begun with a statement of the opening theme in the dominant, as is the case in Mozart's sonatas or trios K.6–7, 8–9, 10–15 and 26–31, and works in a similar vein by Honauer, Schobert, Eckard and Raupach which Mozart knew and arranged into the '*pasticcio*' concertos, K.37, 39, 40 and 41 in 1767.

KÖCHEL[6] deest: SONATA FRAGMENT IN C MAJOR

This fragment (incipit shown in example 8.2) is found on the same folio as a final chorus and preceding recitative added *c.*1771 to the Passion Cantata, *Wo bin ich bittrer Schmerz*, K.42, originally composed in Salzburg in 1767.[3] Assuming the fragment to be roughly contemporary, it predates the first surviving sonatas, K.279–84, and, given that it extends through twenty-five bars (comprising the first subject, transition and opening of the second subject), it allows us a glimpse, at least, of Mozart's likely idiom between the four sonatas just discussed, K.Anh. 199–202 (*Köchel*[6] 33d–g), and the set of 177–5.

K.400 (*KÖCHEL*[6] 372a), ALLEGRO IN B FLAT MAJOR

Among the early editions of the Allegro in B flat are those by André (1826) and Potter (*c.*1838).[4] Only the first ninety-one bars were completed by Mozart; the remaining fifty-seven were added (presumably after the composer's death, and perhaps specifically for the André print) by Abbé Maximilian von Stadler (1748–1833). Stadler's 'literal' completion commences just after the beginning of the recapitulation and consists largely of straightforward repetition or transposition of Mozart's exposition material, along with a reworked transition. The annotations 'Sophie' and 'Constanze' [Weber] at bars 71–2 doubtless refer to Mozart's future bride and her youngest sister. According to Otto Jahn[5] the Allegro therefore originated in 1781, at which time Mozart was lodging in the Weber household under the watchful eye of his formidable future mother-in-law, Caecilia Weber, as he related in a letter to his father of 25 July that year.[6] The style of the music also fits quite well with such a date. Its virtuoso piano writing matches that of the series of Viennese piano concertos beginning with K.413, 414 and 415 written for performance in the capital shortly after the composer's removal there from Salzburg. Within the exposition are passages suggestive of tutti-solo layout. The scalic runs

Example 8.3   Mozart, incipit of fragment in F, K.590a

with punctuating crotchet chords in bars 27–32, for instance, are immediately repeated with the parts inverted – an obvious accommodation of an antiphonal concerto texture to solo means (the divisions of the sections are even reinforced by cadential minim trills over an Alberti bass in bars 32 and 42, a texture commonly found at the end of the 'solo' exposition in a concerto first movement). Likewise unusual in Mozart's sonata Allegros, yet found in the Viennese concertos, is the device of beginning the development with a straightforward statement of the main opening theme in the dominant (bars 58 ff.).

K.ANH. 29 ($KÖCHEL^6$ 590a), F MAJOR, C, 7 BARS; 30 ($KÖCHEL^6$ 590b), F MAJOR, ₵, 15 BARS; 37 ($KÖCHEL^6$ 590c), F MAJOR, 6/8, 33 BARS; 31 ($KÖCHEL^6$ 569a), B FLAT MAJOR, ₵, 19 BARS

These four items are all on a twelve-stave Viennese paper which Alan Tyson has dated to 1788.[7] This is the year of the F major Sonata, K.533 and 494, to which the first three fragments probably relate. Mozart gave no tempo mark to the brief fragment, K.590a, though its character is that of an Allegro; it might perhaps have been a first attempt at the opening movement of K.533. While it is hard to infer much from such an ephemeral sketch as this, it might be worth pointing out that with its rising arpeggios and harmonic repetition at the supertonic degree from bar 4, K.590a foreshadows the opening strategy of K.576, completed in July 1790. Transposed and recast into 6/8 metre, this fragment might have provided Mozart with the germ of an idea for the latter work (example 8.3). The character of K.590b

Example 8.4   Mozart, incipit of fragment in F, K.590b

seems appropriate either to a first movement or a finale. Assuming, for the moment, that K.590a–c were indeed drafts for the first movement of K.533, it is instructive to trace the stages in the evolution of its opening paragraph. In relation to K.590a, K.590b retains the phrase-structure (*thesis – antithesis*), working with a descending arpeggio, answered by rising scale-steps in contrast to K.590a's rising arpeggio and falling scale.[8] At this point, Mozart still clings to the harmonic strategy of supertonic repetition (bar 4), a feature he would ultimately abandon in the opening of K.533, along with the pattern of cadential closure (dominant close, rhymed with tonic close, is replaced in K.533 with an unaccompanied melody, leading to a definite tonic close at bar 4).[9] K.590b (example 8.4) foreshadows Mozart's eventual disposition in K.533 quite closely, however, incorporating inversion of the two-part contrapuntal texture – the opening treble line is transferred to the bass at bar 8, extending to the end of the fragment (compare K.533, bars 1–16). K.590c is evidently an attempt at a 6/8 sonata-rondo finale. At its close the fragment is clearly heading for a cadence in G (the dominant of the dominant), carefully prepared by the diminished-seventh arpeggios with which it breaks off: almost certainly the movement, had it been completed, would have continued with an episode in C, ultimately recapitulated in the tonic, F.

Mozart's eventual finale was a reworking of the already published Rondo in F, K.494, to which a substantial new imitative episode was added – an apparently deliberate adjustment to conform to the contrapuntal idiom of the first movement.[10] Given that there are quite detailed parallels between the structure of Mozart's opening Allegro and his eventual choice of finale, we may justifiably

Example 8.5   Mozart, incipit of fragment in B flat, K.569a

suppose that the assimilation of the finale to the idiom of the first movement was part of his original plan. That it proves possible to identify similarities of approach between the first movement of K.533 and K.590c strengthens the potential association of this fragment with the sonata:

(1) K.590c opens with a *thesis–antithesis* of paired four-bar phrases as follows: $A_{V\text{-close}}$ $A_{I\text{-close}}$ |(lower octave): $A_{V\text{-close}}$ A′(sequential extension). This could be resolved into an eight-bar phrase-pattern initially repeated at the lower octave, and continuing differently. The opening of K.533 is quite similar, also involving repetition of the opening theme (likewise arranged as *thesis–antithesis*), and involving (slightly different) repetition at the lower octave (from bar 9): $A_{I\text{-close}}$ B | (lower octave): $A_{I\text{-close}}$ B (modified continuation).

(2) K.590c continues beyond bar 12 with sequential treatment of a fragment of its opening bar. The Allegro of K.533 continues similarly at bar 15 with repetition of the figure at bar 13 (originally bar 5), followed by fragmentation to bar 18.

(3) The chromatic descent at bars 26 ff. of K.590c is similar to the harmonic progressions of bars 78 ff. of the Allegro of K.533.

K.569a, written, as already noted, on the same paper-type as K.590a–c, displays similar tonal thinking and textural planning to K.590a and b. Its opening is immediately treated to a supertonic repetition (bar 4), while from bar 8 it is transferred to the bass (example 8.5). The key (B flat), though, makes it unlikely that this fragment was related at any stage to K.533. K.569a was evidently conceived in relation to a projected sonata in B flat. Perhaps it slightly predates the other fragments, K.590a–c, in which Mozart subsequently experimented further with some of its ideas, but now in terms of a sonata in F: the descending quaver scale in thirds (bar 2 of K.569a) is very similar to bars 2 and 3 of K.590a, suggestive of a link of some kind.

K.312 (*KÖCHEL*[6] 590d), SONATENSATZ IN G MINOR

This is the longest and most important of the fragments to be discussed in this chapter. First published in 1805[11] as a complete movement (the work of an anonymous nineteenth-century editor, who appended everything after the first chord of bar 106 – where Mozart broke off – to the end of the movement, consisting of 178 bars), K.312 appeared subsequently in the Breitkopf & Härtel *Gesamtausgabe*[12] and has been included in a number of later editions of Mozart's Sonatas.[13] The 'Sonatensatz in G minor' has long been known to pianists, and still finds its way onto the concert platform from time to time.

Currently in the Bodleian Library, Oxford,[14] the autograph is in an album of composers' autographs (including other examples by Haydn and Beethoven) collected in 1836 by Felix Mendelssohn for presentation to his future bride. Mendelssohn purchased the Mozart fragment from the Viennese collector, Aloys Fuchs (1799–1853). In this manuscript, Mozart's hand ceases after the D major chord at the start of bar 106, mid-way through the development, following which is a continuation in a different (unidentified) hand (and a much lighter ink), consisting of a four-bar link leading back to G minor for the recapitulation (indicated simply by the shorthand '21 Tact/ da Capo'), and a reworked transition extending in total to 145 bars (the ending is not that of the 1805 edition, but breaks off in mid-phrase before the reprise of Mozart's original closing theme). The disposition of music across the folios of the manuscript is as follows:

f.8   bars 1–75 Exposition and beginning of development (Mozart)
f.8^v bars 76–106^1 Development (Mozart)
      bars 106^1–[109] Link to recapitulation and da capo indication (nineteenth-century hand)
f.9   blank
f.9^v bars [131 – 45] Recapitulation retransition (nineteenth-century hand)

In successive editions of *Köchel* the fragment has been assigned variously to 1778 (*Köchel*[1]), late 1774 (*Köchel*[3] – numbering revised to K.189i);[15] and summer 1790 (*Köchel*[3] supplement – numbering revised to K.590d). The revisions of Köchel's original date were both made by Einstein in his work for the third edition (1937) and its supplement (1947). His last revision (placing the work in 1790) has recently been confirmed by Alan Tyson, whose investigation of the watermark evidence has shown that K.312 did indeed originate in 1790 or thereabouts: 'The paper-type was first used by Mozart in the middle of his work on *Così fan tutte*, and was then available to him up to the end of his life. So the fragment [K.312] dates from 1790 or 1791.'[16] Allied to this is some stylistic evidence. K.312's development section shares several common features with the B flat major Sonata, K.570 (February 1789), another 3/4 sonata-form Allegro movement, in particular, the diversionary block-chord harmonic progression taking the music away from the expected key into a more remote region (C minor in K.312; D flat major in K.570), and the sequential ascent that follows (K.312, bars 83 ff.; K.570, bars 84 ff.) – in each case based on a subsidiary figure (of identical length and type) from the exposition and ending with a prominent augmented-sixth resolution.

Why Mozart abandoned such a promising movement is unclear. Perhaps he intended a straightforward recapitulation similar to that of the anonymous 1805 print, in which only minimal adjustment of exposition material was required, and, feeling that he had composed enough of the movement to be able to pick up the threads at a later date, left it alone (and never subsequently returned to it). This would place the fragment in a similar category to other works begun in the late 1780s, such as the B flat major Concerto, K.595, the D major Quintet, K.593 and (perhaps) the Clarinet Concerto, K.622, that remained but sizeable fragments for a considerable time, as Alan Tyson has plausibly demonstrated (the only significant difference being that Mozart ultimately completed these works).[17]

PART THREE

STYLE

CHAPTER NINE

Eighteenth-century views of sonata form

How would Mozart have answered the question: 'What is sonata form'? Given the predominance of sonata form in Mozart's solo sonatas (all but two first movements and a significant number of finales and even slow movements employ it), we are justified in considering this question in isolation before turning to more detailed investigations of individual sonatas. Naturally, Mozart's use of sonata form was not limited to the solo sonatas, nor, indeed, to instrumental music, whether for domestic or public consumption. It was a way of organising tonal space that evidently proved more attractive to him, his contemporaries and immediate successors than any other. It was flexible enough to accommodate few or many themes of great variety in length, character and articulation; simple or complex harmonies and key-relations; regular or irregular phrase-groups (or combinations of them); light or dense textures in manifold alternations; single or diverse 'topics'; small or great dimensions, and so on. Above all, perhaps, it could accommodate a vast range of affective representation, from the humble to the grand – from the unpretentious language of scales and arpeggios in the first movement of Mozart's C major Sonata, K.545 ('für Anfänger'), at one extreme, to the epic public statement of the first movement of Beethoven's 'Eroica' symphony at the other. Interestingly, neither of these movements corresponds to the 'textbook plan' of sonata form familiar from many primers on form intended for examination use.[1] It is the purpose of this chapter to review briefly the dichotomy that exists between 'modern' textbook descriptions of sonata form and those of eighteenth-century writers and to illustrate the form as understood and explained by Mozart and his contemporaries within individual movements of Mozart's solo sonatas. Having arrived at an understanding of eighteenth-century appreciations of sonata structures, we will be better placed to appreciate Mozart's procedures.

Sonata form as described by most nineteenth- and twentieth-century theorists is a three-section design consisting of exposition, development and recapitulation of two principal themes, labelled respectively the first and second subjects. This tradition derives from the third volume of Adolph Bernhard Marx's *Die Lehre von der musikalischen Komposition*.[2] Marx, who is probably responsible for the term 'sonata form', takes an overtly thematic approach shaped, to some extent, by the work of Beethoven, in which thematic contrast (not necessarily between just two themes) became increasingly the generator of large-scale form.[3] This approach is at odds with all eighteenth-century theoretical descriptions, which propose a two-section division of the form, the first of which equates to the exposition in Marx's plan, the second of which incorporates both development and recapitulation. Heinrich Christoph Koch, for instance, explains the sonata design thus:

the first allegro of the symphony . . . has two sections which may be performed with or without repetition. The first of these consists only of a single main period [the 'exposition'], and contains the plan of the symphony; that is, the main melodic phrases are presented in their original order and afterwards a few of them are fragmented . . . The second section consists of two main periods, of which the first [the 'development section'] tends to have greatly diverse structures . . . The last period of our first allegro [the 'recapitulation'], which is devoted above all to the main key, most frequently begins with the [opening] theme in this key, but occasionally may also start with another main melodic idea . . . Finally, the second half of the first period which followed the V-phrase in the fifth [= dominant key], is repeated in the main key and with this the allegro ends.[4]

No prescription is made as to the number of themes to be incorporated (though, as will be noted in due course, several writers suggest or imply that the first section – the exposition – should contain both opening and contrasting themes). Usually each of the two sections is repeated, the derivation from the earlier 'developed' binary form being obvious. All eighteenth-century writers are agreed that the generating element of the form is the contrast of *tonality* (not theme). During section one the tonic key is established and then replaced by a close relative (normally the dominant – or mediant in the case of a minor tonic); section two begins with an exploration of tonal space in the region of the related key and concludes with a restatement of the section one material (normally, but not always, in its entirety) in the original tonic. There is a rhetorical (and sometimes dramatic) element to all this, according to which the tonic material within section one could be seen as the basic proposition of a disputation, which is then refuted by further material (not necessarily a new theme) in the related key; the counter-proposals are then explored in detail during the opening part of section two; and the supremacy of the opening proposition is symbolised in the closing part of section two by (normally) two important events – the return of the initial theme in the tonic and the restatement of the related key material within the realm of the tonic (which remains in force subsequently until the end of the movement).[5]

This tonal, rather than thematic, view of the sonata form can account quite happily for the many diverse approaches to the form found in the first movements of Mozart's piano sonatas. This can easily be seen by examining two constrasting examples of the 'first section [consisting] only of a single main period' (Koch's terminology for the exposition)' and 'first main period' of the 'second section' (the development section). In the G major Sonata, K.283, for instance, the opening section (bars 1–22) moving from tonic to dominant features only one main theme (whose consequent part is repeated from bar 10) and a scalic transitional figure. Thereafter, starting out from the new key of D, Mozart introduces at least four themes (bars 23, 31, 35 and 45), each of which is treated to either repetition or embellishment. In the C major Sonata, K.309, the exposition structure is quite different. Its exposition introduces at least ten distinct themes, of which five or six occur in the opening section (bars 1–32). Likewise, the structure of each development section (the 'first main period' of the 'second section' in Koch's description) is quite different. That in K.283 introduces a wholly new theme (bar 54), and continues without further reference to any exposition material; that in K.309 is founded exclusively on exposition material, specifically on the main opening theme and on the closing idea first sounded at bar 54. In each sonata the 'last period' (recapitulation) 'begins with the [opening] theme in [the main] key', and is 'devoted above all to the main key', and in particular, 'the second half of the first period which followed the V-phrase in the fifth [= dominant key], is repeated in the main key' (K.283, bars 90 ff.; K.309, bars 127 ff.). Each movement conforms to the description given by Koch and yet preserves a distinctive structure.

Marx's post-Beethoven view of sonata form and that of the eighteenth-century theorists set quite different agendas. Crudely stated, for Marx, the threefold division of the form into exposition, development and recapitulation centred on what the composer did with his contrasting themes (statement, working-out and restatement). According to this agenda sonata form comprised a series of harmonic, tonal, and textural devices for supporting thematic presentation and, especially, opposition. According to the eighteenth-century agenda almost the reverse was true: theme (not necessarily more than one) occupied a subsidiary role as an agent in the balanced presentation and resolution of tonally opposed forces. Theory only ever being idealised practice, we may assume the true position to have lain somewhere between these two extremes, neither theme nor tonality being supreme, but rather co-existing in an elegant equipoise. Several eighteenth-century theorists refer to sonata Allegro movements as being analogous to a well-delivered oration in which the point(s) to be argued and the techniques for doing so were in satisfying balance. It is clear that, for many eighteenth-century theorists, theme actually occupied a crucial position in the conception of form, but influencing the immediate continuity of the structure, rather than creating its large-scale coherence.

A review of the quite copious literature on melody published during the second half of the century shows that theme, while regarded as perhaps the main thing to be appreciated by the listener, was nonetheless of primarily local significance as an element of musical discourse.[6]

This is the impression given by Koch and Galeazzi, both of whom draw attention to the coordination of thematic events with the tonal progress of a movement. Thus, for example, Koch differentiates in his description of a sonata exposition between 'rushing and sonorous phrases' (which characterise the opening paragraph) and 'a more singing phrase' (which he associates specifically with 'a modulation into the most closely related key . . . ', that is, what would later come to be known as the 'second subject').[7] This accords with Galeazzi's account of the form, dating from 1796:

the Characteristic Passage or Intermediate Passage [the 'second subject'] is a new idea, which is introduced, for the sake of greater beauty, towards the middle of the first part. This must be gentle, expressive, and tender . . . and must be presented in the same key to which the modulation was made [i.e. the dominant, or other related key within the exposition].[8]

While such a pronounced contrast is present in some of Mozart's sonatas (K.284, 309, 311, 457 and 576), in the majority of such cases there is no such clear distinction (K.280, 310, 333, 570, for instance). This illustrates another difficulty that the thematic view of sonata form encounters in relation to eighteenth-century repertory. To be fair, Koch's statement occurs in the course of his description of 'Symphony', though, in common with all eighteenth-century theorists, his description of movement forms is attached to a general discussion of genres, and should not be taken to refer exclusively to the symphonic genre.

In the recapitulation, Galeazzi likewise agrees with Koch that the return of the tonic key should normally be timed to arrive together with a restatement of the opening theme (as in the case of Mozart's K.283 and 309, discussed above), but might on occasion be co-ordinated with a secondary theme:

The Reprise [recapitulation] succeeds the Modulation ['development section']. However remote the Modulation is from the main key of the composition, it must draw closer little by little, until the Reprise, that is, the first Motive of Part I in the proper natural key in which it was originally written, falls in quite naturally and regularly. If the piece is a long one, the true Motive in the principal key is taken up again . . . but if one does not want to make the composition too long, then it shall be enough to repeat instead the Characteristic Passage ['second subject'] transposed to the same fundamental key . . . [9]

Something akin to this actually happens in the first movement of the D major Sonata, K.311, in which the reprise of the opening subject (Galeazzi's 'true Motive in the principal key') is substantially delayed until the end of the movement is in sight (bar 99). It is preceded by what Galeazzi terms the 'Characteristic Passage' (bar 78[3]), now 'transposed to the . . . fundamental key', but this is not the start of the 'Reprise', which occurs at bar 58 with an unusual subdominant restatement of a theme originally sounded at bar 28. In this movement, then, neither the tonal nor thematic views can adequately explain the unfolding of the form, since there is neither a regular tonic recapitulation nor a regular thematic ordering. Nevertheless, the tonal explanation comes closest, since from bar 99 the material from 'the second half of the first period which followed the V-phrase in the fifth [=dominant key], is repeated in the main key'.[10]

One further piece of evidence in favour of the tonal view of eighteenth-century sonata form is actually related to a specific Mozart sonata movement, K.284. Johann Georg Portmann's *Leichtes Lehrbuch der Harmonie, Composition, und des General-Basses*

(Darmstadt, 1789) includes a sonata movement in D major that is overtly modelled on the first movement of K.284, not thematically, but in its key-scheme which Portmann represents diagrammatically.[11] Tonality, not theme, is regarded as the main issue here, especially as regards the harmonic conduct of the development section and the recapitulation. The division of the whole form into tonal sections is shown by punctuation marks, a comma separating harmonic areas within each of the large divisions of the movement, a semicolon separating the end of the development from the beginning of the recapitulation, and full stops the ends of the two main sections (the exposition and the end of the entire movement). As Beth Shamgar points out this hierarchy is revealing:[12] Portmann's use of only a semicolon at the end of the development clearly indicates that, for him, the whole movement consisted of just two large sections, of which the second corresponds to Koch's description quoted earlier. An adaptation of Portmann's scheme is shown below (lower case letters refer to minor keys):

[Exposition:]	D,	E,	A.	:‖:	a,	B,	e,	F♯,	b;	[1]
[or:]					g♯,	C♯,	f♯,	e,	C♯,	F♯;	[2]
[or:]					f♯,	B,	e,	D,	B,	e;	[3]
[or:]					e,	A,	D,	C,	A,	d;	[4]
[then:]			d,	A,	B♭,	F,	G,	e,	A,		[5]
[followed by:]			D,	A,	D.	:‖					[6]

In broad tonal terms, K.284's movement comes quite close to Portmann's diagrammatic scheme. Bars 1–60 are fairly represented by line [1][13] but Mozart then continues into F♯ minor and E minor before arriving at D minor in bar 66. From here to the end of the movement Mozart's piece is in broad agreement with Portmann's lines [5] and [6]. In examining Portmann's various alternative key-schemes for development sections, one is again reminded of Koch's remark that 'The second section consists of two main periods, of which the first [the 'development section'] tends to have greatly diverse structures' and also of Galeazzi: 'However remote the Modulation is from the main key of the composition, it must draw closer little by little, until the Reprise, that is, the first Motive of Part I in the proper natural key in which it was originally written, falls in quite naturally and regularly'. In each of Portmann's schemes (lines [1], [2], [3] or [4], followed by line [5]) the music steadily approaches the tonic, strongly implying that, in both Portmann's 'model sonata' and Mozart's movement on which it is based, the thematic material was subsidiary in overall importance to the tonal pattern, which was capable of supporting a wide diversity of surface elaborations.

Marx's later thematic description of sonata form might best be treated as a *prescription*, of overtly didactic intent.[14] By contrast, eighteenth-century theoretical descriptions of the form treat it as a *convention* according to which a composer presented his ideas, and according to which the listener understood them. Such a groundplan admitted considerable flexibility in detail. It implies a recognised (and recognisable) sequence of musical events in which the external and internal features of the form are not in conflict ('Form' as opposed to 'Content'); indeed, according to such a 'conventional' approach external and internal features were inter-dependent.

The 'conventional' presentation of musical ideas in a logical sequence was analogous to the teaching and practice of oratory, as expressed in the various manuals of rhetoric written by, for example, G. F. Meier and J. C. Gottsched[15] – an analogy pursued by more than one music theorist during the classic period. References to oratory in the work of Mattheson and Forkel were made in a general sense in chapter 1.[16] In a much more specific sense, both Mattheson and Forkel applied the accepted divisions of an oration to the analysis of musical form. Forkel, for instance, offered the following:

one of the main points in musical rhetoric and aesthetics is the ordering of musical ideas and the progression of the sentiments expressed through them, so that these ideas are conveyed to our hearts with a certain coherence, just as the ideas in an oration are conveyed to our minds and follow one another according to logical principles. Accordingly, this is the basis of the necessity that, in a work of art

(1) a main sentiment
(2) similar subsidiary sentiments
(3) dissected sentiments . . .
(4) contrasting and opposed sentiments

must all obtain. When ordered in an appropriate manner, these elements are thus to the language of sentiments the equivalent of that which in the language of ideas . . . are the well-known elements still preserved by good, genuine orators – that is *exordium, propositio, refutatio, confirmatio*, etc.[17]

Elsewhere, Forkel offers the following rhetorically inspired divisions of a musical form:[18]

Exordium	Introduction
Hauptsatz	Main theme
Nebensätze	Secondary themes
Gegensätze	Opposing (contrasting) themes
Zergliederungen	Dissection (fragmentation) of themes
Widerlegungen	Refutations
Bekräftigungen	Reiterations/confirmations
Conclusion	Conclusion

While this sequence is indebted to that of Mattheson's *Kern melodischer Wissenschaft*[19] it also derives from that outlined in, for instance, Meier's *Anfangsgründe*, and which are the 'general laws by which thoughts, in all aesthetic elaborations, must be ordered'.[20] Johann Friedrich Daube likewise refers to 'proper ordering of a few melodic elements, their manipulation, and their correct placement' as a vital factor in a work's comprehensibility.[21] This correspondence between this typical *dispositio* of an oration and sonata form may be expressed as follows:

Part 1

(Exordium)	(Introduction)
Hauptsatz	Exposition
Nebensätze	
Gegensätze	

Part 2

Zergliederungen	Development[22]
Widerlegungen	
Bekräftigungen	Recapitulation
Conclusion	Coda

It should be pointed out here that no exclusive claim is being made for a link between the arrangement of an oration and sonata form. The division of an oration into subsidiary parts implies a flexible structure that first posits something, then adduces contrasting ideas, then engages in argumentation before reasserting the centrality of the main thought and coming to a conclusion. Clearly, such a flexible structure admits of many and varied interpretations or applications. Musically, it can apply to episodic forms such as are found in Mozart's slow movements (K.457; K.570; K.576, for instance) and rondo finales (K.281; K.309–11; K.331; K.545, for instance), as well as sonata forms without development (K.332, Andante). Variations (K.284, finale; K.331, first movement) represent a special case. In a sense, since the theme, in some guise, is progressively embellished the variation set is obsessively to do with the opening theme; yet there remains the defining element of contrast between successive variations, though this is not a *structural* contrast but one inherent in the quality of figurative development.[23]

The essential prerequisite for an analogy of rhetoric and music is a perception in contemporary writings that music was, in some sense, a language. Fortunately, evidence is readily available in the work of many eighteenth-century theorists.[24] Mattheson, for instance, calls music an 'oration in sound' ('Klang-Rede'); Quantz describes music as an 'artificial language'.[25] A detailed comparison is made by Forkel:

In good musical composition, harmony and melody are as inseparable as the truth of ideas and the correctness of expression are in language. Language is the garb of ideas, just as melody is the garb of harmony. In this respect, one can imagine harmony as the logic of music, for it relates to melody as does logic, in language to expression.[26]

While eighteenth-century rhetorical convention can prove a valuable tool for analysing contemporary musical form on a detailed level, it is important to keep its broader contexts in mind. All writers concur in regarding the sequence of Exordium, Hauptsatz, Nebensätze, etc. as a *means to an end*, rather than an end in itself. This aim was aesthetic, rather than purely technical; the ultimate purpose of those who aspired to the skill of oratory was, according to Quantz, 'to make

themselves the masters of the hearts of their listeners, to arouse or still their pas-
sions, and to transport them now to this sentiment, now to that'.[27]

A rhetorically-inspired view of music, while unfamiliar today, was standard in the
eighteenth century. Following on from detailed instruction in grammar, school-
boys such as Joseph Haydn and Leopold Mozart went on to study rhetoric, principally through the latin texts of Aristotle, Cicero and Quintilian.[28] Leopold
Mozart attended the Gymnasium and the Jesuit Lyceum in Augsburg, providing
him with a thorough grounding in grammar; given that his subsequent university
education at Salzburg included philosophy (in which he graduated with
commendation in 1738) and law, we may assume that he gained a detailed acquaintance of the standard principles of argumentation and of Roman law, and particularly of so-called *forensic*, or judicial rhetoric, that is, the species of oratory devoted
to prosecuting or defending a legal case. Leopold was a man of wide learning. He
owned microscopes, was a subscriber to Grimm's *Correspondance Littéraire*, and, in
preparation for the writing of his treatise on violin-playing, *Versuch einer gründliche
Violinschule* (Augsburg, 1756),[29] immersed himself in the study of rhetorical textbooks, as is shown by letters he wrote to the Augsburg publisher, Johann Jakob
Lotter, on 9 June and 28 August 1755, requesting, for example, copies of the works
of Johann Christoph Gottsched.[30] In the charming 'Short history of music' with
which Leopold prefaced his treatise he mentions by name theorists, both ancient
and modern, with whose works he was evidently acquainted – a list that makes
impressive reading, and which, in nodding towards the principal writings of the
established theoretical canon, both strengthens its own position within that canon
and at the same time creates the impression that the *Violinschule* was the work of
an author of wide-ranging scholarship.[31] All of this might be regarded as a mar-
keting ploy, but was in fact an accepted part of the scholarly etiquette of the time,
an expected appeal to tradition by which the ostensible merits of a new work were
introduced. In this respect, Leopold was following the advice of Quintilian,
according to whom it was the duty of an orator to make extensive study of the
existing canon.[32] For our purposes, the 'Short history of music' further demonstrates that Leopold was indeed a man of considerable learning, for whom a thorough grounding in such theoretical texts was an essential foundation for the proper
understanding of music in both its written and practical aspects. Some of this learning we may reasonably suppose he passed on to his son. At the very least, we may
note that Wolfgang was raised in a household in which learning was respected, by
an erudite father whose own education had incorporated a detailed study of
grammar and rhetoric, philosophy and law, and who took a keen interest in music
theory. Leopold's list of approved musical theorists reveals something of the breadth
of his scholarship:

Glarean, Zarlin, Bontemps, Zacconi, Galilei, Gaffur, Berard, Donius, Bonnet, Tevo, Kircher, Froschius, Artusi, Kepler, Vogt, Neidhardt, Euler, Scheibe, Prinz, Werckmeister, Fux, Mattheson, Mizler, Spiess, Marpurg, Quantz, Riepel, and others whom either I do not know or whose names do not occur to me at the moment; all these are men who by their writings on music have earned great credit in the scientific world. But these are only theoretical writings. He who seeks practical authors can find hundreds of them if he searches the dictionaries of Brossard and Walther.[33]

Leopold does not specify any particular works, simply their authors, several of whom wrote more than one important treatise. Werckmeister, for example, was responsible for several works on temperament, as well as the *Harmonologica Musica* (Frankfurt and Leipzig, 1702); Caspar Prinz wrote two treatises entitled *Compendium Musicae* (Guben, 1668; Dresden, 1689); of the many treatises by the medieval writer, Jehan des Murs, Leopold perhaps knew of the *Musica speculativa secundum Boetium* (1323), which draws heavily upon Boethius's *De Institutione Musica*. Athanasius Kircher's most widely-read volume was *Musurgia Universalis*, but Leopold might have known others of his works: his reference to Artusi was not, for instance, to the famous *L'Artusi, overo Della Imperfettioni della Moderna Musica* (Venice, 1600), but to the less familiar *L'Arte del Contrapunto* (Venice, 1586). Gaffurius, Glareanus and Zarlino each wrote copiously on theory, though in each case it is fortunately possible to specify which of their works Leopold had in mind, since elsewhere in his treatise he makes specific reference to Gaffurius's *Practica Musicae* (Milan, 1496) and *Theorica Musicae* (Milan, 1492); to Glareanus's *Dodecacordon* (Basel, 1547) and to Zarlino's *Le Institutione Harmoniche* (Venice, 1558) and *Dimonstratione Harmoniche* (Venice, 1571).[34] In addition to more modern authors (Mattheson, Marpurg and Scheibe are mentioned, among others) Leopold was acquainted with treatises from Greek antiquity: by Ptolemy (presumably the *Harmonicorum*),[35] Aristoxenus (either his *Harmonica* or *Elementa Rhythmica*).[36] Probably Leopold knew these works, and those of Pythagoras, through Marcus Meibom's *Antiquae Musicae Auctoris Septem Graece et Latine* (Amsterdam, 1652).[37] Meibom's edition contains Aristoxenus's *Harmonica* (and Quintilian's *De Musica*, an extract from which Leopold quotes on the reverse of the title-page of his violin treatise). His knowledge of Ptolemy's *Harmonicorum* was perhaps gained through Johannes Kepler's *Harmonices Mundi* (Linz, 1619), which draws upon Ptolemy. Possibly a significant quantity of Leopold's understanding of more recent theory was digested at second hand rather than through direct acquaintance with such works as Leonhard Euler's *Tentamen Novae Theoriae Musicae* (St Petersburg, 1739) and Johann Mattheson's *Der vollkommene Capellmeister* (Hamburg, 1739). Sizeable extracts from both works (along with others by Johann Adolph Scheibe and Meinrad Spiess) appeared in Lorenz Mizler's Leipzig periodical, *Neu-eröffnete musikalische Bibliothek* (1739–54). Mizler (1711–78) founded this periodical as a means of circulating material among a corresponding society of musical scholars, the 'Societät der musikalischen Wissenschaften', a society limited to twenty members and including Bach, Handel and Telemann. Leopold was proposed for membership by Mizler, but for some reason this was never granted. Especially important for Mizler was the rhetorical work of his former university professor in Berlin, Johann Christoph Gottsched, whose widely-read *Versuch einer Kritischen Dichtkunst* (Leipzig, 1730),[38] was serialised in the *musikalische Bibliothek*. Perhaps this was Leopold's earliest acquaintance with Gottsched's writing; in 1755, as noted above, he sought out copies of several of Gottsched's works. While he may have been reliant on Mizler's *musikalische Bibliothek* for some of his theoretical understanding, he certainly owned copies of Johann Joseph Fux's *Gradus ad Parnassum* (Vienna, 1725) and one or more of Joseph Riepel's *Anfangsgründe zur musikalischen Setzkunst* (Regensburg and Vienna, 1752) and *Grundregeln zur Tonordnung insgemein* (Frankfurt and Leipzig, 1755).[39]

This then, is the theoretical atmosphere within which Wolfgang Mozart grew up at home in Salzburg. While there is no direct documentary evidence detailing the kind of musical and general education he had from his father we may hazard a guess, in the light of Leopold's own school and university background, added to his continuing intellectual pursuits during the 1740s and 1750s, that he would have done his best to pass on something of the same pedagogical tradition to Wolfgang – especially as the boy had no 'formal' schooling. Assuming this to be the case, and assuming a central role for rhetoric in Leopold's *Weltanschauung*, we next need to examine the hierarchical structure of rhetoric.

The main Greek and Latin texts by Aristotle, Cicero and Quintilian, noted above, are in general agreement regarding the divisions of this hierarchy. In some sense, the Roman treatises all derive from Aristotle.[40] Occasionally there are differences in detail (such as the order in which the various divisions and sub-divisions are discussed) but only rarely are there differences in substance.[41] There are likewise distinctions in exact terminology, and Quintilian devotes a section of his treatise to the need for consistency in this respect.[42] Neither of these casts any ambiguity on the actual structure of an oration as understood in the Greek and Roman world, and as transmitted, through the middle ages, renaissance and baroque eras, to the Enlightenment.

The highest level was that of *species*, and had three sub-divisions, forensic, deliberative and epideictic.[43] Forensic oratory was that species devoted to the actual prosecution or defence of a legal case, and received the most extended treatment in all the rhetorical texts. Deliberative oratory was that species devoted to debate, in which the eventual outcome was dependent on the strength of the case presented. Epideictic oratory – sometimes called panegyric – was that species devoted to the extolling of personal virtue (or, indeed, vice). In epideictic speeches the merits of a ruler, philosopher, poet, or other famous person were stated and developed. On the next level came the five *partes* of an oration: invention (*inventio*), arrangement (*dispositio*), style (*elocutio*), memory (*memoria*) and delivery (*pronuntiatio*).[44] These were the technical and practical means by which an oration was structured. The second category, arrangement, was typically divided into six parts: introduction (*exordium*), statement of facts (*narratio*), proposition (*propositio*),[45] proof (*confirmatio*), refutation (*refutatio*), and conclusion (*peroratio*).[46]

SPECIES

| Forensic | Deliberative | Epideictic |

PARTES

Invention   Arrangement   Style   Memory   Delivery

Introduction   Statement of Facts   Proposition   Proof   Refutation   Conclusion

In Cicero's *De Oratore*, Crassus recalls his schooling in rhetorical species in the following terms:

. . . some [species of rhetoric] have their place in courts of justice, others in deliberations; while there was yet a third kind, which was to do with the extolling or reviling of particular persons . . . there were prescribed commonplaces [*locos*] which we were to employ in the law-courts where equity was our aim; others for use in deliberations, all of which were to be arranged for the benefit of those to whom we might be giving counsel; and others again in panegyric [*in laudationibus*], wherein the sole consideration was the greatness of the individuals concerned.[47]

Interconnections exist between all three species of rhetoric. The techniques of deliberative oratory, by which a speaker could argue persuasively for or against a particular point at issue, and epideictic, by which the virtues of a person could be described, might form important stages in the conduct of a particular forensic case, leading to a verdict. Both of the two former species were important elements in the armoury of a forensic orator, of course. Quintilian, indeed, was of the opinion that all three species 'contain the whole of rhetoric, since each of them requires *invention, arrangement, expression* [style], *memory* and *delivery*'.[48] In short, while the functions of each species differed they held certain techniques in common. In musical applications of rhetoric it is important to be aware not only of different functions but of appropriate techniques. For instance, in a piece of music the forensic and deliberative species are inappropriate, since no question of accusation or defence arises, neither is the conclusion in doubt.[49] Persuasion is common to all rhetorical species,[50] but whereas in the forensic and deliberative species the aim of the speaker was to persuade his listeners towards a certain course of action, in epideictic rhetoric the speaker's main purpose was to impress his ideas upon the minds of his audience, without seeking to persuade them towards any particular course of action. In one sense, epideictic is a type of *display* which achieves its aim by means of rhetorical eloquence. It is in this broad sense that rhetoric may most fruitfully be applied to music. Since all tonal music is, in one sense, a foregone conclusion, its attributes – principally, the hegemony of the tonic key, but also such features as periodicity –

already known and not at all in doubt, epideictic is clearly the appropriate rhetorical species to apply. According to Aristotle: 'The epideictic style is especially suited
to written compositions, for its function is reading'.[51]

Turning next to the *partes* of an oration, it soon becomes clear that, in compositional terms, only the first three (invention, arrangement and style) apply in any
specific sense. Memory related to the orator's, poet's or composer's remembered
store of past examples of orations, poems or compositions. In this sense, *memoria* has
to do with 'influence', which was the subject of chapter 2. Delivery, on the other
hand, had to do with the 'performance' of an oration rather than its composition;
musically, this is the preserve of performance practice, rather than actual composition. This leaves the three stages of invention (the initial inspiration, the thematic
material upon which a piece is based, for example), arrangement (the organisation
of the material into sections, that is, the outward structure of a movement: sonata
form, binary, rondo and so on) and style (the detailed elaboration of each phrase),
which Cicero describes as follows:

Invention is the discovery of valid or seemingly valid arguments to render one's cause plausible. Arrangement is the distribution of arguments thus discovered in the proper order.
Expression [style] is the fitting of the proper language to the invented matter.[52]

The preparation of a musical 'oration', according to Forkel, consisted of just these
three stages:

(1) *Erfindung* – the creation of basic melodic ideas (the *inventio* of an oration)
(2) *Ausführung* (or *Anordnung*) – the *planning* of the movement, in which the basic ideas
undergo *preparation*, that is, they are put into an order and are elaborated and varied (the *dispositio*, or *elaboratio* of an oration)
(3) *Ausarbeitung* – the actual *composition* of the movement, in which the fine detail of the
themes, harmonies, phrases, periods, etc. is worked out (the *elocutio* of an oration)

Within this threefold scheme, the convention of a sonata form, as described by
the various eighteenth-century writers, equates to stage 2, the *Ausführung*, or
preparation. This was the convention to which the composer adhered. Once this
was determined in outline, the real work of composition pertinent to the individual movement (the shaping of themes, their fragmentation and combination within
a development section, the textures, etc.) was begun. At this point the techniques
of *figurae* appropriate to *Melodielehre* (as taught, for instance, by Mattheson and
Koch), and *Kontrapunktlehre* (as taught, for instance, by Fux and Albrechtsberger)
came into play.[53] These successive stages in the evolution of the musical oration will
next be examined in order. In chapter 10 the inspiration that lay behind the oration
is considered. Chapter 11 looks at the actual design of sonata form movements, episodic forms and variations. Finally, chapter 12 investigates some aspects of the
detailed 'elaboration' (*elocutio*) of these works.

CHAPTER TEN

Pre-compositional choices – the rhetorical *inventio*

At first sight, *inventio* seems a simple concept, namely, the invention of musical themes subsequently worked out according to the different rhetorical *partes* of *dispositio* (arrangement) and *elocutio* (style or expression) during the course of a piece or movement. Applied to a finished piece of music, discussion of *inventio* appears to be little more than a definition of, for example, its principal and contrasting themes. In Mozart's K.333, for instance, the *inventio* in bars 1–38 consists of the opening theme and the secondary theme (in the dominant) that enters at bar 23. The 'fleshing-out' of these bars by means of large-scale tonal planning through strong cadences on B flat in bar 10 (a rounded tonic opening period, from which the remainder of the exposition can diversify), C major in bar 22 and F major in bar 38, a generally slow and uniform rate of harmonic change, speeding up towards these structurally defining cadential divisions, periodic phrasing, phrase-repetition (bar 10[4]; bar 31), internal repetition involving both transposition and decoration (bars 14[4]–22), sequence (bars 1–4; bars 27–9), and so on, belong to the realm of *dispositio* and *elocutio*. It is tempting to view the work in such conceptually separated terms: first the invention (the stuff of 'inspiration'), next the composition.

However, the matter is not so simple. Quintilian's discussion of *inventio* dwells upon the relationship between *invention* and *judgement*, a concept, he says, that some teachers of rhetoric have added to the three traditional *partes* 'on the ground that it is necessary first to *invent* and then to *exercise our judgement*'.[1] Quintilian's main question is whether invention exists as an independent entity or only in close association with the techniques with which is is developed. If it is not independent, what is it dependent on? Transplanted into the realm of musical composition, this question asks: Does a composer invent a theme and then work it out, or does he only invent themes that he knows from experience will prove suitable for the kind of treatment he has in mind within a particular piece?

Cicero lays great stress on the relationship between the material and its treatment,[2] suggesting that, in the realm of music, the composer does not simply invent a theme and then develop it according to the rules of art but thinks of these two aspects as inter-dependent. He will consider the type of discourse to be undertaken in the piece in conjunction with the type of theme to be invented for that purpose. Neither element is entirely divorced from the other:

. . . it does not follow that everything which is to be said first must be studied first; for the reason that, if you wish the first part of the speech to have a close agreement and connexion with the main statement of the case, *you must derive it from the matters which are to be discussed afterwards* [my italics]. Therefore when the point for decision and the arguments which must be devised for the purpose of reaching a decision have been diligently discovered by the rules of art, and studied with careful thought, then, and only then, the other parts of the oration are to be arranged in proper order [introduction, statement of facts, division, and so on].[3]

The theme in a musical composition, therefore, is not to be devised solely as a thing in itself but with an eye to what it might become during the course of the piece or movement.

Aristotle also considers invention. For him, invention is the finding of 'artistic proofs', and is discussed in terms of reasoning by syllogism and induction.[4] A key passage in his *Rhetoric* describes two particular types of 'proof':[5]

Now that which is persuasive is persuasive and convincing either at once and in and by itself, or because it appears to be proved by propositions that are convincing.

Aristotle is distinguishing between two levels of persuasion here, 'primary' and 'secondary'. The former resides in the idea in itself; the latter in a higher sense, supported by subsidiary 'propositions that are convincing' (in other words, a syllogism). In musical terms this suggests that a musical idea may be convincing either in a 'primary' sense (that is, by itself, as a plain statement), or else in a 'secondary' sense (in the course of development, in combination with another theme or themes). This secondary sense is analogous, perhaps, to the syllogism, in that, through the combination of recognisable themes ('propositions') a further mental construct – which we call 'counterpoint' – results. A couple of examples will make this clear.

Mozart's B flat Sonata, K.281 (1774–5), begins with a theme that is a direct statement 'convincing . . . at once and in and by itself'. It does not, for example, combine with other elements in the exposition or development, but contributes to the musical discourse as a 'primary' statement, sounded twice in immediate succession at the opening of the exposition and recapitulation, and once more (in the dominant) towards the beginning of the development. In Mozart's later B flat Sonata, K.570 (1789), the opening theme is initially stated in octaves (that is, another 'primary' theme, 'convincing . . . at once and in and by itself'), but in the later course of the movement is combined with a distinctive quaver countertheme (bars 41 ff.; bars 101–30; bars 171 ff.). From the combination of these two propositions (theme and countertheme) Mozart constructs a significant proportion of his development, a structural feature which we appreciate as a higher level of organisation than a straightforward, single, thematic presentation, a satisfying portion of the musical discourse that 'appears to be proved by [two separate] propositions that are [individually] convincing'. Mozart seems, then, to have designed the opening theme of K.570 not simply as a theme in itself but as one that can engage with other thematic elements to produce a 'convincing' whole. Nor is contrapuntal combination the only 'syllogism' in K.570. Mozart effects the return to the recapitulation by further development of the quaver countertheme (itself a product of Mozart's melodic 'invention'), combined with the harmonic strategy of sequence (bars 117 ff.). Seen in terms of Aristotle's artistic proofs, two separate propositions (a melodic element and a harmonic element) are combined at this important structural turning point to produce a third (sequential organisation – like counterpoint, a mental 'construct') 'persuasive . . . because it appears to be proved by propositions that are convincing'.

So much for the inter-relationships between invention, arrangement and expression (style). Before proceeding to a more detailed examination of the arrangement as a *parte* in its own right, it is worth pausing to consider the concept of *inventio* in isolation. What was the process by which a theme was 'invented'? While this might appear to be the indefinable product of the artistic inspiration, it is possible, to some extent, to progress back one stage further than the written evidence of the score, even when, as in Mozart's case, sketches – for the sonatas, at least – scarcely exist. Through a knowledge of eighteenth-century theories of melody, it is possible to propose hypothetical 'reductions' of melody, to recover the possible *Urlinien* (to appropriate a Schenkerian term) that lie behind Mozart's themes.[6]

A number of eighteenth-century treatises make a distinction between *simple* melody and *figured* melody. The latter builds upon the former, resulting in melodic decoration (that is, figured melody) of a simple underlying pattern – one that could legitimately be traced back to the species counterpoint demonstrations in Fux's *Gradus ad Parnassum* (1725).[7] It is incorporated in a number of eighteenth-century treatises to varying degrees, the most extreme being Koch's *Versuch einer Anleitung zur Composition* (1793)[8] in which a simple eight-bar melody is extended into an entire movement of thirty-two bars entirely by melodic decoration and repetition. Between these extremes lies Johann Georg Portmann's *Leichtes Lehrbuch,*[9] which gives an illustration of the application of embellishment to a simple melodic progression similar in complexity to that found in some of Mozart's sonatas. Several examples and their hypothetical *Urlinien*, are shown in example 10.1. The first three, all from slow movements, are straightforward cases of embellishment of simple melodic originals. Examples 10.1a and 10.1b, from K.283 and K.311, respectively, need no further comment here; example 10.1c, the principal theme within the secondary key-area in K.309, is slightly more complicated, in that it seems to have originated from a 'third species' suspension chain in two-part counterpoint.

In other cases the initial *inventio* appears to have been harmonic rather than melodic. Two cases involving strong opening arpeggio figures are the first movements of K.457 in C minor and K.576 in D. Reducing the melodic components of these arpeggios to block chords shows that in the former case the *inventio* was a progression I: V: I (bars 1–9[1]), while in the latter it was I: ii: I (bars 1–9[1]). The very notion of a harmonic *progression* as *inventio* impinges upon the element of tonal planning, a compositional feature that falls more properly within the realm of the next of the three relevant rhetorical *partes, dispositio* (arrangement), and neatly illustrates the interaction between the levels of *inventio* and *dispositio* discussed by Quintilian,

Example 10.1
(a) Hypothetical *inventio* of K.283, 1st movement (opening)

(b) Hypothetical *inventio* of K.311, 2nd movement (opening)

(c) Hypothetical *inventio* of K.309, 2nd movement, bars 40 ff.

(d) Hypothetical *inventio* of K.311, 1st movement (opening)

(e) Hypothetical *inventio* of K.279, 2nd movement (opening)

Cicero and Aristotle, noted above. Such an overlap extends also to planning of phraseology of opening themes such as those of K.311 in D (first movement) and K.279 (second movement). In each case the repetition within the opening phrase is arguably part of the original *inventio* (represented melodically in examples 10.1d and 10.1e), and yet is a compositional *technique* that properly belongs to the level of *dispositio*.[10]

One final area in which *inventio* and *dispositio* overlap to some extent is progressive embellishment within a movement. In the second movement of K.309, for example, each successive reprise of the main theme is treated to embellishment (compare, for instance, bars 1/ 17/ 45; 9/ 25/ 65). Now in each of these locations, the original *inventio* is still present (as a 'latent' *Urlinie*, that generates each reprise), and yet the progressive nature of the embellishment is really a factor within the *dispositio*.[11]

CHAPTER ELEVEN

Dispositio: rhetoric and design

DISPOSITIO (ARRANGEMENT, DESIGN)

The traditional division of the rhetorical *dispositio* was into the six categories of *exordium* (introduction), *narratio* (statement of facts), *propositio* (proposition), *confirmatio* (proof), *refutatio* (refutation) and *peroratio* (conclusion), categories which were applied to the arrangement of a 'musical oration' (*Klang-Rede*) by Mattheson and later copied by Forkel, as noted in chapter 9. Before proceeding to a detailed interpretation of Mozart's sonatas according to such an approach, it is important to warn against too *literal* an application of rhetoric (most especially, perhaps, of the parts of the arrangement, developed in rhetoric primarily for legal prosecution and defence). This was conceded by Mattheson himself, following a review of *Kern melodischer Wissenschaft* in Lorenz Mizler's *Neu-eröffnete musikalische Bibliothek*, in which it was claimed that Mattheson had confused *exordium*, *narratio* and *propositio* by applying each of these terms to the same melody.[1] Mattheson's response incidentally shows that he equated the outline of a musical 'form' with the conduct of 'melody':

Marcello [the composer of the aria which Mattheson had quoted as a demonstration of rhetoric in music] . . . has given as little thought to the six parts of an oration in composing the aria I published in the Kern, as in his other works; but one concedes that I have quite plausibly shown how they must be present in the *melody* [my italics] . . . Experienced masters proceed in an orderly manner, even when they do not think about it . . . it would be very pedantic indeed if one were to look for all these elements in their particular order in every *melody* [my italics] and seek to apply them . . . A musical oration has a great deal more liberty [than a verbal oration]; hence in a melody there might be something similar among the exordium, the narratio, and the propositio, so long as they are made different from one another by keys, by being made higher or lower, or by similar marks of distinction.[2]

In this reply, Mattheson demonstrates no little skill in the application of rhetoric, since his counter-argument is founded on the same proposition as that which had underlain Mizler's own attack, namely the suitability of Mattheson's analogy between musical disposition and the various rhetorical partitions of *exordium*, *narratio*, and so on. Mattheson is able to demonstrate that, while Mizler can see no further than the terms themselves, for Mattheson they are merely *means to an aes-*

thetic end: the 'persuasion' of the listener, through the techniques of rhetoric, of the artistic merits of a particular piece. Mattheson never intended the division into *exordium, narratio, propositio, confirmatio, refutatio* and *peroratio* to straitjacket the composer (or analyst), he believed merely that these foundations of rhetorical eloquence could, by analogy, provide a suitable conceptual framework for the appreciation of music. It is in this spirit – and especially with respect to the implicit *melodic* generation of musical form – that the following discussion of Mozart's sonatas is undertaken.

All of the main authorities on rhetoric discuss these categories in detail, especially Quintilian, who draws liberally on the oratorical theory and practice of Cicero. Aristotle, Cicero and Quintilian, while drawing clear distinctions between the three species of rhetoric, nevertheless devote the substance of their discussions of these six categories of *exordium, narratio, propositio, confirmatio, refutatio* and *peroratio* to their proper application in forensic rhetoric, that is, rhetoric in the 'live' judicial context of prosecution and defence. Aristotle, however, makes it clear that epideictic rhetoric – that which, for our musical purposes, is the most useful species – may legitimately borrow techniques from forensic rhetoric.[3] Occasionally procedures outlined by one of the classical authors with respect to forensic (or even deliberative) rhetoric have been imported to the following discussion where relevant, but the principal guide has been epideictic rhetoric, and its associated techniques.

The discussion of arrangement in Mozart's sonatas is based in part on the rhetorical sequence of *exordium, narratio, propositio, confirmatio, refutatio* and *peroratio*, as proposed in Mattheson's work. However, some adaptation is necessary. While it is possible to account for his reversal of the traditional order of proof and refutation as an adaptation to the hierarchy of tonic and subsidiary keys in eighteenth-century music, it is unclear what he felt would be the musical equivalent of *propositio* or *refutatio*. Is, for example, the latter to be equated with the contrasting theme of a secondary key-area within the exposition, or else with contrasting material in the ensuing development section? In which case, is *confirmatio* associated with the appearance of the main theme in the development or else the beginning of the recapitulation – representing a 'confirmation' of the tonic key together with (usually) a reprise of the main theme? What, then, of the *peroratio*? Is this merely a coda? If so, this is difficult to square with Cicero's assertion that the *peroratio* is 'a passage in which matters that have been discussed in different places here and there throughout the speech are brought together in one place and arranged so as to be seen at a glance'.[4] Mozart's codas tend to emphasize just one thematic idea. That at the end of the sonata-form finale of K.332 in F is a straightforward quotation of bars 22–35 earlier in the movement. That of the first movement of K.331 takes up a theme newly introduced at the beginning of the development (and not employed elsewhere in the movement); in the Andante cantabile of the same sonata a coda was added evidently as an afterthought in the first edition, acting as a balancing phrase in the tonic major to the conclusion of the central (minor) episode. In the finale of the B flat Sonata, K.333, Mozart appends a coda that weds the shape of the main theme to a cadential progression that features strong subdominant colouring. The first movement of the C minor Sonata, K.457, concludes with a fresh stretto presentation of the main theme before continuing with repetitions of a (new) cadential idea descending into the lower register of the piano at the end. The concept of *peroratio* as proposed by Cicero and others might, then, be analogous to the recapitulation in that 'matters that have been discussed in different places here and there throughout the speech [that is, in various keys] are brought together in one place [the tonic]'. Such was the conception of Forkel, as expressed in a passage suppressed from his *Allgemeine Geschichte* that has recently been cited for the first time in a scholarly work by Marc Evan Bonds.[5] Forkel regards the sonata form as a two-section structure, which may be partitioned rhetorically approximately as shown above in chapter 9 (p. 105). According to Forkel:

As the first part of a sonata is ordinarily much shorter than the second, there is no true elaboration, fragmentation, etc. in the first part; instead, it comprises, just as in the introduction to an oration, only a preliminary presentation and mention of the main intention and goal of a musical work. The second part, on the other hand, comprises: 1. The *Hauptsatz* transposed, or in the key of the dominant. 2. Fragmentation of the *Hauptsatz*. 3. Various doubts against it, along with a refutation and resolution of the same. 4. Yet another confirmation through the presentation of the *Hauptsatz* once again in a varied form, as in a secondary key related to the tonic. 5. A conclusion that now moves to the tonic, just as the harmony had moved to the dominant in the first part. The movement now ends in this fashion.

In such a scheme, the exposition material of a sonata form equates to the *exordium* and *narratio* of an oration; the remainder of the movement consists of (i) the development, comprising the musical *confirmatio* and *refutatio* (there being no need here, as was required in a speech, for a separate *propositio* or *partitio*, announcing the various points to be 'disputed', intervening between the *narratio* and *confirmatio*); and (ii) the recapitulation, serving as a 'summing up' of the previous tonal and thematic discourse. Though Forkel named no particular source for his rhetorical partitioning, it is close to the two-part structure of rhetoric proposed by Aristotle in his discussion of arrangement: 'A speech has two parts. It is necessary to state the subject, and then to prove it.'[6] The 'first part' of Forkel's scheme is the 'statement of the case', the 'second part', the 'proof'. This is quite a plausible template for sonata form, capable of supporting both thematic and tonal explanations of the 'narrative' and 'treatment' in particular cases as well as general situations. Within a sonata exposition, for instance, subsidiary and transitional themes can be regarded as 'digressions' within the *narratio*, to be included (perhaps) in the subsequent *refutatio* (development). Thematic and tonal divergences within the recapitulation (*peroratio*) may be regarded as analogous to the techniques of amplification and embellishment admitted by the classical authors in the rhetorical peroration, or summing up.[7] Quintilian remarks of the peroration that 'the most attractive form of peroration is that which we may use when we have an opportunity of drawing some argument from our opponent's speech'.[8] The marshalling of contrary arguments to the support of one's own propositions was one of the crowning achievements of a skilled orator. A musical parallel to this rhetorical device is obvious: within a recapitulation, of course, the most significant structural feature is the *adaptation to the tonic of material originally sounded in a different key*. Such a rhetorically-inspired model, if not too literally applied, can reveal some interesting perspectives on music, as I hope to show in the following discussion of Mozart's piano sonatas.

EXORDIUM

'The Introduction is the beginning of the discourse; by it the hearer's mind is prepared for attention'.[9] At first glance, the *exordium* would seem to be largely inapplicable to Mozart's piano sonatas since, unlike the 'Dissonance' Quartet, K.465, for instance, or the Violin Sonata in B flat, K.454, the 'Prague' Symphony, K.504 or that in E flat, K.543, none of them opens with a slow introduction. Only the Fantasia in C minor, K.475 stands as a prefatory gesture to the Sonata in the same key, K.457, but this is of quite a different order, evidently written independently of the sonata, and capable of standing alone as a separate piece.[10] All the other sonatas begin with a presentation of their main material: in rhetorical terms, the *narratio* (statement of facts).

The *exordium* cannot be dismissed so perfunctorily, though. Aristotle, having described the various divisions of a speech,[11] notes that 'the *exordium* and the epilogue (*peroratio*) are merely aids to memory'. This suggests that the function of an introduction is to set the *context* for what follows. In musical terms, this equates to the setting of the 'frame-of-reference' within which the piece is to be understood, such as its key, speed, and phraseology, that is, those elements of the classical language through which the composer will seek to persuade the listener during the course of the movement. Temporally, there is no division between the *exordium* and the *narratio*. Both happen simultaneously in the opening bars of a piece or movement, *which therefore have a dual purpose*: the sounding of the main thematic material by which the piece obtains its specific identity; and (less obviously) the linguistic 'frame-of-reference' of the movement or piece in question. Musically, therefore, the *exordium* need not temporally precede the main section; it is separate from the *narratio* only in regard to the type of information it conveys. The *narratio* of Mozart's G major Sonata, K.283, first movement, is its right-hand theme; its *exordium*, or context (stated simultaneously), consists of its 'G major-ness' (expressed by strong tonic–dominant–tonic chord progressions within a stable harmonic rhythm), its periodic phrasing, its melody-and-accompaniment texture and its minuet character. Other contexts occurring at the start of other Mozart sonatas include block chords or unisons, suggesting a 'quasi-orchestral' texture (K.280; K.284; K.309; K.311); the refined cantabile, normally associated with the dance or vocal aria (K.282; K.332; K.545; K.570); opposition of different 'affects', normally a bold opening gesture, juxtaposed with a 'pathetic' answering phrase (K.309; K.576).

Sometimes, as in K.309, the signals provided by the *exordium* are more complex: in addition to its combination of 'quasi-orchestral' texture and 'opposing affects' is its irregular periodicity (2+5 bars, stated twice), another 'frame-of-reference' that prepares the attentive listener for what follows. All authors are agreed that the *exordium* should not draw too much attention to itself, so detracting from the effectiveness of what follows. According to Cicero the *exordium* 'brings the mind of the listener into a proper condition to receive the rest of the speech. This will be accomplished if he becomes well-disposed, attentive and receptive. Therefore one who wishes his speech to have a good *exordium* must make a careful study beforehand of the kind of case which he has to present.'[12] Quintilian further suggests the manner in which this should be achieved:

The old rule still holds good that no unusual word, no overbold metaphor, no phrase derived . . . from poetic license should be detected in the *exordium* . . . The style of the *exordium* should not resemble that of our purple patches nor that of the argumentative or narrative portions of the speech, nor yet should it be prolix or continuously ornate; it should rather seem simple and unpremeditated.[13]

The successful musical *exordium*, then, will be one that sets out, by means of its opening material, a clear and simple agenda, catching the listener's attention and acquainting him with the fundamental issues of tonality, tempo, periodicity and so on; and which has a clear connection with the character of the movement as a whole. In both respects, it is hard to fault Mozart. In such openings as K.283 the *exordium* is simple and direct, and is completely in keeping with the character of the rest of the first movement. Elsewhere, the *exordium* proposes a more complex context. That of K.309 has already been noted in passing; another example is that of K.310. The 'frame-of-reference' presented by its opening material includes confirmation of the A minor tonality by regular alternations of tonic and dominant chords, *but over a pedal A*, suggesting from the outset a kind of repressed disquiet (the dominant-seventh chords do not sound on their own, as part of a root-progression I-V-I, but clash with the tonic note, A, so creating harmonic tension). This is reinforced by the throbbing close-position quaver chords in the left-hand along with subtle chromatic inflections in the melody. All this uneasiness eventually boils over at bars 58–70 in the development, which feature dissonant suspension chains that project the initial chordal clash onto the level of full-scale tonal conflict; a wildly undulating semiquaver pedal-point in the bass; and grating semitonal clashes (now between full chords, rather than single notes). Mozart's *exordium* in this magnificent movement is organised so as to 'bring the mind of the listener into a proper condition to receive the rest of the [movement . . . in keeping with] the kind of case which he has to present'. Its technical features are entirely in conformity with the advice of Cicero and Quintilian in that they concisely set out the 'frame-of-reference', clearly prefiguring the essence of the movement as a whole, while not detracting from its impact by including gestures of too extraordinary a nature at the beginning.

That there is more than one way to organise an *exordium* is confirmed by both
Cicero and Quintilian, who each describe two manners: an *introduction* (a direct
appeal to the listener) and *insinuatio* (an indirect, or subtle, appeal, in which the
nature of what is to follow is gradually outlined, as if by stealth).[14] In his path-break-
ing article on the Ricercare as *exordium*, Warren Kirkendale[15] distinguishes between
Cicero's two species, demonstrating an analogy between the rhetorical *introduction*
and *insinuatio*, and the two common types of Ricercare: the first equates to a direct,
chordal opening while the second, an imitative structure, becomes lodged by
degrees in the listener's consciousness through successive entries of the imitative
theme in each of the polyphonic parts ('by dissimulation and indirection [it] unobtrusively steals into the mind of the auditor').[16]

None of Mozart's sonata movements begins imitatively, though, in contrast to
the direct chordal or melodic opening (analogous to Cicero's *introduction*), are openings such as that of the rondo finale of K.281 in B flat which only gradually affirms
the tonic key, beginning sequentially with progression into B flat from the supertonic degree, C minor. Another type of *insinuatio* is the harmonically unsupported
opening of K.533 in F (first movement); the first accented downbeat features an
accented passing note, B flat, the tonic, F, not being at all firmly stressed until the
introduction of chordal underpinning in bar 5 – an event delayed by further repetition (bar 3) of the bare opening melody and prolonging the tonal ambiguity in the
phrase. Yet another case is the beginning of the finale of the C minor sonata, K.457,
insinuatio here being due to the persistent rhythmic syncopation throughout the
theme. Occasionally, despite a direct thematic statement there remains the sense that
the opening phrase is introductory, as in the finale of the C major Sonata, K.330,
whose *piano* opening is recapitulated, *forte*, with confirmatory arpeggiated semiquavers in the lowest register of the piano.

NARRATIO: THE EXPOSITION

Narratio, in the species of epideictic rhetoric, is a concept that requires careful handling. It is not to be regarded as a statement of something alleged to have happened
(as in legal cases), and requiring 'proof' and 'refutation'. As Aristotle states: 'narrative [in this sense] only belongs in a manner in forensic speech . . . in epideictic . . .
speech how is it possible that there should be a narrative as it is defined, or a refutation . . . ? . . . The necessary parts of a speech are statement . . . and proof. These
divisions are appropriate to every speech [in all three species, forensic, demonstra-
tive and epideictic], and at the most are four in number – exordium, statement,
proof, epilogue . . . .'[17] Aristotle makes a distinction here between narrative in the
forensic sense of διηγησις ('statement of facts') and προθεσις ('setting forth' of
material). As applied to a 'musical oration', the *narratio* clearly refers to the 'setting
forth' of material within the opening section of a movement or piece, and most
immediately to the initial statement of the main thematic material. As noted in the
previous section, in Mozart's sonatas this almost always occurs at the very opening,

a rhetorical practice recommended by Cicero.[18] Aristotle, Cicero and Quintilian all discuss the appropriate length of a *narratio*.[19] All touch on the need for brevity and clarity of exposition in which the contributing elements are defined at no greater length than strictly necessary (and without clumsy repetition) and are distinguished from each other. Whereas the author of *Ad Herennium* warns against digression from the main point, Cicero (*De Inventione*, I.xix) draws a distinction between a type of *narratio* incorporating a plain statement and another that includes an appropriate digression.[20] Both types are encountered in Mozart's sonata openings. That of K.279 in C, for instance, consists of a straightforward statement, as do those of K.332 and K.545. Opening statements of episodic structures tend also to be of this type (the finales of K.309, K.311, K.310 and K.570, for example). A digression to contrasting material before a reprise of the opening is characteristic of the first movements of K.309, K.311, K.310 and K.576. Another type of digression involves an immediate extension of the opening material, as in the first movement of the B flat Sonata, K.333, in which, having stated the main theme, Mozart continues with it by means of fragmentation, transposition and repetition (bars 4–10), before restating it (in the lower octave) as the beginning of his transition to the second key-area. This technique is not confined to opening themes. It occurs also during the finale of the early Sonata in G, K.283 (bars 41–64, in which the continuation commencing at bar 57 extends the idea of bar 41). Seen in the context of epideictic rhetoric, such digressions are not beyond the bounds of decorum. Aristotle's extended treatment of this species includes copious illustrations of permissible digressions within the narrative;[21] likewise, the author of *Ad Herennium*.[22] Indeed, variety within this species was expected. Both Cicero and pseudo-Cicero mention a type of narrative 'wholly unconnected with public issues . . . recited or written solely for amusement, but [which] at the same time provides valuable training . . . This form of narrative should possess great vivacity, *resulting from a variety of materials* [my italics].'[23] Within a sonata-form exposition, of course, there is built-in tonal variety, since the principal ingredient is modulation away from the tonic to a related key. Mozart's polythematic sonata expositions are entirely in keeping with this expectation; indeed, viewed in rhetorical terms, 'digression' is their chief motivation. In the following discussion, therefore, no attempt is made to pursue 'latent' connections between motives; instead, the pursuit of contrast as a guiding principle within an exposition (*narratio*) is the aim.[24] A still broader agenda for 'digression', of course, is the concept of a *modulation out of the main key* within the exposition as a whole, from tonic to dominant (or relative major).

Some basic strategies may be observed in Mozart's sonata expositions. On average the first movements and finales contain seven or eight distinct themes, of which, in the main, the majority will belong to the secondary key-area (dominant, in the case of major-key movements; relative major in minor-key movements). The first movement of the C major Sonata, K.330, contains three or four contrasting themes within its opening paragraph (outlining the tonic key, and then introducing the dominant)[25] and no fewer than six within the secondary key-area. That of the B flat

Sonata, K.333, is similar, with three themes in the first section (bars 1–22) and six in the second (bars 23–63). In the first movement exposition of the C minor Sonata, K.457, Mozart places just two themes in the tonic region, while there are six in the secondary key-area (the relative major). That of K.576 in D is likewise weighted in favour of the secondary key-area, which has four or five themes as opposed to just two distinct ideas in the opening tonic section. Nor is this practice restricted to first movements. Within the sonata-form finale of the C major Sonata, K.279, the opening tonic section (bars 1–16) contains two themes, while the remainder of the exposition has at least six.

Some expositions maintain a more equal thematic balance between the two main key-areas. In the first movement exposition of K.279 Mozart places four themes in the tonic region and six in the dominant. Two other cases in which this is apparently true are the first movements of K.332 in F and K.570 in B flat. However, the balance of themes between the primary and secondary key-areas in these two expositions is complicated to some extent by their unusual tonal schemes. In both expositions the opening section incorporates a significant tonal digression: to the relative minor (D) and subdominant (E flat) respectively. If the themes entering at bar 23 of K.332 and bar 23 of K.570 were designated to the secondary key-area then the balance would be significantly different. That this is not the case is suggested by their transitional character. Each involves significant sequential movement culminating in the arrival of the secondary dominant key. Such an interpretation is also supported by the rhetorical rationale of digression within the exposition/*narratio*, which positively encourages diversity, not only of theme but of treatment (in this case, tonal digression within an otherwise stable area).

It is not always easy to determine the number of themes in each section, such is the fertility of Mozart's melodic imagination. Sometimes the proliferation of themes results from mere embellishment, as in the first movement of K.330 in C, at bar 9 (decorating the figure at bar 5). Elsewhere a self-contained section may be subdivided into two or three discrete thematic ideas, as in the finale of K.279 at bars 46–50; the first movement of K.284 in D (at bars 34–8, over a dominant pedal); or that of K.333 in B flat (at bars 23–30).

Another movement exhibiting sub-divisions of themes is the finale of K.332 in F. Its energetic opening theme contains two elements: the first emphasises fundamental triadic steps with chromatic touches; the second (end of bars 3 ff.) gives added prominence to the chromatic D flats (example 11.1a). The passage beginning at bar 22 supports three connected and yet sharply-characterised ideas (example 11.1b). While these thematic sub-divisions contribute in an important way to the unfolding of the narrative they do so on a relatively superficial level. Much more important here is the exposition's tonal design which has implications for the structure of the remainder of the movement, and particularly its closing section (*peroratio*). Mozart's exposition incorporates two significant tonal digressions: at bar 36, following a tonic full-close, there begins a new theme in the relative minor (just as in the first movement and likewise of transitional nature); the

Example 11.1

(a) Mozart, Sonata in F, K.332, finale, bars 1–6

(b) Mozart, Sonata in F, K.332, finale, bars 22–35

secondary key-area (bars 50 ff.) begins unusually in the dominant minor, C major not arriving until bar 65. By inserting these two key-digressions between the fundamental tonic–dominant axes Mozart so seriously upsets the expected proportions of the exposition as to weaken its stability, an issue addressed subsequently in the recapitulation where the original thematic sequence is revised as shown below:

Exposition	*Recapitulation*
Bars 1–22^1	Bars 148–169^1 [=1–22^1]
Bars 22–35	Omitted (see below, bars 232–45)
Bars 36–90	Bars 169–226^1 [= transposition of 36–90 followed by new extension, bars 226–32^1]
	Bars 232–45 [=insertion of 22–35]

As can be seen the finale is skilfully rounded-off by the quirky exposition codetta, reinforcing the tonic at the close of the movement as it had earlier rounded-off the movement's opening tonic paragraph to which it clearly serves as a long-range counterbalance. By withholding it during most of the recapitulation, Mozart makes its eventual appearance doubly satisfying both in terms of its immediate tonal significance and as an aspect of the broader planning of the movement.[26]

Within his slow-movement sonata forms Mozart's themes are of an altogether more *cantabile* character than those found in opening or closing Allegros. There is also rather less contrast in character between the initial themes of the tonic and dominant key-areas. In the first movement of K.284, for instance, there exists an unmistakable contrast between the strident opening gesture and that at bar 22. Similar contrast may be observed between the corresponding themes in the first movements of K.309 (bar 1: bar 35), K.311 (bar 1: bars 16–17) and K.457 (bar 1: bar 36). This clearly fits Galeazzi's description, quoted earlier, of 'a new idea, which is introduced, for the sake of greater beauty, towards the middle of the first part. This must be gentle, expressive, and tender'. No such wide contrast exists between, for instance, the opening theme of K.283 and the theme at bar 9, commencing the dominant key-area. They share, in addition to an obvious *cantabile* manner, a similar texture (especially the density of the accompaniment and the quantity of rhythmic movement), a similar rate of chord change, accentuation and register. However, within the narrower limits imposed by the *cantabile* idiom, Mozart succeeds in injecting considerable melodic variety. The corresponding tonic and dominant themes in the Andante cantabile of K.333 display variety of rhythmic profile, accompaniment texture, accentuation and phraseology (2 + 2 bars, as opposed to a through-composed four-bar opening: example 11.2). In addition to this, the harmonic rate of change at bars 14–17 is in subtle contrast to that of the near-uniform crotchets of bar 1 – a factor which, co-ordinated with the changes in key and register, contributes to the light and airy grace of the passage. Similar is the diversity of design in the corresponding themes of the slow movement of K.310: once again there is contrast of rhythm, register, chord rhythm and accentuation, added to which is a striking change of texture, incorporating inversion of the polyphony at bar 17.

Example 11.2   Mozart, Sonata in B flat, K.333, 2nd movement, principal themes

One further remarkable point of design within Mozart's slow-movement sonata structures is their tendency towards progressive decorative embellishment, principally by means of passing-notes, appoggiaturas and neighbour-notes (frequently with added chromatic inflection), both in a local context (the immediate embellishment of the opening theme of K.310's Andante cantabile from bar 4, for example) and in a larger structural sense, as the expositions unfold. The continuations of both K.333 and K.310 beyond the commencement of their secondary key-areas show this feature quite clearly. The quality of such decorations is not a matter for discussion here: that topic falls within the sphere of *elocutio* (style). What is notable in terms of *dispositio* is that, for all the consistency of Mozart's melodic writing in these slow movement sonata structures, each successive theme retains nevertheless an individuality that marks it out from its surrounding bars and contributes to the variety that is the touchstone of the epideictic *narratio*.

CONFIRMATIO: THE DEVELOPMENT SECTION

As remarked above, in epideictic rhetoric the 'facts' were taken on trust, there being no actual 'refutation' of material previously stated. Aristotle's opinion was that 'amplification is most suitable for epideictic [rhetoric] whose subject is actions which are not disputed.'[27] Amplification in this sense means the exaggeration or highlighting of the attributes of the material. Some appropriate techniques of amplification (imported from forensic rhetoric) are outlined by Cicero in *De Inventione*;[28] others are given in *Ad Herennium*.[29] Quintilian's thorough discussion of amplification proposes four techniques: *incremento* (augmentation), *comparatione* (comparison), *ratiocinatione* (reasoning), and *congerie* (accumulation).[30] The first and last of these are most appropriate to epideictic oratory. Both are to do with building to a climax, and in this context belong to the rhetorical level of *dispositio* (arrangement).[31] Each has some relevance for the musical organisation of a development section.

Augmentation is a means of building to a climax by the use of exaggerated language, 'most impressive when it lends grandeur even to comparative insignificance'.[32] In musical terms augmentation does not apply, of course, to augmentation

Example 11.3   Mozart, Sonata in C, K.309, 1st movement, bars 69–82

of the rhythmic values of a theme, but to means by which the music is driven forward to a significant, perhaps climactic, point by techniques such as rising or falling melodic and harmonic sequence, highlighting of a fragment of a theme by repetition, a general increase in rhythmic activity and a gradual rise (or fall) in register or dynamic. A development illustrating the use of sequence and fragmentation is that of K.309 in C (example 11.3). Its first section, leading to a conclusive cadence in the relative minor, is based exclusively on the movement's main theme (bars

59–82). Initially, Mozart 'exaggerates' the end of this theme by fragmentation (bars 60, 61, 62); later, he introduces sequential repetition of its leading part (bars 73–6) combined with further fragmentation of its end (bars 76, 77, 78) before resolving the accumulated melodic and harmonic tension with a diminished-seventh arpeggio leading to a perfect cadence in A minor (bars 79–82). Overall, there is a gradual ascent in register and increase in momentum, particularly in the accompaniment, which moves from quavers to semiquavers. In the first movement of K.457 the distinctive change of texture at bar 83 – introducing entries of the main theme in dialogue against triplet quaver patterns, and featuring persistent use of high treble register from bar 87 – shows another way of 'exaggerating' a theme's characteristics.

Accumulation is also climactic in function, 'attained by the piling up of words . . . all the accumulated details [having] but one reference'.[33] Musically, this technique might plausibly relate to a passage such as that in the first movement of K.310, bars 58–70, based exclusively on a derivative of the movement's opening theme ('all the accumulated details [having] but one reference') and moving to a climactic dividing point within the development (bar 70, where the motive and texture change) by successive ascents in register, supported by a clear 'circle-of-fifths' harmonic progression (B-E-A-D) and obsessive repetition of the dotted rhythm and the undulating semiquaver pedal points. Another illustration of this type of structurally focussed accumulation is provided by the development of the first movement of K.284 in D, bars 52–9. The sectionalisation of the development in K.279's first movement is clearly supported by accumulation (example 11.4a). It subdivides into four sections (bars 39–44; 45–7; 48–51; and 51^3–57), each of which is identified with repetition of just one figuration or texture.

Sectionalisation is an important strategy within Mozart's sonata developments. Normally there will be two or more sections, each associated with one particular theme or pattern. Frequently, too, these sectional divisions are coordinated with the significant stages of the unfolding key-scheme, as in K.279, cited above (example 11.4a). Reduced to bare harmonic outline, its opening section is based on the progression shown as a harmonic sketch in example 11.4b, whereas the semiquaver dialogue in its closing section co-incides precisely with the start of the dominant pedal G (bar 51^3). Modulation, as noted by Koch and Galeazzi in their discussions of sonata form,[34] is the rationale of a development section. The commonest modulation schemes in Mozart's sonata developments involve sequences, such as that outlined in K.309; and 'circle-of-fifths' progressions, as in K.576, bars 82–96, moving from F sharp, through B and E to A (bar 92), the last stage of which acts as a dominant pedal (bars 92–8) introducing the recapitulation. Mozart often prefers to modulate as far as the dominant of the relative minor key before moving back to the tonic. Normally this point is reached at the culmination of a section, serving as a preparation for the key that commences the next section.[35] Sometimes the dominant of the relative minor is further emphasised by a complete structural break.[36] In K.576 Mozart binds the two sections of his development together by prolonging this tonal degree (F sharp) between bars 79 and 83, where it doubles as a

Example 11.4

(a) Mozart, Sonata in C, K.279, 1st movement, bars 39–58

Example 11.4(a) (*cont.*)

(b) Mozart, Sonata in C, K.279, 1st movement (harmonic sketch of opening of development)

culmination of the first section and the beginning of the second (in which the phraseology shifts from two-bar groups to three-bar groups). A different tonal scheme is found in the first movements of K.309 and 311, in each of which the first section culminates decisively in the relative minor.[37]

The development sections most frequently end with a dominant pedal, preparing the regaining of the main tonic degree at the beginning of the recapitulation. Several instances of this have already been mentioned in passing. A straightforward example is found in the finale of K.330, bars 86–95. Elsewhere, attention is distracted from the pedal note itself by means of chromatic neighbour-notes, as in the finale of K.283 (bars 160–170). On the other hand, such chromatic accretions can

Example 11.5   Mozart, Sonata in B flat, K.333, 1st movement, bars 86–94

enhance the pedal effect, particularly when they appear to bear as close an affinity to the melodic line as in K.333, bars 86–93 (example 11.5).

The sectionalisation of Mozart's sonata developments is closely bound up with their thematic basis. In this respect a sharp divergence between his practice in quick and slow sonata structures is apparent. Following the central double-bar in slow-movement sonatas he almost always develops material heard previously. This is true of the slow movements of K.279, K.280, K.281, K.283, K.333 and K.533.[38] The exception to this is the Andante cantabile of K.310, in which, at bar 31[3] he introduces an entirely new theme. In sonata Allegros, the developments are frequently based on new material, either in whole or in part. In both first movement and finale of K.283, for instance, the development section is completely unrelated to themes heard in the exposition, as are those of the first movement and finale of K.330.[39] In other cases there is a fairly brief reference to some exposition material, while the remainder of the development is free. The first movement of K.279 (cited previously) is a case in point. It begins with a figure rhythmically related to the opening main theme at bar 1, though after bar 44 there is no further quotation of exposition themes. An identical approach characterises the first movement development of K.333. In K.280 (first movement) the sequence of events is reversed. Here the development begins with new material and continues with a harmonic 'circle-of-fifths' built around the main theme from the secondary key-area (bar 67 – originally sounded at bar 27). The finale of the same sonata treads still another course, beginning with the theme from bar 38 of the exposition, though with a new consequent phrase (bars 82–5) attached; this new consequent becomes the driving force of the second section of this development (bars 90–106). In the opening Allegro con spirito of K.311 Mozart fashions the whole of his development out of the exposition's last two bars.[40] The development of K.332's opening Allegro begins with an entirely new theme, though the majority of it works with the jaunty syncopated idea from bar 56 of the exposition. Finally, while the first movement development of K.576 contains some reference to the opening 'hunt' motive, much of it (including the lead back to the recapitulation beginning at bar 83) relates to the two bars of exposition codetta. Indeed, it is relatively rare in Mozart's sonatas to find a development that rigorously works out the potential of the exposition material. Such is the case in the finales of K.279, K.282, and K.332, and likewise in the first movements of K.309, K.310, K.457, K.533 and K.570.

References to exposition material take two forms: *quotation*, without much actual *development* of the quoted figure(s); or else some kind of *transformation* in which aspects of the exposition material are 'amplified'. Normally, both forms co-exist within a single development. The development of the finale of K.282 in E flat, for instance, begins by quoting the main theme, though within a swiftly modulating harmonic flow. From bar 47 Mozart fragments the opening octave leap (left hand) and places this in rhythmic 'canon' against off-beat falling scale steps (right hand), creating an irresistible tension. In the first movements of K.457 and K.570 there are substantial quotations of exposition themes in more or less unaltered form. At bar 79 of K.457 Mozart quotes in the minor mode the whole phrase from bar 23 of the exposition, and then continues for a further dozen bars with statements of the main theme in its original rhythm, and only minor intervallic alterations (a change of chord position) before he finally fragments its last two crotchets at bars 95–8, preparing for the inflected dominant pause chord at the end of the section. In K.570, following the two chords diverting the tonality into the remote area of D flat, Mozart quotes a lengthy section of the exposition (bars 23–40) virtually unchanged (bars 81–100, shifting to the more familiar tonal degree of D – the dominant of the relative minor, in preparation for the next section in G minor). This continuation takes as its starting-point bars 41–8 of the exposition, but invests this figure with a new contrapuntal context (including invertibility) along with fragmentation and sequence from bar 117. Treating the theme in this way reveals an aspect of its potential not explored hitherto, in a manner analogous to that in which an orator might expand upon one of the issues raised near the beginning of his speech. A further illustration of this type of development is found in the first movement of K.533 in F. Once again, there is some quotation of previous material (the development opens with a version of the main theme, transposed to the dominant minor, and, from bar 125, takes over the principal theme of the secondary key-area). Both these themes, however, are subjected to alteration. In bars 104–6 the main theme is fragmented, and newly combined with a triplet quaver motive perhaps suggested by the last four bars of the exposition, while at bar 127 the secondary theme is given a new crotchet continuation, evidently derived from the left hand of bars 45–6. More significant structurally, though, is the 'amplification' of the contrapuntal texture by means of dialogue (bars 125–33) and then by stretto entries at two crotchets' distance, first at the fifth, then (modified) at the octave. In these ways the contrapuntal texture which underlies much of the exposition, is given more weight. Again the rhetorical analogy (reinforcement of an earlier aspect of the *narratio*) is obvious.

PERORATIO: THE RECAPITULATION.

The author of *Ad Herennium* states that the conclusion of a speech is in three parts: *enumeratione, amplificatione* and *commiseratione*.[41] The last of these (an 'appeal to pity') is also described by Aristotle, Cicero and Quintilian in their discussions of the peroration.[42] These categories clearly applied in the first place to 'live' legal situations, though, as in the case of *exordium, narratio*, and *confirmatio*, techniques from forensic oratory were legitimately imported into epideictic. Two (*enumeratione, amplificatione*) are particularly applicable to a musical environment. The first (summing-up, or recapitulation) is described in *Ad Herennium* as 'recall[ing] the points we have made – briefly, that the speech may not be repeated in its entirety, but that the memory of it may be refreshed'. While recommending brevity in the recollection of such points, Quintilian also urges that 'the points selected for enumeration must be treated with weight and dignity, enlivened by apt reflexions and diversified by suitable figures; for there is nothing more tiresome than a dry repetition of facts'. The second (amplification) is quite frequently found in Mozart's recapitulations, in situations where exposition themes are treated to further development. Normally, such amplification occurs during the recapitulation transition – a section in which Mozart was required, for tonal reasons, to alter that passage in the exposition in which he had formerly modulated one or two degrees sharp of the tonic key.[43] In his responses to this requirement, Mozart sometimes resumes the compositional techniques discussed above in relation to the development section.

One such retransition is that in the first movement of K.576, bars 111–17. These bars, featuring a simple canon at the octave and at a half-bar's distance, are generated from the sextuplet semiquaver pattern that evolves out of the 'hunt' motive (bar 108) and are carried through in a sequence from C, to D, to E, resulting in obvious thematic, harmonic and textural 'amplification'. Further illustrations of amplification in this context are found in the first movements of K.533, bars 153–68, combining sequential restatements of the opening theme with prolonged fragmentation of its second four-quaver group from bar 161, and K.457, bars 118–20, in which Mozart begins with previously untried stretto entries of the main theme and continues to the dominant of C minor at bar 126 with a new idea altogether, replacing that of bars 23 ff. of the exposition (quoted in the development, bars 79–82).[44] Perhaps in order to reinforce still further the tonic key's hegemony over thematic material formerly presented in the dominant (or relative major) towards the end of a sonata-form movement Mozart sometimes introduces amplification within the latter part of his sonata recapitulations. In the finale of K.279, bars 135–47, there is an additional paragraph of imitation featuring the theme originally sounded at bar 22^2, and extensively quoted (in a deliberately unstable tonal environment) at the start of the development. Amplification of former dominant-key material is also found in the first movement of K.280, bars 117–23 – again within a strong tonic context, and utilising a theme that had formed the basis of a 'circle-of-fifths' modulation in the development (bars 67 ff.). An especially memorable amplification towards the end of a movement is found in the first movement of K.333 (bars 142–52). Here Mozart extends the original three-bar pattern of bars 46–8 into a much more substantial section founded on a falling suspension chain and featuring progressive fragmentation and transformation of the right-hand quaver pattern, a shift at bar 149 from minim to crotchet chord changes, and culminating in a decisive tonic cadence in bars 151–2. In this case the extended sequence was almost certainly suggested by the fact that the piano did not stretch beyond f″, ruling out a literal upward transposition of bar 47 from d″ to g″. Mozart therefore had to adapt the shape of this phrase and the resulting reinforcement of the tonic, B flat, in the course of this excursion is a happy marriage of structural sophistication and practical common sense.

Returning to *enumeratio*, the actual recapitulation of earlier themes, Mozart's normal practice is to retain the original order of themes unchanged. This is in accordance with the advice given in *Ad Herennium*: 'we shall reproduce all the points in the order in which they have been presented, so that the hearer . . . is brought back to what he remembers'.[45] In some movements, however, he reorders the exposition material significantly. Perhaps the most striking example is the opening Allegro of K.311 in D, in which the main theme is not recapitulated until bar 99, that is, *after* the reprise of almost all the other exposition material.[46] Thematic reordering is found also in the first movements of K.282 and K.576, in the slow movement of K.279[47] and in the finale of K.332. In the opening Adagio of K.282 the reprise of the main theme does not take place until the very end, in a closing phrase specifically labelled 'Coda' (bar 34). The sequence of events in K.576 is somewhat more complex. In the recapitulation the most significant exposition themes are reordered, as follows:

Exposition	Recapitulation
Bar 1	98
Bar 16	omitted
Bar 28	137
Bar 34	144
Bar 41	121, with embellished repeat, bar 129

Another technique found in some of Mozart's sonata recapitulations is the reprise of one exposition theme in the *tonic minor*. This occurs in the first movements of

K.309 in C (bars 101–9: the opening theme), K.311 in D (bars 83–6: the principal theme of the secondary key-area), K.533 (bars 153–68: the opening theme) and K.570 (bars 181–7: the secondary theme of the secondary key-area). In each case there is significant minor-mode treatment of that theme within the development section. A possible rhetorical explanation for this is found in *Ad Herennium*: '[In the summing-up] the speech must not be repeated in its entirety . . . [but] must take its beginning [i.e. derive] from the division . . . set[ting] forth the points treated in the proof and refutation'.[48] This could be interpreted as follows: 'In the recapitulation the exposition themes must not be literally repeated but must take account of their transformation in the development'. In this sense, Mozart's introduction of the minor mode in the recapitulations of K.309, K.311 and K.533 'takes its beginning' from the development, acknowledging, as it were, its tonal transformations of the exposition material.

Two movement-types remain to be considered under the category of arrangement: variations and episodic forms (ternary designs – including minuets and trios – and rondos). In addition, there is the Fantasia, K.475, composed separately from the C minor Sonata, K.457, but evidently intended to precede it. All have quite clear rhetorical analogies.

VARIATIONS

Two variation sets are included among the piano sonatas: the finale of K.284 in D; and the first movement of K.331 in A. Mozart was a noted composer of piano variations, indeed they were among his most popular published works.[49] Virtually all of Mozart's surviving piano variation sets are free-standing pieces, reflecting the close association between variations and 'live' improvisation, in which a given melody (suggested, perhaps, by a member of the audience at a *salon*) would be subjected to progressive embellishment.

The plan of each of the variation movements, K.284 and K.331, is outlined below:

K.284: finale[50]

Theme   Binary form, A (8 bars) + B (9 bars), with repeat of each half; simple
        melody and accompaniment texture
Var.1   Florid triplet decoration of right hand melody
Var.2   Triplet decoration transferred to left hand (with semiquaver counter-
        theme); tendency towards alternation of the hands in dialogue
Var.3   Florid right-hand semiquavers
Var.4   Semiquaver decorations transferred to left hand; right hand returns to a
        simpler melodic statement (with occasional embellishment)

Var.5   Double-thirds introduced as a countertheme; texture inversion at bar
         V:13/98
Var.6   Hand-crossing, with semiquaver pattern providing the chordal filling
Var.7   *Minore*, in which the texture returns to that of theme (right hand) and
         accompaniment in 'pathetic' *empfindsamer Stil*
Var.8   Octaves; texture inversion in each half (bars VIII:4/140; VIII:13/149)
Var.9   Counterpoint; textural variety from phrase to phrase; texture inversion;
         octave figure retained from var.8 (bars IX:4/157; IX:12/165)
Var.10   Tremolando countertheme to *cantabile* melodic statements; frequent tex-
         tural inversion
Var.11   Adagio Cantabile: through-composed[51] with ornate melodic decoration
         over Alberti-style bass[52]
Var.12   Allegro: through-composed[53] ; metre shifts to 3/4; considerable textural
         variety from phrase to phrase (bars XII:1/222; XII:9/230)

K.331: first movement[54]

Theme   Binary form, A (8 bars) + B (10 bars), with repeat of each half; simple
         melody and accompaniment texture
Var.1   Light embellishment of right-hand melody in semiquavers, featuring
         chromatic neighbour-notes
Var.2   Triplet semiquaver accompaniment pattern in Alberti-bass style; trans-
         ferred to right hand in melodic context (bars II:5/41; II:17/53)
Var.3   Uniform semiquaver texture in both hands (melody/ accompaniment),
         occasionally breaking into octaves
Var.4   Hand-crossing, with semiquaver pattern providing the chordal filling;
         texture changes to simple melody and accompaniment texture at bar
         IV:9/81, returning after four bars to the cross-hands texture
Var.5   Ornate right-hand embellishment of melodic outline with demi-semi-
         quaver accompaniment in Alberti-bass style
Var.6   Metre shifts from 6/8/ to 4/4; frequent change of figuration (bars
         VI:1/109; VI:5/113); additional coda, bars VI:19/127 to the end).

In both sets of variations the original phrase-structure of the theme and its harmonic foundation are generally preserved, though the outline of the original
melody does not remain easily detectable for long.

Finding suitable rhetorical analogies to the variation genre is complicated somewhat by the fact that variations inhabit a no-man's land on the margins of *dispositio*
and *elocutio*. Fundamental to the design of any set of variations is the idea of progressive embellishment of the original theme, the detailed quality of which is properly a feature not of *dispositio* (arrangement) but of *elocutio* (style). On the other
hand, there are clear strategies of external design, most appropriately considered at
this stage as part of the rhetorical *dispositio*. This ambiguity requires careful handling.

Elaine Sisman, in her thoroughly absorbing study of Haydn's variations,[55] has developed a rhetorical model for the composition of variations, taken from a variety of sources, including Erasmus's influential treatise, *De duplici copia rerum ac verborum commentarii duo*[56] and *Ad Herennium*. Erasmus's treatise is devoted to the acquisition of stylistic elegance in speech or writing (though especially the former), an essential ingredient of which is the ability to describe the same thing in a myriad of different ways in order to avoid the 'ugly fault' of identical repetition of words or phrases. From *Ad Herennium*, Sisman takes the figure of 'refining' (*expolitio*):

Refining consists in dwelling on the same topic and yet seeming to say something ever new. It is accomplished in two ways: by merely repeating the same idea, or by descanting upon it. We shall not repeat the same thing precisely – for that, to be sure, would weary the hearer and not refine the idea – but with changes . . . in the words, in the delivery, and in the treatment.

Our changes will be verbal when, having expressed the idea once [in its primary form], we repeat it once again [adding heightened figures of speech] . . . [the delivery has to do with the tone of voice assumed in performance, and does not relate to actual *composition*] . . . The third kind of change . . . will take place if we transfer the thought into the form of Dialogue . . . putting into the mouth of some person language in keeping with his character . . . or into the form of Arousal [stirring the hearer by an appeal to his emotions] . . . But when we descant upon the same theme, we shall use a great many variations. Indeed, having expressed the theme simply, we can subjoin the Reason,[57] and then express the theme in another form . . . next we can present the Contrary[58] . . . then a Comparison and an Example[59] . . . and finally the Conclusion.

A related rhetorical technique is 'Dwelling upon the Point', which 'occurs when one remains rather long upon, and often returns to, the strongest topic on which the whole cause rests.'[60] Quintilian, quoting Cicero's remarks in *De Oratore*, notes that 'great effect may be produced by dwelling on a single point, and amplifying the facts in course of statement, with a view to making our audience regard the point which we amplify as being as important as speech can make it . . . we may employ digressions and then . . . make a neat and elegant return to our main theme.'[61]

Taken together, these rhetorical models provide a fruitful starting-point for the study of variations. However, they must be treated with some caution, since the discussions of 'refining' and 'dwelling upon the point' occur in sections of these treatises dealing with aspects of *elocutio*, not *dispositio*,[62] while Erasmus's treatment of 'copiousness' was intended explicitly to foster the acquisition of good style in speech, and derives in part from Quintilian, who describes 'copiousness' as 'wealth of thought or luxuriance of language'.[63] At first sight, an obvious analogy exists between Erasmus's 150 different ways of saying 'Your letter pleased me mightily', or his 200 ways of saying 'I will remember you as long as I live'[64] and Mozart's six 'different ways of saying' the opening phrase of K.331 (example 11.6). Yet Erasmus's purpose was to provide a model not of a finished speech, but rather of a *fund of stock phrases to be drawn upon in such a speech*, and therefore belongs to the level of *elocu-*

Example 11.6 Mozart, Sonata in A, K.331, 1st movement, openings of theme and successive variations

(a)

(b)

(c)

(d)

(e)

(f)

(g)

tio, not *dispositio*. Likewise, Quintilian's discussion of 'dwelling upon the point' (occurring as part of an extended treatment of 'figures of thought and speech'[65]) is specifically directed towards the production of a temporary *effect* which this *figure* produced on the audience at a certain point in a speech: a *figure* is not a *structure*.[66] Turning to the figure of 'refining' (*expolitio*), it is difficult to see how the procedure of 'descanting' can have any very wide application to the structure of variations.[67] What is a 'reason' in this context? Or a 'contrary'? Or a 'comparison'? Perhaps 'refining' is best viewed in the same way as Erasmus's *copia*, namely, as '[a] means of training for skill in style . . . advantageous[ly] practiced in exercises divorced from a real cause'.[68] In her structural analysis of the variation finale of Haydn's Sonata in A, Hob.XVI:30, Sisman applies instead the figures of *periphrasis* ('a manner of speech used to express a simple idea by means of a circumlocution')[69] and what she describes as *pleonasm* ('the addition of superfluous words for purposes of decoration and emphasis')[70] to acccount for the decorative characteristics of successive variations.

More widely applicable, I believe, to the variation genre is the rhetorical device known as the *trope*, discussed by the author of *Ad Herennium*[71] and, in greater detail, by Quintilian.[72] It is described by Quintilian as 'the artistic alteration of a word or phrase from its proper meaning to another . . . some *tropes* are employed to help out our meaning and others to adorn our style . . . the changes involved concern not merely individual words, but also our thoughts and the structure of our sentences.'[73] Clearly, a *trope* was regarded as a flexible device of language, ranging, in its potential impact, from the purely local (embellishment) to the structural (alteration of meaning; structure of sentences). This flexibility, crossing the boundary between *dispositio* and *elocutio*, makes the *trope* a suitable rhetorical model for a genre such as variations, which, as mentioned above, achieve an ambiguous fusion of 'arrangement' and 'style'.

Quintilian's discussion of *tropes* begins with the *metaphor*, which he considered to be the most beautiful type. 'It adds to the copiousness of language by the interchange of words . . . On the whole, *metaphor* is a shorter form of *simile* . . . in the latter we compare some object to the thing which we wish to describe, whereas in the former this object is actually *substituted for the thing*' [my italics].[74] Applied to variations, each successive variation of the theme is a *metaphor* for that theme, a new term 'substituted' for it. To take a specific example, variation 1 of K.284 *represents* the original theme quite closely, in that the outline of the original melody is still discernible and its phrase-structure is retained exactly. Its triplet movement 'adds to the copiousness of language'. A different *metaphor* is texture inversion, transferring the *metaphor* of the theme from right hand to left, a device appearing first in var.2 and found more frequently towards the end of the set (vars.5, 8, 9 and 10); another is counterpoint (vars.5 and especially 9), in which the original texture (theme and Alberti-bass accompaniment) is replaced by such 'substitutes' as canon (var.9, bar IX:4/157), later becoming canon by inversion (bar IX:12/ 165), or else dialogue emphasised by register separation (var.2; var.6) or 'voicing' (var.8). Yet another kind of *metaphor* is harmonic, as in the case of the chromatic sequence following the theme's central double-bar. In vars.3, 5, 6, 7, 9, 10, 11 and 12 the original harmonic content of this passage is changed (though its sequential context remains clear).[75] All of these *metaphors* stand as substitutes for the initial statement, exercising a kind of 'commentary' on it.

Equally important, in the view of Quintilian, is the quantity of the *metaphor*: 'a *metaphor* must not be too great for its subject . . . excess in the use of *metaphor* is also a fault.'[76] Here, perhaps, it is possible to criticise Mozart for an excessive application of figurative melodic ornament in his variations. Typically, after a variation or two, we virtually lose sight and sound of the original theme. While its outline is still present in vars. 1 and 2 of K.284's finale, for instance, by var.3 it is all but impossible to detect due to the sheer delight in figuration for its own sake. From this point on, the resemblances to the opening theme become increasingly remote, the most extreme point in this process being var.11 (discussed further below).

In using *metaphors* in sequence, care must be taken not to 'mix' them. According to Quintilian:

it is all-important to follow the principle [of Cicero, a passage from whom he quotes] and never to mix your metaphors. But there are many who, after beginning with a tempest, will end with a fire or a falling house, with the result that they produce a hideously incongruous effect [destroying] the charm of language by the extravagant efforts [they] have made to attain it.[77]

There is an obvious analogy here between the avoidance of mixed metaphors in oratory and the maintenance of a consistent (and therefore coherent) pattern of figuration throughout each single variation – a basic technical resource in eighteenth-century variations. In K.284, each variation introduces a distinctive and persistent pattern (be it a figuration, such as vars.1 and 2 or a texture, such as vars.6 or 9) that characterises every phrase. This principle holds good for K.331 too, though here with an additional refinement. Mozart's 6/8 theme is twice reprised: first, following an imperfect cadence at bar 4 and again during the second section, at bar 13.[78] In each subsequent variation, Mozart makes a distinction between these two thematic reprises by means of a change of figuration: in each case, the second reprise returns to the pattern with which that variation began. The fact that Mozart felt it necessary to round-off each variation with such a return reflects a concern for coherence. Had he left each variation 'open-ended' that coherence would have been weakened in a manner analogous to that deplored by Quintilian in orators who, by mixing their metaphors 'produce a hideously incongruous effect [destroying] the charm of language by the extravagant efforts [they] have made to attain it'.[79]

Another species of *trope* discussed by Quintilian appears to be a valid rhetorical model for variation: *hyperbole*.[80] This was a *trope* of 'adornment', which he describes as 'an elegant straining of the truth . . . employed indifferently [i.e. variously] for exaggeration or attenuation.'[81] *Hyperbole* may employ *metaphors*, singly, or in combination, to work up to a climax of expressive intensity; while primarily a figure of embellishment it also has *structural* significance. Quintilian quotes an especially eloquent example of *hyperbole* from Cicero:

What Charybdis was ever so voracious? Charybdis did I say? Nay, if Charybdis ever existed, she was but a single monster. By heaven, even Ocean's self, methinks, could scarce have engulfed so many things, so widely scattered in such distant places, in such a twinkling of the eye.[82]

In this passage, the *metaphors* pile up in a mounting succession, overstating the case for dramatic effect. It is quite easy to draw an analogy between this kind of heightened speech and a piece of music such as var.11 of K.284's finale. Here Mozart piles up a succession of increasingly ornate phrases distinguished by progressive rhythmic division, supported by a huge variety of melodic embellishments either composed, or added as ornaments, the effect of which is similar in its saturation to the extract of Cicero quoted above. One has the sense that such high-flown, hyper-expressive language is almost *too* much to bear, though it forms an impressive climax to the set, following which the change to a rather more earthy concluding minuet (var. 12) provides necessary relief, indeed, resolution. Perhaps Mozart transgresses good taste in this imposing façade. Certainly one sympathises with Quintilian's remark that 'although every *hyperbole* involves the incredible, it must not go too far in this direction, which provides the easiest road to extravagant affectation.'[83]

EPISODIC FORMS

Twenty of Mozart's sonata movements are in some kind of episodic form, that is, a form involving digression(s) away from and periodic returns to an opening statement. Normally the opening statement is capable of standing as a self-contained tonal unit, beginning and ending in the tonic key. The digressive section or sections separating recurrences of this statement provide diversity of key, melody and sometimes phrase-structure, register and texture. Reprises of the opening statement are either plain or decorated; often (as in the second and third movements of the B flat Sonata, K.570) they are contracted. Episodic forms included in the following discussion comprise simple rondos, so-called sonata rondos, and minuet-trio couplings. A schematic table of episodic movements found in the sonatas is given below (table 11.1).

In column 2 the alternating sections are represented by A B A [C . . .] A, in which A denotes the opening statement while B, C and so on, denote intervening episodes. Superscript Arabic numbers (A^1, A^2) indicate varied reprises; superscript Roman numbers (B^I, B^{IV}) indicate a reprise of an episode in a different key (normally the tonic) from that in which it first appeared. Where individual sections are themselves internally subdivided this is indicated by lower-case letters within round brackets, for instance: (|: a :|: b :|).

From table 11.1 no 'typical' procedure can be inferred. In sonata rondo finales significant divergent episodic material is normally reprised within the tonic towards

Table 11.1. *Episodic structures in Mozart's Sonatas*

K.	Structure	Remarks
281/iii	ABAC(|:a:|:b:|)ADA¹B¹A	'Rondeau'. The first reprise of A is curtailed at bar 43. A brief cadenza is inserted between B and A (bar 43). A=bars 1–27, with transitional theme beginning at bar 18; B = bars 28–43; C = bars 52–70; D=90–113; B¹ = bars 124–42. At bar 114 it occurs against a prolonged dominant trill (followed by texture inversion).
282/ii	A(|:a:|:b:|) B(|:a:|:b:|) A(|:a:|:b:|)	Minuet I; Minuet II; Minuet I da capo
284/ii	A(a a¹)BA¹CB^IV A² + coda	'Rondeau en Polonaise'. A=bars 1–16; B = bars 17–30; C = bars 47–52; B^IV=bars 53–69; coda introduced by interrupted cadence at bar 85. Varied reprises of A become progressively more ornate.
309/ii	A(a a¹)A¹B a² B¹ A²	A = bars 1–16; A¹ = bars 17–32; B = bars 33–43, with subsidiary theme at bar 40; a²=bars 44–52; B¹ = bars 53–64; A² = bars 65–79.
309/iii	ABA¹CB¹A²	A sonata rondo, in which there is no central reprise of A (marking the 'recapitulation') – instead, C flows into the tonic reprise of B. The concluding A is extended into a coda. A = bars 1–39 (with subsidiary transitional motive beginning at bar 19); B = bars 40–92 (with subsidiary motives at bars 53, 66 and 77); A¹ = bars 93–115; C = bars 116–142; B¹ = bars 143–188; A² = bars 189–252.
310/iii	ABA¹C(|:a:|:b:|)A²B¹	An unusual rondo structure in which the symmetry is provided not by a reprise of A, but of the opening two sections (AB, bars 1–106) at the end (A²B¹, bars 175–252). The movement approaches monothematicism (the principal derivatives being at bars 29 and 64, with related motives at bars 37 and 72). Contrast of theme and mode is provided by the central section, C (bars 143–74). The reprise of AB exploits the similarities between themes to create ambiguity in the order of events: are bars 203–10 a reprise of bars

63 ff., or bars 29 ff. (with texture inversion)? Likewise, are bars 211–25 a modified reprise – again featuring texture inversion – of bars 72–86, or are bars 211–18 a reprise of bars 45 ff.? Whichever is the case, the following passage (bars 226 ff.) takes as its starting-point bars 56 ff., so that some reordering undoubtedly occurs.

311/ii ABA^{1}B^{1}A^2+coda

A sonata rondo without central episode. A = bars 1–16; B = bars 16–39; A^1 = bars 40–52; B^1 = bars 52–74; A^2 = bars 75–86; coda = bars 86–93.

311/iii ABA^{1}CA^{2}B^{1}A^3

A sonata rondo with central episode (relative minor). A= bars 1–40 (with subsidiary ideas at bars 16 and 28); B= bars 41–85 (with subsidiary ideas at bars 56, 69 and 75); A^1 = bars 86–118; C = bars 119–73 (ending with cadenza); A^2 = bars 173–205; B^1 = bars 206–248; A^3 = bars 248–69.

330/ii A(|:a:|:b:|)B(|:a:|:b:|)A(ab)[+coda]

The final coda (bars 60–4) is not present in the autograph but was added to the 1784 print, presumably to provide a degree of symmetry with bars 36–40, ending the middle episode.

331/ii A(|:a:|:b:|) B(|:a:|:b:|) A(|:a:|:b:|)

Minuet; Trio; Minuet da capo

331/iii A(|:a:|:b:|) B(|:a:|:b:|:c:|:a:|)AB(|:a:|)+ coda

'Rondo Alla Turca'

333/iii ABACA^{1}B^{1}A^2+coda

A = bars 1–23, ending with imperfect cadence, and incorporating subsidiary transitional idea at bar 16; B = bars 23–40, with prominent closing figure at bar 36; A = bars 41–64, with modified close at bars 60 ff.; C=bars 64–111, including extended 'development' of the principal theme of A at bars 90 ff.; A^1 = bars 112–48, incorporating extension of the transitional figure (originally bar 16); B^1 = bars 148–72, including cadenzas (bars 171–2 and 198–9) and further 'development' of the main theme of A (bars 173 ff.) and the closing figure of B (originally bar 36: cf. bars 179 ff.); A^2 = bars 200–14; coda = bars 215–25, featuring subdominant colouring.

Table 11.1 (*cont.*)

K.	Structure	Remarks
457/ii	ABA¹CA²+coda	A = bars 1–7; B = bars 8–16; A¹ = bars 17–23; C = bars 24–40; A² = bars 41–7; coda = bars 47–57. The textual revisions made during the course of composition, revealed by the recently rediscovered autograph, are dealt with in chapter 6.
457/iii	ABA¹CB¹A¹C¹+coda	A= bars 1–45, featuring subsidiary ideas at bars 16 and 26; B = bars 46–102, in the relative major, E flat, and featuring prominent subsidiary idea at bar 74, and important closing figure at bar 90 (developed later in the coda, bars 289 ff.); A¹ = bars 103–45, with modified closure at bar 143–4; C = bars 146–66; B¹ = bars 167–220, with modified ending, leading to A¹ = bars 221–74 (identical with bars 103–45), leading into C¹, still in the subdominant, and closing into extended coda (bars 289–319), developing the closing figure of B (originally bars 90 ff.) and affirming the tonic, C minor.
533/iii	ABA¹CA²D(‖:a:‖:b:‖) A³B¹+coda	A revised text of the F major Rondo, K.494, composed in 1786 and published in 1788. See chapter 7. A = bars 1–12; B = bars 13–38; A¹ = bars 39–50; C = bars 51–82; A² = bars 83–94; D = bars 95–116, followed by three-bar link to A³ = bars 120–131; B¹ = bars 132–175, incorporating a substantial contrapuntal passage (bars 143–69) inserted between bars 142 and 170, bars which, in the original form of the Rondo, K.494, were contiguous; coda = bars 176–87, with main theme reprised in low register.
545/ii	A(‖:a,a¹:‖)B(‖:b,a¹:‖)CA+coda	A = bars 1–16; B = bars 17–32; C = bars 33–48; A = bars 49–64; coda = bars 64–74.
545/iii	ABACA+coda	A = bars 1–8 (repeated); B = bars 9–20; A = bars 20–28; C = bars 28–52; A = bars 53–60; coda = bars 60–73. All subsequent reprises of A omit the initial repeat.

570/ii	A(|:a:|:b:|)B(|:a:|:b:|)aC(|:a:|:b:|)a+coda	Reprises of A are all curtailed, ceasing after a single statement of its first four bars. A = bars 1–12; B = bars 13–27, concluding with three-bar extension; a = bars 28–31; C = bars 32–43, concluding with four-bar extension; a = bars 44–7; coda = bars 48–55.
570/iii	A(aba)B(|:a:|:b:|)C(|:a:|:b:|)a+coda	A = bars 1–22; B = bars 23–44, concluding with two-bar extension; C = bars 45–62, featuring prominent chromaticism and concluding with six-bar extension; a = bars 63–70; coda = bars 71–89, incorporating prominent references to motives from B and C.
576/ii	A(aba)B(aba)A(aba)+coda	A = bars 1–16; B = bars 17–43; A = bars 44–58; coda = bars 59–67.
576/iii	$ABA^1CB^1A^2$+coda	A sonata rondo. A = bars 1–25; B = bars 26–64; A^1 = bars 65–94; C = bars 95–116, developing material from A contrapuntally; B^1 = bars 117–62, featuring new continuation from bar 152, leading to final reprise of A^2 (= bars 163–77); coda = bars 178–89.

the end of the movement (as in K.576), though this is not always the case (K.457). The expected contrasts of tonality (dominant; relative major/ minor; subdominant) occur in the contrasting sections. Sometimes reprises of the opening section are curtailed, sometimes not. Reprises are sometimes embellished, sometimes not. The only constant is the idea of a recurring theme separated by contrasting sections. As noted previously, the rhetorical figure known as 'dwelling upon the point' may, according to the author of *Ad Herennium*, 'employ digressions and then . . . make a neat and elegant return to our main theme'. In so far as this description implies a structure formed from digression from and return to a central theme, 'dwelling upon the point' proves a suitable – if generalised – rhetorical model for the design of Mozart's episodic forms.

One feature that unites many of Mozart's episodic movements is their tendency, despite the inherent principle of *contrast*, to transplant material between contrasting sections, especially towards the end. The result is a sense of inter-connection between ostensibly disparate elements of the structure and consequently an enhanced feeling of overall cohesion. A simple illustration of this occurs in the rondo finale of the C major Sonata, K.545. During the first episode (bar 12) Mozart 'quotes' an extract of the movement's opening theme; a slightly longer 'quotation' occurs within the second episode also (bar 44).These cross-references undoubtedly give an added dimension to what would otherwise be a rather lightweight piece. At the end of the slow movement of K.457 Mozart 'quotes' a fragment from the first episode (bars 54–5; cf. bars 13–14). Further examples of direct melodic 'quotation' are found in the finale of the C major Sonata, K.309, which 'quotes' a prominent tremolando pattern from the first episode (originally bars 58 ff.) towards the end (bars 217–27), and the Andante con espressione of the D major Sonata, K.311, whose first episode (in the dominant) 'quotes' the movement's opening theme at bar 25.[84] Melodically, such 'quotations' can be developmental, rather than literal, such as that at bars 91 ff. of the finale of K.333. Here, Mozart treats the central episode as a kind of 'development section', working with the movement's opening theme.

Cross-referencing between episodic sections is not confined to the melodic sphere. Occasionally this takes on a tonal or harmonic aspect. An example is the coda to the Andante of K.576 in which, following the tonic reprise of bars 44–59, the texture and rhythm (though not the actual melodic shape) of the central F sharp minor episode are absorbed within the tonic, A major. In the slow movement of K.545 harmonic cross-references occur between the coda and the central episode. Bars 65–7 and 70–1 provide clear aural reminiscences of the harmonies at bars 39–40 and 43–4 of that episode, reproducing the progression from melodic chromaticism to structural harmonic chromaticism (that is, the enhancement of the dominant degree, D in the bass by adjacent chromatic neighbour-note motion). Another illustration occurs within the slow movement of K.570: bars 36–7 (the second episode) recollect the falling-step chromaticism of bars 17–20 (the first episode).[85]

Is there any rhetorical explanation for this procedure? A plausible candidate is the device known as *synecdoche* (συνεκδοχη), described in *Ad Herennium* and by Quintilian.[86] Quintilian includes *synecdoche* in his section on *tropes* of 'meaning' (that is, after *metaphor* and before such '*tropes* of adornment' as *periphrasis*), indicating that, in his view, *synecdoche* was a device with implications for the 'structure' of the speech, rather than of purely local concern. He describes it as follows: '*synecdoche* has the power to give variety to our language by making us realise many things from a part, the *genus* from a *species*, things which follow from things which have preceded'.[87] Considered as a term within a musical oration, *synecdoche* seems to cater satisfactorily for the instances of cross-reference outlined above. A melodic quotation stands for the whole of the previous section in which it originally formed a part ('making us realise many things from a part . . . things which follow from things which have preceded'), while the quotation in the coda of the Andante of K.576 of the middle episode's rhythm and texture represents 'the *genus* [that is, the contrasting key of F sharp minor, now resolved within the tonic] from a *species* [the textural and rhythmic signals of that foreign tonality].'

FANTASIA IN C MINOR, K.475

The Fantasia in C minor, K.475, was intended to stand as an introduction to the C minor Sonata, K.457, composed the previous year.[88] In rhetorical terms, such an introduction was termed an *exordium*. If regarded in this way, Mozart's Fantasia takes on a new meaning. According to the author of *Ad Herennium* the *exordium*'s purpose was 'to enable us to have hearers who are attentive, receptive, and well-disposed'.[89] According to this author there were two kinds of *exordium* a 'direct opening' and a 'subtle approach',[90] a point confirmed by both Cicero and Quintilian, who each describe two manners: an *introduction* (a direct appeal to the listener) and *insinuatio* (a more sophisticated appeal, in which the case is put 'by dissimulation and indirection unobtrusively [stealing] into the mind of the auditor').[91]

The restless tonal and harmonic structure of Mozart's Fantasia, with its rapidly shifting textures, and alternation of free improvisatory passages with more stable, periodic ones such as the D major aria (bars 26–35) and the B flat sarabande (bars 86–124), strongly suggests that it belongs to the second type of *exordium*, the *insinuatio*. Its structure is in no sense predictable in advance, unlike the outlines of, say, a sonata-form movement, or a binary dance movement, or some other type of ternary or episodic form. It evolves according to no familiar plan. Instead it makes its impact 'by dissimulation and indirection unobtrusively [stealing] into the mind of the auditor', who has nothing against which to measure or plot its unfolding. The structure may be represented as follows:

Section	Bars	Key	Remarks
1	1–25	C minor	Unstable, chromatic area; bars 1–18 outline descending chromatic scale in bass, stretching from tonic to dominant degrees: C B B flat A A flat G G flat/F sharp G; thereafter the G functions not as a dominant, but as a chromatic neighbour to F sharp, which persists to the end of the first section.
2	26–35	D major	Aria in two sections, each repeated, with reprise of opening cantabile theme at bar 32 in a higher register; ending chromatically inflected, D – D sharp in the bass, leading onwards.
3	36–85	Unstable	Begins on the dominant of A minor, and ends with a dominant seventh chord of B flat, traversing G minor, F major/minor, D flat and G flat/F sharp major; the F sharp (bar 73) initiates another chromatic descent, before serving as a chromatic neighbour note (bars 78–81) to F (bar 82), in a manner analogous to the relation of G–F sharp at the end of section 1; a subsidiary, *cantabile*, theme in F enters at bar 58.
4	86–124	B flat	Sarabande character
5	125–160	Unstable	Features tremolando figurations; the harmonies move rapidly, but according to circle-of-fifths schemes; again, an upper chromatic neighbour-note (A flat, bars 136–40) plays a role (this time indirect) in the formation of a structural pitch (G, the dominant), leading onwards.
6	161–76	C minor	Curtailed reprise of section 1, without full chromatic descent from tonic to dominant; upper chromatic neighbour-note motion A flat-G prominent.

If Mozart's *exordium* is to be interpreted as an *insinuatio*, in what specific ways does it proceed 'by dissimulation and indirection . . . into the mind of the auditor'? It operates on every level by *ambiguity*. In section 1 the sense of tonality is destabilised by two important factors: the angular opening theme, featuring chromatic steps that weaken its underlying triadic profile, C-E flat-G-C-B; and the lack of tonic-dominant-tonic progressions, which would confirm the central key. While there are localised fifth-progressions at bars 6–7 (A flat to D flat) and bars 10–11 (B to F sharp), neither is clinched by a return to the initial term that would define a temporary key. Elsewhere, the progressions at bars 8–9, 12–13 and 14–15, moving by semitone steps, obscure, rather than clarify, the tonality.

Only in bars 18–19 does a tonic-dominant-tonic progression occur, alternating D and G in such a way as to suggest G as the stable dominant degree in a piece ostensibly in C minor. Yet even this is an illusion: it is an upper neighbour-note preparation for F sharp (secured in bars 21–2 by means of the outward resolution of an augmented-sixth, G-B-D-E sharp, onto an F sharp chord). Even this diversion is not the end of the story. The repeated F sharps in bar 25 suggest a dominant preparation for the arrival of B major (or minor), but are re-interpreted instead as the mediant degree of D major in which the following aria is cast.

That such a remote degree – F sharp, a tritone away from the tonic, C – should turn out to be the most stable region within section 1 is, literally, ironic. Irony, or *illusio*, was a technique well-known to rhetoricians. It is a *trope*, described by Quinitilian as follows:

> . . . that class of allegory in which the meaning is contrary to that suggested by the words, involves an element of irony, or as our rhetoricians call it, *illusio*. This is made evident to the understanding either by the delivery, the character of the speaker or the nature of the subject. For if any one of these three is out of keeping with the words, it at once becomes clear that the intention of the speaker is other than what he actually says.[92]

Within the tonal system as inherited by Mozart, the structure of a piece was governed by a widely-understood hierarchy of chord-relationships, acknowledged by composers, theorists and listeners, among which the strongest was that which linked the dominant chord to the tonic. In the regulation of tonal structure, the elevation of the dominant chord to the status of an opposing tonality within the hierarchy was a normal procedure, while the status of a chord constructed on a tritonal degree was aberrant. Mozart's choice of F sharp as the most stable region within section 1 of the C minor Fantasia is therefore ironic, in the true rhetorical sense, in that, structurally, its 'meaning is contrary to that suggested' by both the preceding bars (which seemed to establish the 'expected' dominant degree, G) and the normal tonal hierarchy (the 'aberrant' becoming, temporarily, the 'norm').

The rhetorical model of the *exordium* helps us to deal with broader issues in the Fantasia, too. The idea of *insinuatio*, in which a point is made subtly, by stealth, rather than in a direct statement, relates not only to local gestures of melody or chord progression, but to the overall balance of the structure. The two most extended stable tonal sections, in D (section 2) and B flat (section 4), are not in the expected keys of the dominant and relative minor, but in keys founded, respectively, a whole-tone higher and lower than the tonic, C. Just as the tritonal degree of F sharp is not part of the normal tonal hierarchy, neither are the major modes of the supertonic or the flattened seventh. In terms of the prevailing classical hierarchy of tonality, then, relatively remote domains are given unexpected structural prominence and, collectively, serve to undermine the traditionally central function of dominant-tonic polarity. When it is finally established, towards the end of the Fantasia, C minor can hardly be regarded as the 'central' key of the piece.

Bars 167–72 at the end of the Fantasia are derived from bars 16–18 of section 1. They stand in relation to that moment in a manner analogous to the eventual recapitulation *within the tonic* of a dominant-key episode in a sonata rondo (or else, of secondary key-area material within a sonata form). Had the earlier section actually cadenced in the dominant, G, the tonic recapitulation of bars 167–72 would have been just another illustration of a familiar classic period tonal strategy – something taken for granted, in fact. Yet here, this is not quite the case. The dominant degree, G, was not the final destination of section 1: rather, it was a preparation for F sharp. This unsettling tonal sequence is not resolved at the end of the Fantasia. The quotation of bars 16–18 in a tonic reformulation is only a *partial* resolution of the earlier conflict, indeed, it is more a reminder than a resolution. Consequently, C minor is not at all strongly established: its long-postponed appearance merely reveals the hitherto absent context for what has already taken place. Yet this is not a weakness, for the Fantasia is, after all, only the *exordium*, a preface to the *narratio* which follows in the Sonata. Had Mozart confirmed C minor too strongly at the close he would have jeopardised the Fantasia's introductory function by making it too convincing a tonal organism in its own right. As an *exordium*, the Fantasia is a shining example of Mozart's feeling for proportion and restraint. It retains the interest (rendering the hearers 'attentive, receptive, and well-disposed') without detracting from the impact of the 'speech' itself.

CHAPTER TWELVE

The rhetorical *elocutio*

This chapter draws analogies between the 'syntax' of Mozart's sonatas and the rhetorical *elocutio*, that is, the detailed construction of sentences and the shaping of language by *figurae*. *Elocutio* (style or expression) is considered at length in all the major rhetorical texts of classical antiquity. The acquisition of good style was regarded as the pinnacle of an orator's training. At its most basic, *elocutio* required of an orator first, a good command of grammar and secondly, presentational 'polish'. Cicero, regarded by his contemporaries as one of the most polished of speakers, recommended that especial care be taken to avoid ugly juxtapositions of words:

it is important to pay attention to this matter of order of words . . . it produces a well-knit, connected style, with a smooth and even flow; this you will achieve if the ends of the words join onto the beginning of the words that follow in such a way as to avoid either harsh collision or awkward hiatus.[1]

A musical equivalent of this is care in the part-writing (correct resolution of dissonances, and so forth) and in the harmonic progression (avoiding such solecisms as 'dead' beats, in which there is no harmonic change from a weak to a strong beat, for example). Careful regulation of these elements 'produces a well-knit, connected style, with a smooth and even flow' by ensuring that successive melodic and harmonic terms are connected 'in such a way as to avoid either harsh collision or awkward hiatus'. In example 12.1, from the finale of K.311, smooth continuity of the melodic line is assured by the judicious balance of movement by step and by leap; by correct connection of the quaver D in bar 44 with the following crotchet C sharp (fulfilling the demands of the counterpoint); and by the application of decorative non-harmonic pitches on predominantly weak parts of the beat or bar. Harmonically, the chord progressions are grammatically 'correct', and, when the phrase is repeated, varied; the balance of relative stasis and momentum steers the phrase forward towards the cadence in bar 48; and the relationship between the leading melodic part and the bass-line makes good two-part counterpoint. In all respects this is a 'polished' statement, one which combines a mastery of both grammar and eloquence.

When examining the rhetorical and musical *elocutio*, it is essential to keep in mind that in this context, rhetorical *figurae* apply to the adornment of a structure, not to

Example 12.1   Mozart, Sonata in D, K.311, finale, bars 44–51

the design of the structure itself. Aristotle, the author of *Ad Herennium*, Cicero, and Quintilian all make a clear distinction between stylistic adornment and structural significance. Aristotle clearly separates his consideration of style from that of arrangement within Book III of his *Rhetoric*,[2] while in *Ad Herennium* and in Quintilian's *Institutio*, figures are divided into two categories, thought and speech.[3] Cicero makes a wise distinction between that which is expressed and the means by which it is expressed:

there is an almost incalculable supply both of figures of speech and figures of thought . . . but there is this difference between the figurative character of language and of thought, that the figure suggested by the words disappears if one alters the words, but that of the thoughts remains whatever words one chooses to employ.[4]

The rhetorical *elocutio*, then, consists of 'the embellishments which the line of thought can employ to explain the meaning'.[5] Musically, this comprises the embellishment of a theme by various means, of which two are fundamental, *decoration* (the addition of non-harmonic tones) and *development* (for instance, sequential repetition or fragmentation). Before proceeding to a review of these figurative techniques, however, we need to investigate the sentence-structure within which they occur, that is musical *periodicity*.

PERIODICITY

A useful rhetorical model for periodicity is found in book III of Cicero's *De Oratore*. In the context of a section on rhythmic style[6] he observes that Greek orators of the school of Isocrates had 'thought that in speeches the close of the period ought to come not when we are tired out . . . but by the arrangement of the words and of the thought', borrowing from poet-musicians in injecting a 'rhythmical cadence' given by 'the modulation of the voice and the arrangement of the words in periods'.[7] The musical equivalent of this is surely the division of a passage into melodic 'periods' rounded-off by (harmonic) cadences. One of Cicero's recommendations for the coordination of metre and thought within a speech bears a striking resemblance to the discussion of phrase-organisation by one of the most important of eighteenth-century musical theorists, Johann Kirnberger. Cicero's recommendation is to 'let your habitual practice in writing and in speaking be to make the thoughts end up with the words' (that is, sense coordinated with sentence). Kirnberger's analogy between music and speech notes that:

in speech one comprehends the meaning only at the end of the sentence [especially, of course, in the German language, where the verb comes at the end] . . . The same is true of music. Not until a succession of connected notes reaches a point of rest [a cadence] at which the ear is somewhat satisfied does it comprehend these notes as a small whole . . . This break or resting point can be achieved either by a complete [perfect] cadence or simply by a melodic close with a restful harmony, without a close in the bass [some kind of imperfect or interrupted cadence][8]

Periodicity, clearly a crucial issue in later-eighteenth-century musical language, was discussed in great detail by Joseph Riepel, one of whose treatises was owned, as noted previously, by Leopold Mozart, and which, therefore, may have been used by Leopold in the musical instruction of his son.[9]

According to Riepel, the normal preference was for symmetrical, balanced phrases in units of two or four bars. He devotes some attention to the construction of irregular groupings, up to as many as nine bars (which he regards as being an aggregation of a four- and a five-bar group). Riepel's discussion hinges on cadential articulation of phrases, especially on tonic (*Grundabsatz*) and dominant (*Quintabsatz*) degrees, and indicates tonic or dominant termination, respectively, with black or white squares above the phrase-ends of his examples. Subdivision of a phrase (*Einschnitt*) is explained (2 + 2 bars; 4 + 4 bars, and so on, including irregular subdivisions such as 3 + 2 bars) as well as the symmetrical balance of phrases to form larger continuities (4 + 4 bars, for instance). In Riepel's view any local irregularity (a five-bar phrase, for example) was best 'smoothed out' by repetition, resulting in a larger symmetry (5 [= 3 + 2] + 5 bars, and so on). Having defined various types of phrase, whether including a modulation or not, Riepel goes on to explain some methods of transforming these by means of repetition (perhaps in sequence) of an initial or internal figure, by inserting a figure within what would otherwise be a regular phrase (usually of four bars), by expansion of the end of a phrase, or else by reiteration of the cadence for extra emphasis.[10] Many of these theoretical formulations are reflected in Mozart's sonatas.

Riepel's illustrations of phrase-structure frequently employ the minuet. An example of a perfectly regular periodicity, featuring four-bar phrases, is Minuet II in the E flat Sonata, K.282. Its opening section (up to the double-bar) is sixteen bars long, divided as 4 + 4 + 4 + 4 bars. Each of these four-bar phrases is built up by internal repetition of motives, and the cadential closure is weak in all but the last (bars 15–16/ 47–8).[11] Minuet I of K.282 has an opening section of twelve bars with irregular subdivision, 4 + 6 + 2 bars. The first four bars are constructed from sequential repetition (up a step) of a two-bar unit; the six-bar phrase that follows is itself sub-divided 1 + 1 (a repetition of the opening bar) + 2 + 2 bars (cadential); the additional two bars reiterate the cadential closure in the dominant.[12] The Minuet of K.331 begins with a ten-bar section, subdivided 4 + 6 bars. The leading four-bar phrase features internal motive-repetition (bars 2 and 3), while in the ensuing six-bar phrase three successive bars (6–8) repeat the same motive. These three bars could be regarded as an insertion within the middle of the phrase (structured 1 + 3 + 2 bars).[13] 'Smoothing-out' of local irregularities by immediate repetition also occurs in the first-movement exposition of K.309 in C. Its fourteen-bar opening section is constructed as 7 [=2 + 5 (=3 + 2)] + 7 bars, exactly fulfilling Riepel's prescription for the treatment of irregular phrases.[14] Mixture of regular and irregular phrase-lengths is employed at the opening of the G major Sonata, K.283 (whose dance 'topic' is the Minuet). Its opening section is subdivided 4 + 6 + 6 bars; the irregularity created by following a four-bar opening by a six-bar continuation is counterbalanced by repetition of the latter at bars 10^1–16^1. The six-bar phrase results from internal 'expansion' (prolonging the pitch D in bars 6 and 7, as shown in the hypothetical skeleton previously shown in chapter 10 (example 10.1a), perhaps reflecting Mozart's initial *inventio* for the phrase). One of the most eloquent examples of expansion at the end of a phrase is found in the Adagio of the F major Sonata, K.332. A cadence on F in the middle of bar 16 is postponed by the ensuing decoration (example 12.2), eventually arriving in bar 19.

Initial irregularities are not always diluted by repetition, however. The Adagio of K.457 begins with a three-bar phrase, followed by an embellished repeat that is extended to four bars, making a seven-bar section. Elsewhere a regular phrase length of four bars is irregularly sub-divided. The Andantino beginning at bar 86 of the C minor Fantasia, K.475, for instance, creates a four-bar phrase in a memorably 'lop-sided' fashion by shifting the accentuation of a two-beat motive from strong-to-weak (bars 86–7) to weak-to-strong (bars 87–8).

FIGURES AND THEIR APPLICATION

Melodic figures (*figurae*) were familiar to composers and music theorists throughout the eighteenth century. Classifications of *figurae* and descriptions of their use are to be found in the writings of Mattheson, Scheibe, Spiess and Riepel, theorists whose works were known in the Mozart household. Mattheson, writing in *Der vollkommene Capellmeister*, noted that, in devising expressive melodies, figures imported from rhetoric were particularly useful to the composer.[15] Musical 'figures' were by no means new to the eighteenth century. A substantial quantity of baroque musical theory had stressed their importance, beginning with the publication in 1606 of Joachim Burmeister's *Musica Poetica*, a work which proposed for the first time an

Example 12.2　Mozart, Sonata in F, K.332, 2nd movement, bars 13–18

analogy between various ornamental musical 'figures' and the *figurae* of classical rhetoric.[16] The composers and theorists of the classic period inherited an already mature tradition of *Figurenlehre*, the application of which seemed entirely natural. Forkel's discussion of rhetorical figures in the *Allgemeine Geschichte der Musik*[17] discriminates between two sorts of figures, which equate to the 'figures of thought' and 'figures of speech' in *Ad Herennium* and Quintilian's *Institutio*, previously mentioned in chapter 11 in relation to the variation genre. While the former influence the detailed musical continuity, the latter serve to adorn that structure. In the Andante amoroso of Mozart's B flat Sonata, K.281, for example, the reprise of the opening theme at bar 59 is embellished by the addition of triplet semiquaver neighbour-notes. In the 'Rondeau en Polonaise' of the D major Sonata, K.284, Mozart decorates each recurrence of the rondeau theme, for instance, with triplet quavers at bar 9, and with semiquaver and demisemiquaver roulades at bar 70. Thematic reprises within the slow movement of K.309 in C become exceedingly ornate.[18] In

Example 12.3   Mozart, Sonata in C, K.330, 2nd movement, hypothetical original conception of bars 8–12

such contexts, the musical figures are a means of adornment, what Quintilian calls 'gestures of language'[19] that make the speech more eloquent. Other figures, 'figures of thought', may be equated with techniques of musical development, and influence the musical continuity.

Some of the principal terminology relating to the *figurae* found in eighteenth-century texts is as follows:

Dispositio	the arrangement of the principal ideas (*figurae*)
Propositio	statement (normally of the first main idea)
Confirmatio	reinforcement of an idea
Antistrophe	a consequent phrase or balancing continuation of a melodic idea
Antithesis	an opposing idea (such as a 'second subject' in a sonata form)
Distributio	the fragmentation of a figure (also called *Zergliederung*)
Gradatio	sequential repetition (also called *Versetzung*)
Variatio	embellishment of an idea
Apostrophe	introduction of a different 'topic' (which may also incorporate a significant change of texture, such as counterpoint, within a piece)
Confutatio	resolution of a phrase, or section, or movement (usually clinched by a decisive cadence)

This account of rhetoric in Mozart's sonatas concludes with several case-studies, beginning with two examples of thematic construction, and continuing with two varied sonata developments, before turning to the analysis of an extended passage.

K.330: ANDANTE CANTABILE

In this slow movement Mozart takes great care to vary the sequential repetition of phrases. Even when, as at bars 28 ff., the melodic sequence is exact, the harmonic underpinning is subtly changed. Beginning at bar 8 is a phrase whose *inventio* might originally have been somewhat as shown in example 12.3 in which the sequence is

Example 12.4   Mozart, Sonata in D, K.311, 2nd movement, underlying melodic profile
of bars 17–24

exact. What Mozart actually wrote retains the balanced periodicity of that hypothetical original but alters the order of events in that only the closing part of the
figure in bars 8–9 is sequentially repeated: in bar 10 what was originally the end of
a figure becomes (sequentially) the beginning of a new continuation cadencing at
bar 12. The positioning of expected events within the successive phrases is here
subtly reversed. A rhetorical technique applicable in this context is the *trope* known
as *hyperbaton*, defined by Quintilian as 'the transposition of a word to some distance
from its original place, in order to secure an ornamental effect.'[20] In achieving this
elegant design, Mozart has merged *gradatio* (sequence) with *distributio* (fragmentation) and *variatio* (variation).

K.311: ANDANTE CON ESPRESSIONE

The very beautiful subsidiary theme beginning at bar 16 of the slow movement of
K.311 is constructed from a series of one-bar figures closely related by rhythmic
profile (especially the syncopation in the middle of each of its first six bars).[21] On
the other hand, these bars are characterised by melodic diversity. Its effect, though,
is not one of fragmentation but of unbroken continuity – an effect in part attribut-
able to the rhythm but also to an underlying melodic unity revealed by regarding
the theme as an *allegory* (a series of *metaphors*)[22] in which each successive bar is a
metaphor for the basic descending minim outline (Mozart's probable *inventio* for the
phrase), shown in example 12.4. The melody gains continuity through the
accumulation of these inter-related one-bar *metaphors*, each of which relates additionally to the basic scale-descent that underlies the phrase. It succeeds as a unity
because of its sophisticated coordination of these musical elements. Undeniably,
though, Mozart's theme possesses a special quality of refinement, of elevation that
goes beyond mere technical description, a quality recognised by classical authors –
and in the eighteenth century – as the 'sublime'. One of the most popular texts of
classical antiquity in Mozart's day was the incomplete *On the Sublime* by pseudo-
Longinus.[23] In chapter 32 of pseudo-Longinus's treatise is a description of a succession of *metaphors* that captures something of the quality of Mozart's theme: 'the
onward rush of passion has the property of sweeping everything before it . . . it does
not allow the hearer leisure to consider the number of metaphors, since he is carried
away by the enthusiasm of the speaker'.[24]

Example 12.5   Mozart, Sonata in A minor, K.310, 1st movement, underlying suspension chain in bars 58–70

TWO DEVELOPMENT SECTIONS: K.310 AND K.311

The development sections of the D major Sonata, K.311 (1777) and the A minor Sonata, K.310 (1778) provide interesting illustrations of Mozart's application of rhetorical *figurae*. In both sonatas the developments truly 'develop' material from their expositions (unlike some of the 1774–5 sonatas, whose much briefer developments often proceed independently of the main exposition themes). That of K.311 is based exclusively on the exposition's closing-figure (*confutatio*, consisting of falling quavers followed by rising melodic cadence at bars 38–9). Its opening (bars 40 ff.) takes this as its *propositio* and begins by applying *gradatio* (descending sequence), forming an eight-bar paragraph. Within each element of the *gradatio* Mozart first fragments the new *propositio*, imitating just its falling quavers, while at the end (bar 43) he combines the antecedent and consequent. The following section extends the *propositio*'s antecedent quavers by *gradatio*, this time against a falling chain of suspensions implied by the right hand semiquaver tremolandos, reaching F sharp minor by the end of bar 51, after which the figure is further fragmented to four quavers, reaching B minor in bar 55. Bars 56–7 employ *aposiopasis* (a complete breaking-off of the narrative flow, represented here by unexpected chord progressions, through which the music lurches towards the subdominant (G), preparing for the ambiguous entry of the recapitulation, in which the original thematic order is reversed). Notice that each significant stage in the progress of the development (bars 40–7; 48–51; 52–5; 56–7) is marked-off by the application of a particular rhetorical technique.

In the A minor Sonata, K.310, *distributio* (*Zergliederung*) is applied in a more sophisticated way. Beginning at bar 50 with a statement of the entire opening *propositio* in C major, Mozart proceeds to isolate just the prominent dotted quaver-semiquaver rhythm from its first bar, which stands at the head of a sequentially modulating contrapuntal passage lasting until bar 70. As in K.311, this passage combines the techniques of *distributio* and *gradatio*. But there is a further level of 'argumentation' on which the sophisticated orator is seeking to 'persuade' his hearers here. The descending steps of the *gradatio* outline a suspension chain (example 12.5), a texture employed within the second theme-group of K.310's exposition (bars 28 ff.) and to which it retrospectively refers. In other words, Mozart combines two disparate elements of his exposition: a theme associated with the first subject group and a texture originating in the second subject group. At bars 86–93 of the recapitulation Mozart returns to this combination of *Hauptsatz* and *Gegensatz* elements, transferring the theme to the left hand with the suspension tremolandos above in a texture almost identical to bars 48–51 of K.311.

K.576 – SLOW MOVEMENT

Despite an outward appearance of simplicity, this Adagio conceals a degree of rhetorical complexity, with regard to the coordination of melody and harmony, entirely typical of Mozart's late style. Its form is simple ternary, the middle section of which lasts from bar 17 to bar 43 in the predictable key of the relative minor (F sharp). Beginning in bar 17 there is a marked change of idiom and texture (*apostrophe*) as well as tonality, while at bar 43 there is a return to the 'topic' of the opening bars (which, with characteristic economy, are repeated note-for-note until bar 59, followed by a short coda).[25] The *dispositio* of the movement is thus clear and straightforward. Its detailed *elocutio* is a different matter altogether. During the course of the Adagio of K.576 Mozart reinterprets the melodic and harmonic content of his opening *propositio* in a sophisticated way which has a bearing on the unfolding of the overall form. At bar 9, following a tonic close, he continues with a secondary idea, or *antistrophe*, setting out a new register and exploring new tonal space (E). What follows, however, is a repositioning of the opening *propositio* (bar 13) as the *closing* cadential portion of the phrase, confirming the tonic and the end of the *Hauptperiode* in bar 16. Rhetorically, the reinterpretation of the original opening figure as the closing part of a phrase upon repetition is known as *epiphrasis*. But Mozart is not content to restrict the application of his rhetoric merely to localised melodic/periodic matters. He underpins this melodic *epiphrasis* with new chromatic harmony, whose part-movement postpones any sense of harmonic resolution until the beginning of bar 14, so combining the appearance of melodic *resolution* of the *antistrophe* at bar 13 with harmonic *instability*. This amounts to a new rhetorical gesture (that is, a dislocation of melodic and harmonic elements), utterly at odds with the previously predictable balance of phrase and cadence, and suggestive of a level of expression not so far disclosed. This strategy justifies the unusually passionate continuation of Mozart's central *Gegenperiode* (bars 17–43) which maps out the contrasting tonal space of F sharp minor by means of chromatic chords (the local dominant, C sharp, is repeatedly prefixed by an augmented-sixth chord, d–b sharp) and vigorous demisemiquaver figuration.[26] During the later reprise of the entire *Hauptperiode* the same dislocation of melodic and harmonic arrival recurs (bars 56–7), this time subverting the apparent restoration of melodic, harmonic, periodic and tonal balance after the chromatic upheavals of bars 17–43 and justifying the continuation beyond the tonic cadence in bar 62. Why should

Mozart have done this? He could easily have retained the original harmony from bar 1 or bar 44 at this point, ending the movement with the tonic close at bar 62. One reason may be that he felt a more conclusive resolution of the Adagio's tonal tensions was required, in which the melodic material of the contrasting *Gegenperiode* was restated within the tonic region, as indeed happens in the coda (bars 62–7). By bringing together elements of the piece formerly kept separate (the *propositio* of the *Gegenperiode* subsumed within the tonality of the *Hauptperiode*), Mozart's coda makes a fitting *peroratio*, analogous to the means by which an orator subsumed contrary positions within his central *thesis*. Viewed in these terms, Mozart's choice of chord progression at bars 13–14 amounts to much more than a simple reharmonisation: it serves to open up latent tensions implicit within the melodic chromaticism of the *propositio* (bars 3 and 6, for instance), which are subsequently addressed in the course of the Adagio.

K.533: ANDANTE – A RHETORICAL ANALYSIS

A movement that illustrates *figurae* combined at several simultaneous levels is the Andante of the F major Sonata, K.533 and 494 (1788). It is in sonata form and its rhetorical arrangement of figures utilises several of the standard melodic *figurae* noted by eighteenth-century theorists. It follows the sequence of *Haupt- Neben-* and *Gegensätze* within the exposition and continues with dissection (*distributio*) and combination of these thematic elements in the development before their expected *Bekräftigung* in the recapitulation; the recapitulation ends with a *conclusion*.

The *Hauptsatz*, or principal key-area begins with a standard four-bar melodic *propositio* concluding in the tonic, B flat and continuing with an *antistrophe* whose main features are the tied upbeat (contrasting with the characteristic downbeat of the *propositio*) and its chromatic lower neighbour-note approached from the third above. From bar 11 there is a restatement (*repetitio*) of the initial material whose transition to the dominant is secured by a sequential passage (*gradatio*) based on a decoration of bar 9 (bars 19–22). The second key-area (*Gegensatz*) in which the main theme from bar 1 serves as a bass in a rising sequence (*gradatio* again), contains an *antistrophe* (contrasting idea) at bar 33 which progresses to a concluding figure (*confutatio*) at bar 42. It is in his development that Mozart reveals his genius for persuasive oratory by means of complex, yet economical rhetorical delivery. He begins by combining a fragment (*distributio*) of the main exposition theme (*propositio*, left hand) with the second group's *antistrophe* (right hand), two *propositiae* that are kept separate during the exposition, but whose relationship is here clearly demonstrated, so advancing the argument a stage further. Later at bar 59, following an *aposiopasis* (a complete breaking-off of the narrative flow) is a mixture of *distributio* and *gradatio* in relation to a particular thematic figure, the *antistrophe* (originally from bar 4 of the piece, that continues from the opening *propositio*). The left hand of bar 59 takes up the *antistrophe* figure and fragments it (*distributio*) to just three beats; over the course of the next dozen bars Mozart indulges himself with extensive application of sequence (*gradatio*), repeating the fragmented figure sequentially ten times within a rising chromatic context ending with a more conclusive *aposiopasis* on the dominant seventh of B flat, preparing for the tonic restatement of the opening *propositio* at bar 73 (the start of the recapitulation).

Rhetoric is the art of persuasion. It is also a science. A definition of the precise admixture of these two attributes was often attempted in the classical treatises,[27] though it proved elusive. All writers were agreed, however, that the successful orator was one who convincingly combined the *partes* of *inventio*, *dispositio* and *elocutio*, as discussed in the previous chapters. Clearly, this power of persuasion required of the orator a firm command of the arguments and the eloquence with which to present the case. In music, as in words, this requires a harmony of idea and expression.

Such a synthesis of idea and expression in Mozart's music was apparently sensed by the anonymous English reviewer of K.309–11, in the edition by Götz (Mannheim), which appeared in *The European Magazine and London Review* in September 1784:

Upon a review of these *Sonates*, we find in them a considerable degree of merit: fancy, taste and judgement unite through the work, and distinguish Mr. Mozard as a fertile and judicious composer . . . Many master-strokes discover themselves, and shew us real Genius led by the hand of Science.[28]

The foregoing discussion has approached Mozart's piano sonatas from the rhetorical point of view in order to illuminate facets of their style that may otherwise escape notice. Rhetoric is, of course, but one among many valid critical techniques, and no special claim is made for its superiority over rival methodologies. Mozart's sonatas, like all his music, appeal on many levels, and no avenue of analytical enquiry can claim omnipotence. Mozart himself seems to have been aware of the multiplicity of meanings that his works achieved, when he wrote to his father about the three piano concertos, K.413–15, observing that they were

a happy medium of what is too easy and too difficult; they are very brilliant, pleasing to the ear, and natural, without being vapid. There are passages here and there from which connoisseurs alone will derive satisfaction; but these are written in such a way that the less learned cannot fail to be pleased, though without knowing why.[29]

This combination of qualities, this 'Genius led by the hand of Science', is as vital to our modern sensibilities as it was for those of Mozart's contemporaries, and is surely one of the touchstones of his enduring greatness.

Notes

1 The solo sonata in context

1 Translation from W. S. Newman, *The Sonata in the Classic Era*, 3rd edn (New York and London, 1983), p. 23. Original German text in J. G. Sulzer, *Allgemeine Theorie der schönen Künste*, II/2 (Leipzig, 1773–5), pp. 688–9. The early chapters of Newman's comprehensive study (especially pp. 19–58) are basic to an understanding of the emerging classical sonata.

2 J. C. Gottsched, *Auszug aus des Herrn Batteux schönen Künsten aus dem einzigen Grundsätze der Nachahmung hergeleitet* (Leipzig, 1754), pp. 207 and 189. The original French publication appeared in Paris in 1746; facsimile edn (Geneva, 1979).

3 *Mimesis* as a theory stems from Aristotle, especially his *Poetics*. For an English translation by M. E. Hubbard, see D. A. Russell and M. Winterbottom (eds.), *Classical Literary Criticism* (Oxford, 1972; rev. 1989), pp. 51–90.

4 For a concise review of this issue, citing works by Mattheson, C. P. E. Bach, Quantz, Forkel and Koch, see Carl Dahlhaus, *Esthetics of Music*, translated by William Austin (Cambridge, 1982; repr. 1995), chapter 4.

5 J. A. Hiller, *Wochentliche Nachrichten und Anmerkungen, die Musik betreffend*, 1 (Leipzig, 1766), p. 308 [Blainville]; 2 (Leipzig, 1767), pp. 293–8 and 3 (Leipzig, 1768), pp. 111–15; 119–25; 142 [Rousseau]. For a detailed study of the infiltration of French attitudes in German musical aesthetics see Bellamy Hosler, *Changing Aesthetic Views of Instrumental Music in Eighteenth-Century Germany* (Ann Arbor, 1981), pp. 1–13 *passim*.

6 See *Anderson*, no. 25, 1 April 1764, in which Leopold describes Grimm as 'a great friend'.

7 On 15 September 1773 (*Briefe*, no. 297), Leopold wrote to his wife mentioning two music textbooks that he had lent to a Herr Klieb[e]nstein; these are J. J. Fux, *Gradus ad Parnassum* (Vienna, 1725) and Joseph Riepel, *Anfangsgrunde zur musikalischen Setzkunst*, vol. I (Regensburg and Vienna, 1752). Elsewhere (for instance, *Anderson*, no. 308, 11 June 1778), he refers to a number of other theoretical textbooks on music which he clearly knew, including (in chronological order, rather than the order given by Leopold in his letter): Jean-Philippe Rameau, *Traité de l'Harmonie reduite à ses principes naturels* (Paris, 1722; 4th edn 1772); J. A. Scheibe, *Der critische Musicus* (Leipzig, 1738–40, repr. 1745); J. Mattheson, *Der vollkommene Capellmeister* (Hamburg, 1739); (probably) J. le Rond D'Alembert, *Eléments de musique théorique et practique, suivant les principes de M. Rameau* (Paris, 1752), of which a German translation, *Herrn D'Alemberts . . . systematische Einleitung in die musikalische Setzkunst, nach den Lehrsätzen des Herrn Rameau*, was produced by F. W. Marpurg (Leipzig, 1757); F. W. Marpurg's own *Historisch-Kritische Beyträge zur*

Aufnahme der Musik (Berlin, 1754–78); and C. P. E. Bach, *Versuch über die wahre Art, das Clavier zu Spielen* (Berlin, 1759–62). In addition to Leopold's subscription to Grimm's *Correspondance Littéraire*, mentioned above, he had studied philosophy and law at the University of Salzburg; he had keen literary interests and sought out copies of works such as Gottsched's *Ausführliche Redekunst* (Augsburg, 1736) – see *Briefe*, vol. I, nos. 2, 4, 5, 8, and 12 (all of 1755). See also Nicholas Till, *Mozart and the Enlightenment* (London and Boston, 1991), pp. 9–16.

8 It is worth recording, at this point, that Aristotelian *mimesis* was only one theory among several prevalent towards the end of the eighteenth century. For a perceptive discussion of some alternative models, see M. H. Abrams, 'From Addison to Kant: Modern Aesthetics and the Exemplary Art,' in R. Cohen (ed.), *Studies in Eighteenth-Century British Art and Aesthetics* (Berkeley, Los Angeles, London, 1985), pp. 16–48. Two models are discussed, the 'contemplative' and the 'heterocosmic', in each of which the art work is regarded as an end in itself, rather than a means to an end (such as the 'moral improvement' of the perceiver). Such a 'concept of the contemplation of a self-sufficient artistic object [the art work] as the manifestation of selfless love' (Abrams, 'From Addison to Kant', p. 23) has obvious theological or, alternatively, neo-Platonic, resonances. Among Abrams's sources for this stance are Karl Philipp Moritz's *Schriften zur Aesthetik und Poetik* (Berlin, 1785) and Immanuel Kant's *Critique of Judgement* (Berlin, 1790), along with several of Joseph Addison's essays in *The Spectator* (see Abrams, 'From Addison to Kant', notes 24–5). In such an aesthetic view '[t]he Platonic Absolute, and Augustine's God, have been displaced by a human product, the self-sufficient work of art' (Abrams, 'From Addison to Kant', p. 24). According to Moritz, indeed, the art work 'creates its own world, in which . . . everything is, in its own way, a self-sufficient whole' (quoted by Abrams, p. 26).

9 Sonatas were obviously played in the Mozarts' home in Salzburg. In *Anderson*, no. 139, 18 August 1771, and no. 192, 21 December 1774, Leopold Mozart writes to his wife about sonatas by Rutini, [J. C.] Bach and Paradies that Nannerl played, years after she had been paraded around the palaces of the European nobility; she evidently continued to play sonatas for herself and her family at home in Salzburg (see also note 31 below). Mozart did occasionally perform his solo sonatas in concerts. At Augsburg on 22 October 1777 he played K.284 in D in the concert-room of Prince Fugger von Babenhausen, an event advertised the day before in the *Augsburgische Staats- und Gelehrten-Zeitung* and reviewed enthusiastically the following week (Deutsch, *Doc.Biog.*, pp. 166–8). This concert was not a solo recital, however, but a miscellany containing in addition the concertos K.242 in F (for three claviers) and in B flat, K.238 of January–February 1776, along with some other, probably improvised, piano solos. In a letter to Leopold of 17 October 1777 Mozart explained that this was to be 'a sort of concert in Count Fugger's drawing-room' (*Anderson*, no. 225), but, in fact, the *Augsburgische Staats- und Gelehrten-Zeitung* advertised tickets for the performance, price thirty Kreuzer or one florin, depending on the location of the seat. Performances of solo sonatas are not documented in any of Mozart's public concerts in Vienna during the 1780s, though documentation for these is admittedly incomplete. See appendix 1 of Mary Sue Morrow, *Concert Life in Haydn's Vienna: Aspects of a Developing Musical and Social Tradition* (New York, 1989). On the basis of such programmes as survive, it would seem that when Mozart included examples of his solo piano music in his public concerts (subscription series) these were mainly fugues, fantasias and variations – often improvised – rather than sonatas.

10 Wq. 63/5; H.74. An edition may be found in M. Frey (ed.), *Sonatenbuch der Vorklassik* (Mainz, 1949), no.3.

11 Johann Mattheson, *Der vollkommene Capellmeister* (Hamburg, 1739) and *Kern melodischer Wissenschaft* (Hamburg, 1737); Johann Philipp Kirnberger, *Die Kunst des reinen Satzes in der Musik*, 3 vols. (Berlin and Königsberg, 1774–9); Johann Joachim Quantz, *Versuch einer Anweisung die Flöte traversière zu spielen* (Berlin, 1752); Johann Nikolaus Forkel, *Über die Theorie der Musik* (Göttingen, 1777) and *Allgemeine Geschichte der Musik* (Leipzig, 1788); Heinrich Christoph Koch, *Versuch einer Anleitung zur Composition*, 3 vols. (Leipzig, 1782–93) all give consideration to musical expression, form or performance in rhetorical terms. A detailed consideration of Mozart's sonatas from the rhetorical standpoint is attempted in part III of the present study.

12 *Briefe*, vol. I, nos. 2 and 8.

13 Mattheson, *Kern melodischer Wissenschaft*, p. 128. Translation from Marc Evan Bonds, *Haydn's False Recapitulations and the Perception of Sonata Form in the Eighteenth Century*, Ph.D. dissertation (Harvard University, 1988), p. 114. Chapter 2 of Bonds's thesis is a detailed study of the rhetorical conception of classical musical form, highly recommended for its inclusion of the original German language texts alongside English translations. His thesis feeds into Bonds's more recent *Wordless Rhetoric: Musical Form and the Metaphor of the Oration* (Cambridge, Mass., 1991) which is a more extensive study of musical rhetoric through the eighteenth and nineteenth centuries.

14 Forkel, *Allgemeine Geschichte der Musik*, vol. I, p. 50; translation again from Bonds, *Haydn's False Recapitulations*, p. 138. In his *Musikalischer Almanach für Deutschland auf das Jahr 1784* Forkel applied a rhetorical approach to the analysis of the first movement of C. P. E. Bach's Sonata in F minor, Wq. 57/6; H.173, one of the *Kenner und Liebhaber* sonatas published in 1781 (though it was actually composed in 1763). See Bonds, *Haydn's False Recapitulations*, pp. 139–40. The detailed applications of rhetoric to musical form will be examined again in chapter 11.

15 C. H. Blainville, *L'esprit de l'art musicale* (Geneva, 1754), pp. 117–18. Cited in M. R. Maniates, 'Sonate, que me veux-tu? The enigma of French musical aesthetics in the eighteenth century', *Current Musicology*, 21 (1969), pp. 117–40, at p. 129: 'le chant tient ses beautés de la nature, comme de la première main, et que la symphonie les a qu'en seconde'.

16 Jean-Jacques Rousseau, *Dictionnaire de Musique* (Geneva, 1767; Paris, 1768; facsimile reprint Hildesheim, 1969).

17 Rousseau, *Dictionnaire de Musique*, p. 297. Translation from Peter Le Huray and James Day, *Music and Aesthetics in the Eighteenth and Early Nineteenth Centuries* (Cambridge, 1981), p. 110.

18 Le Huray and Day, *Music and Aesthetics*, p. 93.

19 Article 'Expression', p. 211. Cited in Maniates, 'Sonate', p. 128.

20 D'Alembert and Diderot (eds.), *Encyclopédie ou dictionnaire raisonné des sciences, des arts et des métiers*, 17 vols. (Paris, 1751–65), vol. VI, p. 315a: 'Un concert, une sonate, doievent peindre quelque chose, ou ne sont que bruit, harmonieux, si l'on veut, mais sans vie'. Cited in Maniates, 'Sonate', p. 127.

21 Lacombe, *Le spectacle des beaux-arts* (Paris, 1758), p. 255. Cited in Maniates, 'Sonate', p. 126.

22 Translation from Le Huray and Day, *Music and Aesthetics*, p. 126.

23 'Instrumental music [can] subsist apart [from words] because it may be so managed as to

resemble conversation'; see W. P. D. Wightman and J. C. Bryce (eds.), *Adam Smith – Essays on Philosophical Subjects* (Oxford, 1980), p. 191

24 Smith, *Essays*, p. 205. See also Peter Jones, 'The Aesthetics of Adam Smith', in H. Mizuta and C. Sugiyama (eds.), *Adam Smith: International Perspectives* (London, 1993), pp. 43–62, especially pp. 55–6.

25 Smith, *Essays*, p. 205.

26 Smith, *Essays*, pp. 197–8.

27 David P. Schroeder, *Haydn and the Enlightenment: the Late Symphonies and their Audience* (Oxford, 1990), pp. 136–7.

28 Modern editions: *J. C. Bach Keyboard Music: Thirty-five Works from Eighteenth-Century Manuscript and Printed Sources,* introduced and in part edited by Stephen Roe (Garland; New York and London, 1989); *Joh. Chr. Bach: Klaviersonaten,* ed. Ernst-Günter Heinemann, 2 vols. (Henle; Munich, 1981). Facsimile edition: *J. C. Bach: Twelve Keyboard Sonatas,* with an introduction by Christopher Hogwood, 2 vols. (Oxford, 1973). Mozart thought highly of Bach's keyboard works, and used them in his own teaching; see the letter of 14 February 1778, *Anderson,* no. 286a.

29 Edition: *Georg Christoph Wagenseil: 6 Divertimentos für Cembalo,* Heft I. (Doblinger Verlags 'Diletto Musicale'; Munich, 1975). A number of sonatas by Wagenseil's pupil (and Mozart's friend) František Xaver Dušek (1731–99) survive in manuscript. They are clearly didactic in nature, and were probably written shortly after 1770, when Dušek is known to have become established as a teacher in Prague. See František Xaver Dušek, *Sonate per il Clavicembalo* ed. J. Raček (Supraphon; Prague, 1977).

30 In *Anderson,* no. 256 of 6 December 1777, Mozart notes that Rosa 'is exactly like the Andante'.

31 *Anderson,* no. 243a. Subsequently, in the letter cited in note 30, Mozart states that Rosa played the sonata 'excellently. The Andante (which must *not be taken too quickly*) she plays with the utmost expression.' Nannerl Mozart also played this sonata; Leopold told Mozart on 11 December 1777 that 'Nannerl plays your whole sonata excellently and with great expression' (*Anderson,* no. 259). This observation, taken together with Wolfgang's remarks about exact quantities of *forte* and *piano* to be applied in the Andante, suggests that Nannerl may have been playing the piece on a fortepiano (for which the piece was clearly conceived). No documentary evidence is known for the availability of fortepianos in Salzburg before the end of 1780; see Richard Maunder, 'Mozart's keyboard instruments', *Early Music,* 20 (1992), 215, citing a casual remark of Leopold's in his letter of 4 December 1780 (*Anderson,* no. 369): 'about half past eleven, Herr von Edelbach and three strangers came into the room . . . Your sister had to play them a short piece on the *pianoforte* . . . [my italics]'. The evidence of the Andante of K.309 is not conclusive, but strongly suggestive, unless Nannerl played the piece on the Mozarts' five–octave clavichord, presumably of disposition FF – f''', on which K.309 would (just) be playable.

32 The embellished repeat of this passage poses some fingering problems on the third beats of bars 57 and 58 if a true *legato* in the inner part is to be achieved.

33 Including, for instance, Katharina and Marianna Auenbrugger, to whom Haydn dedicated his six sonatas, Hob. XVI: 35–9 and 20 in 1780.

34 Dedicatee of the Fantasia and Sonata in C minor, K.475 and 457, as published by Artaria in 1785; a reproduction of the title-page may be seen on p. 593 of *Early Music,* 19 (1991).

35 See, for instance, appendix 1 of Morrow, *Concert Life,* for listings of their concerts.

36 H. Wagner (trans., intro. and ed.), *Wien von Maria Theresia bis zur Franzosenszeit: Aus den Tagebüchern des Grafen Karl von Zinzendorf* (Vienna, 1972); A. Orel, 'Gräfin Wilhelmine Thun (Mäzenatentum in Wiens klassischer Zeit)', *Mozart-Jahrbuch* (1954), 89–101; Charles Burney, *The Present State of Music in Germany, the Netherlands and United Provinces*, facsimile of the 1775 London edition (New York, 1969); Karoline Pichler, *Denkwürdigkeiten aus meinem Leben*, intro. and ed. E.K. Blümml, 2 vols. (Munich, 1914), which makes reference to Mozart's attendance at the salons of her father, von Greiner. Further information on Viennese salons may be found in Volkmar Braunbehrens, *Mozart in Vienna*, trans. T. Bell (Oxford, 1991), pp. 142–72.

37 See, for instance, the quotation from Johann Pezzl's *Beschreibung und Grundriss der Haupt-und Residenzstadt Wien* (Vienna, 1809) in Morrow, *Concert Life*, p. 128, in which Pezzl describes the private salons as being 'among the most gratifying enjoyments of this city'.

38 Parisian musical salons – including one attended by Mozart – will be examined below.

39 Deutsch, *Doc.Biog.*, p. 167; we do not know precisely who else attended this gathering, or, indeed, what the Count himself thought of the performance, for in a letter to her husband, dated 31 October 1777 (*Anderson*, no. 232), Mozart's mother described him as follows: 'The Prince of Wallerstein is greatly to be pitied, for he is in the deepest melancholy . . . Wolfgang had a talk with him, but the Prince is so absent-minded that he asked him four or five times about the same thing. He refuses to listen to music.'

40 Burney, *Present State*, pp. 282–5, *passim*.

41 A physician at the Imperial court, whom the Mozarts met during their visit to the capital in late 1767. L'Augier held regular salons at which intellectual and artistic matters were discussed. Among the aristocratic members of this salon was the Duke of Braganza, himself an avid patron of the arts. See *Anderson*, nos. 50, 55, 88 and 182, the last of which discloses that the Mozarts were still friendly with L'Augier in 1773, the year after Burney's description here. For a recent study, see John Jenkins, 'Mozart's Good Friend Dr Laugier', *Music and Letters*, 77 (1996), 97–100.

42 Unknown. Burney remarks elsewhere of his piano pieces that 'they are very original and in a good taste: they shew the instrument much, but his own feelings more' (Burney, *Present State*, p. 221). An entry in Robert Eitner, *Biographisch-Bibliographisches Quellen-Lexicon des Musiker und Musikgelehrten* (Leipzig, 1900–4; repr. New York, n.d.), refers to him as 'Dilettant, um 1772 in Wien lebend', basing his comments on those of Burney.

43 Unknown.

44 Unknown.

45 Unknown.

46 Burney, *Present State*, p. 221.

47 Burney, *Present State*, p. 257.

48 *Anderson*, no. 398, 11 April 1781.

49 *Anderson*, no. 441, 16 January 1782. On this occasion Mozart states that he himself 'improvised and played variations' along with some sonata Allegros by Paisiello; Clementi played his Sonata in B flat, Op.24 no.2, as noted in a handwritten addition to the 1804 Breitkopf & Härtel edition of his piece. On 24 March 1781, Mozart described Countess Thun to his father as 'the most charming and lovable lady I have ever met; and I am very high in her favour' (*Anderson*, no. 395).

50 Detailed biographical summaries of all these patrons may be found in Peter Clive, *Mozart and his Circle* (London, 1993), which usefully gives thorough citations of primary sources. See also H. C. Robbins Landon, *Mozart: The Golden Years* (London, 1989), pp. 108–19.

Baron van Swieten is considered at some length in Edward Olleson, 'Gottfried van Swieten: Patron of Haydn and Mozart', *Proceedings of the Royal Musical Association*, 89 (1962–3), 63–74.

51 Mozart, *Trois Sonates pour le Clavecin ou Pianoforte* (Vienna, 1784).

52 Mozart, *Trois Sonates pour le Clavecin ou Pianoforte. La troisième est accomp: d'un Violon oblg:* (Vienna, 1784).

53 For example, the first movements of K.451 in D, K.453 in G and K.459 in F, all of 1784.

54 *Charles Burney, Music, Men and Manners in France and Italy, 1770*, ed. H. E. Poole (London, 1969), p. 225.

55 M^dme Brillon was described as 'une des plus habiles clavecinistes de l'Europe' in A. Choron and F. Fayolle, *Dictionnaire Historique des Musiciens* (Paris, 1810; facsimile reprint Hildesheim and New York, 1971).

56 This event was recorded in Michel Barthélemy Olivier's famous painting (now in the Musée du Louvre) of 1766, reproduced, for instance, in the article 'Paris § IV.2' in *The New Grove*.

57 *Anderson*, no. 284b, 9 February 1778, in which Leopold also reminds his son of a number of musicians whom they had met in Paris some twelve years earlier, adding: 'I need hardly tell you . . . that *with very few exceptions* you will gain nothing by associating with these people.'!

58 *Anderson*, no. 303.

59 As will be seen in chapter 2, there is actually little to suggest that Mozart knew any of Joseph Haydn's piano sonatas before his removal to Vienna at the beginning of the 1780s. Michael Haydn, however, was a close colleague of the Mozarts in Salzburg.

60 *Anderson*, no. 315.

61 *Anderson*, no. 307a, 29 May 1778. Elsewhere (*Anderson*, no. 309a) he speaks of the Count's 'excellent judgement and . . . real insight into music'.

62 Deutsch, *Doc.Biog.*, p. 185.

2 Stylistic models for Mozart's sonatas

1 In a letter from Verona (*Anderson*, no. 139), Leopold mentions a trio in F by Haydn, who receives no further mention in the surviving family correspondence until 24 April 1784 (*Anderson*, no. 510).

2 See Devriès and Lesure, *Dictionnaire des Editeurs de Musique français*, vol. I, *Des Origines à environ 1820* (Geneva, 1979). Also, A. Weinmann, *Vollständiges Verlagsverzeichnis Artaria & Comp.* (Vienna, 1952); Weinmann, *Wiener Musikverleger und Musikalienhändler von Mozarts Zeit bis gegen 1860* (Vienna, 1956); Weinmann, *Beiträge zur Geschichte des Alt-Wiener Musikverlages. Kataloge Anton Huberty (Wien) und Christoph Torricella* (Vienna, 1962).

3 Barry S. Brook (ed.), *The Breitkopf Thematic Catalogue: the Six Parts and Sixteen Supplements, 1762–1787* (New York, 1966), p. 403.

4 Curiously, the reprint of this volume by Preston of London, *c.* 1780 (reproduced in Christopher Hogwood's facsimile edition, *J. C. Bach: Twelve Keyboard Sonatas* (Oxford, 1973)), is lacking in *RISM A*. It is in the Fitzwilliam Museum, Cambridge, shelfmark 52 B 32 and bears an inscription by the composer; see V. Rumbold and I. Fenlon, *A Short-Title Catalogue of Music Printed Before 1825 in the Fitzwilliam Museum, Cambridge* (Cambridge, 1992).

5 Advertised in a Heina catalogue of that year as *Trois sonates par Amades Wolfgang Mozard* (price, 6 livres); see Devriès and Lesure, *Dictionnaire*, no.39 (for K.26–31) and no.95 (for K.309, 311 and 310). A copy of the latter is in the Bibliothèque Nationale, Paris, shelf-mark Ac.p. 2574.

6 See Deutsch, *Doc.Biog.*, p. 198.

7 *Anderson*, nos. 440 and 441, for instance.

8 *Anderson*, no. 491.

9 *Anderson*, no. 259 of 11 December 1777.

10 Many of Cannabich's symphonies begin with strongly triadic themes, sometimes in unison; see, for instance, his symphonies F-1, E flat-6 and D-11 cited in the thematic index to E. K. and J. K. Wolf (eds.), *The Symphony at Mannheim*, The Symphony, 1720–1840, no. 103, series ed., Barry S. Brook, (Garland; New York, 1984), p. lxv. Cannabich's symphony no. 5 in E flat, published in full in this volume, pp. 285–318, has a triadic tutti opening, *forte*, which continues with lighter contrasting material, leading to an immediate restatement of the *forte* opening; this is similar in outline to the first section of Mozart's K.309.

11 It is perhaps significant also that this sonata, along with the D major, K.311, and the A minor, K.310, was published not in Berlin or Vienna, but in Paris, where chamber and orchestral music by Mannheimers such as Stamitz and Cannabich had for some time been in favour.

12 On this general subject, see Jan La Rue, 'Significant and Coincidental Resemblances Between Classical Themes', *Journal of the American Musicological Society,* 14 (1961), 224–34. Thematic parallels have been pointed out in the past: the opening of J. C. Bach's Sonata Op.17 no.4, in G, has been cited as a possible thematic ancestor of the opening of K.333 in B flat, for example by Philip Radcliffe in his article, 'Keyboard music', in *The New Oxford History of Music*, vol. VII, *The Age of Enlightenment*, ed. E.Wellesz and F. Sternfeld (London, 1973), p. 595. In fact, this opening tag, covering a falling stepwise fourth, is common to several of Bach's sonatas (Op.5 no.5; Op.17 no.6). As will be shown below it is difficult to establish any documentary link between Mozart and Bach's Op.17.

13 Deutsch, *Doc.Biog.*, pp. 12–13.

14 Deutsch, *Doc.Biog.*, p. 16.

15 *Anderson*, no, 55: 'I was told that all the clavier-players in Vienna were opposed to our advancement, with the sole exception of Wagenseil.' *Anderson*, nos. 51, 10 November 1767, and 139, 18 August 1771, disclose that the Mozarts also owned copies of a concerto for two claviers, and a trio for clavier, violin and cello in C by Wagenseil.

16 They had copies of twenty-two of Wagenseil's concertos as early as 1762, as revealed in Leopold's letter to Lorenz Hagenauer on 10 November that year (*Briefe*, vol. I, no.41).

17 Burney, *Present State*, p. 329.

18 Johann Ulrich Haffner, *Oeuvres melées, contenant vi sonates pour le clavessin de tant de plus célèbres compositeurs*, 12 vols. (Nuremberg, 1755–66). Leopold Mozart's sonatas, probably composed between *c.* 1759 and 1763, were printed in vols. V (no. 4), VI (no.5), and IX (no.4). For an edition, see that of M. Seiffert, *Leopold Mozart: Ausgewählte Werke* Denkmäler der Tonkunst in Bayern, Jg. IX, Bd. 2 (Leipzig, 1908), pp. 3, 12 and 22. A listing of all the composers represented in Haffner's widely-circulated anthology is given in A. Wotquenne, *Catalogue de la Bibliothèque du Conservatoire Royale de Bruxelles*, vol. IV (Brussels, 1912), p. 331.

19 By 'developed' binary is meant a movement structured ‖: A :‖: B :‖ in which A comprises (usually) two thematic groups, A^1 and A^2, the second of which is in a new key (usually the dominant); the B section begins with the opening theme (A^1) of the movement in the new key (as in a typical baroque binary form) and later recapitulates some or all of the A^2 music in the tonic key (A^1 is not subsequently recapitulated). This form is common to many mid-century sonata first movements from Paradies, C. P. E. Bach, J. C. Bach, Wagenseil and others; Mozart does not employ it in his solo sonatas, though, all of which (except for the special case of K.545) have full tonic-key recapitulations of both first and second subject groups.

20 See Cliff Eisen, 'The Symphonies of Leopold Mozart: their Chronology, Style and Importance for the Study of Mozart's Early Symphonies', *MJb* (1987–8), 181–93, and especially p. 186 and ex.4.

21 See M. H. Schmid, 'Klaviermusik in Salzburg um 1770', *MJb* (1978–9), 102–12. The manuscripts, labelled A–E by Schmid, are all in the library of St Peter's Abbey, Salzburg, and were evidently compiled for domestic use. Mss. A and B are the work of the Salzburg copyist Raab; the person for whom they were copied is unknown. Steffan (1726–97), a pupil of Wagenseil, became *Klaviermeister* to Archduchess Maria Carolina and Archduchess Maria Antonia at the Imperial Court in 1766. The bulk of mss. A–E contains his work (often unascribed); other composers represented include Dušek, Eckard, Schobert and Joseph Haydn (the variations Hob. XVII:2 and 3, containing, in these copies nineteen and ten variations respectively). Schmid's manuscripts 'D' and 'E' at St Peter's have been allocated the classmarks Ntb 14 and Ntb 10 respectively. In addition to mss. 'A–E' is another manuscript (Ntb 26) consisting of three upright folio leaves containing five more unascribed single movements: Menuetto (C), Allegretto (C), Allegretto (E flat), Allegro scherzande (G) and Allegretto (A).

22 This is the slow movement of the 'Sonata in Es/ per il/Clavi Cembalo/ ò/ Forte Piano/ Del Sigre Steffan'. The sonata exists in manuscript at Kromeríz, Umelecko-historice Muzeum, ms. II.A.295. For an edition, see *Josef Antonín Štěpán (Steffan) Composizioni per piano*, ed. D. Setková [Musica Antiqua Bohemica 70] (Prague, 1968), no.VIII. Further on Steffan's piano music, see D. Setková, *Klavírní dílo J. A. Stepana* (Prague, 1965). Traditionally, Steffan's importance has generally been confined to possible influence on the early sonatas of Haydn; see, for example, B. Wackernagel, *Joseph Haydns frühe Klaviersonaten* (Tutzing, 1975) and A. Peter Brown, *Joseph Haydn's Keyboard Music* (Bloomington, 1986), pp. 189 ff. Wyzewa and Saint-Foix (*Wolfgang Amédée Mozart: sa Vie Musicale et son Oeuvre*, (Paris, 1912–46), vol. II, pp. 167 ff.) considered Steffan's influence on Mozart's early sonatas to have been of great significance (an opinion not generally maintained in later scholarship). Certainly the possibility of direct influence is difficult to uphold with confidence. Mozart may or may not have known of the St Peter's Abbey manuscripts containing Steffan's often unascribed *divertimenti*, although from our knowledge of Leopold's appreciation of Wagenseil's work it may be that the work of his pupil, Steffan, was likewise well-regarded in the Mozart household (though unrecorded). Steffan is nowhere mentioned in Mozart's correspondence, though the latter may have come across his sonatas or *divertimenti* at the salons of Franz Sales von Greiner, whose daughter, Karoline Pichler, was Steffan's pupil. We have it on Pichler's authority that Mozart attended her father's gatherings, though there is no evidence that the two composers actually met.

23 His death, on 22 December 1777, is referred to by Leopold Mozart in a letter to his son

written the same day (*Anderson*, no. 265). See the entry 'Adlgasser, Anton Cajetan' in *The New Grove*. Adlgasser was the author of at least three manuscript music treatises (listed in the article in *The New Grove*); it is not known if Mozart knew of these.

24 Sonatas by Adlgasser and Eberlin appear in vols. IV (no.3), V (no.1), VI (no.3), and VIII (no.1).

25 Though the second main section, immediately following the central double-bar, begins with a statement of this theme in the dominant.

26 See E. J. Simon, 'Sonata into Concerto: a Study of Mozart's First Seven Concertos', *Acta Musicologica*, 31 (1959), 170–85; p. 179 of Simon's article includes a table detailing Mozart's precise movement allocations. Mozart used Schobert's Op.17 no.2; Honauer's Op.1 no. 1, Op.2 nos. 2 and 3; Eckard's Op.1 no.4, and Raupach's Op.1 nos. 1 and 5 (and a movement by C. P. E. Bach). The models for Mozart's *pasticcios* were first identified by Saint-Foix, Wyzewa and Saint-Foix, *Wolfgang Amédée Mozart*, vol. I, pp. 187–9. The source for one movement has still to be identified

27 Koch, *Versuch einer Anleitung zur Composition*, vol. III (Leipzig, 1793), p. 226; discussed in Leonard Ratner, *Classic Music – Expression, Form and Style* (Stanford, 1980), p. 95. See also Elaine Sisman, 'Small and Expanded Forms: Koch's Model and Haydn's Minuet', *The Musical Quarterly*, 68 (1982), 444–75.

28 Honauer's Op.1 set, for example: *Six sonatas for the harpsichord or piano forte* [including two transposed from their 'difficult' keys of E flat and B flat, to D and G respectively] (Welker; London, *c.* 1770), copy in London, British Library, RM 17 d.7 (1); Raupach, Op.1: *Six sonatas for the piano forte or harpsichord* (Welker; London, *c.* 1770), copy in Washington, DC, Library of Congress; Eckard's Op.1 was reprinted in Riga (Latvia) by Hartknoch in 1773 as *Sei sonate per il clavicembalo solo . . . opera I*, copy in London, British Library, i. 61. In the following discussion sonatas from the following published collections are examined: Johann Schobert, *Deux sonates pour le clavecin avec accompagnement de violon*, Op.1 (Longman and Broderip; London, *c.*1780), copy consulted, Oxford, Bodleian Library Mus 173 c.217 (1); *Deux sonates pour le clavecin avec accompagnement de violon ad libitum,* Op.3 (R. Bremner; London, *c.*1770), copy consulted, Oxford, Bodleian Library Mus 173 c.245 (2); *Deux sonates pour le clavecin*, Op.4 (R. Bremner; London, *c.*1770), copy consulted, Oxford, Bodleian Library Mus 118 c.13 (5); *Six sonates pour le clavecin . . . les parties d'accompagnement sonts [sic] ad libitum,* Op.14 (Vendôme; Paris, [1766]), copy consulted, Oxford, Bodleian Library Mus 118 c. S. 173; *IV Sonates pour le clavecin avec accompagnement de violon*, Op.17 (Preston; London, *c.*1780), copy consulted, London, Royal College of Music, LX.B.7.(14); Leontzi Honauer, *Six sonates pour le clavecin . . . livre premier*, Op.1 (Oger; Paris, *c.*1765), copy consulted, Oxford, Bodleian Library Mus 118 b.7; Honauer, *Six sonates pour le clavecin . . . livre second*, Op.2 (Oger; Paris, *c.* 1765), copy consulted, Oxford, Bodleian Library Mus 118 c. H. 44; Honauer, *Six sonates pour le clavecin . . . oeuvre 3*, Op.3 (Oger; Paris, *c.* 1770), copy consulted, Oxford, Bodleian Library Mus 173 c. 224; Johann Gottfried Eckard, *Six sonates pour le clavecin 1er oeuvre* (Petit; Paris, [1763]), copy consulted, London, British Library, h.19, see also E. Reeser, (ed.) *J. G. Eckard: Oeuvres Complètes pour le Clavecin* (Kassel, 1956); Hermann Friedrich Raupach, *Six sonates avec accompagnement de violon . . . oeuvre Ier* (La Chevardière; Paris, [*c.*176 5]), copy consulted, London, British Library g. 645; *IV sonates avec accompagnement de violon*, Op.2 (La Chevardière; Paris, [*c.*1765]), copy consulted, London, British Library RM 17. e. 6 (1).

29 T. de Wyzewa and G. de Saint-Foix, *Wolfgang Amédée Mozart: sa Vie Musicale et son Oeuvre*, 5 vols. (Paris, 1912–46), vol.I, pp. 65 ff.

30 *Anderson*, no. 22; in the same letter Schobert's rival, Eckard, is praised. On 29 May 1778 (*Anderson*, no. 307a), Mozart noted that he had bought some (unspecified) Schobert sonatas in a Parisian music shop, in which he noticed a French translation of his father's *Versuch einer gründliche Violinschule* of 1756.There is no mention of a meeting with Raupach in the Mozart correspondence, though Baron Melchior von Grimm's *Correspondance Litteraire* for 15 July 1766 notes that Mozart and Raupach had improvised together at the piano; Deutsch, *Doc. Biog.*, pp. 56–7.

31 K.6, for example, quotes – almost literally at times – from the opening and closing movements of Eckard's B flat sonata, Op.1 no.1 (Paris [1763]).

32 This same sequence of features recurs in the two sonatas of Schobert's Op.4 and in most of the Op.14 sonatas. As previously mentioned, Schobert's Op.14 sonatas were also published as Op.4 by Hummel of Amsterdam.

33 Honauer's Op.2 no.1, in D, has a well defined transition modulating to a cadential close in E, and preparing for the entry of the second subject group in A; Op.2 no.5, in C minor, moves to B flat before introducing its secondary material in E flat. Eckard's themes are rather less sharply defined than Schobert's or Honauer's, resulting in expositions in which the main elements are melodic embellishment and contrapuntal continuity rather than periodic contrast.

34 Thomas Arne, *VIII Sonatas or Lessons for the Harpsichord* (Walsh; London, 1756).

35 *Anderson*, no. 191, 16 December 1774, and *Anderson*, no. 192, 21 December 1774, both from Munich.

36 Copy consulted, Oxford, Bodleian Library Mus 118 c. P. 30. There is no documentary evidence that Mozart met Paradies while in London, though this may have happened. Paradies (1710–92) was a Neopolitan by birth but had settled in London in 1746. His sonatas were first published by John Johnson; John Welker brought out an edition in about 1770. A Parisian edition, published by the Le Clerc house, survives in London, British Library h. 58.a. Catalogues of music printed by the Le Clerc firm show that between 1752 and 1760, and again in 1762, they were offering unspecified clavecin music by Paradies for sale at nine livres, more than most other piano items in their lists, and perhaps, therefore, indicating a *set* of pieces, namely the twelve *Sonate di Gravicembalo*. See Devriès and Lesure, *Dictionnaire*, nos.131 and 132. If these were Paradies's sonatas, then the Mozarts could have purchased them in Paris rather than London, though the latter seems more likely. At any rate, Paradies's sonatas were available in the Mozarts' library.

37 Including even a twofold statement of the closing theme, which soon becomes a cliché in mid-century sonatas.

38 *Anderson*, no. 327, 27 August 1778.

39 *Anderson*, no. 286a, 14 February 1778 includes mention of an Andante cantabile which Mozart had taught Aloysia Weber; this movement was evidently not from one of Bach's sonatas, none of which contains a movement with this heading. Bach's overture to Galuppi's *La Calamita dei Cuori* (1763) was also evidently a favourite of Mozart's; he drew upon one of its themes in the slow movement of the Piano Concerto in A, K.414 (1782).

40 It is tempting to believe that Mozart became acquainted with these pieces in pre-

publication copies during the London visit; however, it is equally possible that Leopold bought a printed copy at some stage between 1766 and 1772.

41 For a discussion of the editions, and possible instruments intended for the performance of Bach's Op.5 Sonatas, see Richard Maunder, 'J. C. Bach and the Early Piano in London', *Journal of the Royal Musical Association*, 116 (1991), 201–10. Bach's Op.17 *Six Sonatas for the Harpsichord or Piano-Forte* likewise appeared in both French (Paris, 1774) and English (London, *c.*1779) editions. For modern editions of Bach's sonatas see chapter 1, note 28.

42 Whose work Leopold Mozart had criticised in relation to Wolfgang's sonatas for clavecin with violin accompaniment; see *Anderson*, no. 33, 3 December 1764.

43 Maunder, 'J. C. Bach' illustrates some other passages of Op.5 impossible on the harpsichord.

44 On 'topics' in eighteenth-century music, especially those deriving from dance types, see Ratner, *Classic Music*, pp. 9–18.

45 Note especially the chord-sequences in bars 21–4, touching on C minor as a preparatory supertonic for the new key, B flat, reached *via* its own dominant (F) at the end of the passage (bar 28).

46 Mozart's first movement exists in two versions, the original being abandoned towards the end of the development section, and subsequently recast in the form we now know. For the abandoned version, see *Mozart Sonatas I*, p. 140. The different texts will be considered in chapter 3. See also László Somfai, 'Mozart's first thoughts: the two versions of the Sonata in D major, K.284', *Early Music*, 19 (1991), 601–13, which contains a facsimile of Mozart's autograph (now in the Biblioteka Jagiellonska, Kraków).

47 Mozart uses this device again in the first movement of K.309 in C (1777).

48 The original – cancelled – version of K.284 announced its second subject at bar 25 (due to a longer preceding transition), but in the passage under discussion there are no significant differences between Mozart's first and second thoughts.

49 In the light of Mozart's treatment, and particularly his immediate repetition of bars 38–40, one can see that Bach's structure would have benefited from repetition of his bars 31–33, giving a still stronger impact to the closing passage from bar 34. Overall, though, his handling of the form is not far removed from that of Mozart.

50 *Anderson*, nos. 191 and 192.

51 A manuscript copy of Bach's Op.17 no.3 in E flat (including a slow movement not transmitted in the print) is in the Museum Carolino Augusteum, Salzburg, Hs 1789. According to the library catalogue the script is from the second half of the eighteenth century; see Josef Gassner, *Die Musikalien-Sammlungen im Salzburger Museum Carolino Augusteum* (Salzburg, 1962). Probably the copy was made locally, but there are no identifiable markings connecting it to the Mozarts.

52 *Anderson*, no. 307a, of 29 May that year, mentions a visit to a music shop there to buy sonatas by Schobert for a pupil. He could have come across Bach's latest set on a similar occasion.

53 K.310 in A minor was actually written in Paris during the early summer of 1778, and might therefore have post-dated Mozart's acquainatnce with Bach's Op.17 set, though its dimensions are far broader than any of Bach's pieces.

54 *La Boehmer* is a binary form movement which Bach assigned to the year 1754 in his *Nachlass-Verzeichniss*, published posthumously by his widow in 1790. He printed it in the *Musikalisches Mancherley* (Berlin, 1762–3), along with other, similar, character-pieces

(a genre that he abandoned soon afterwards); see Darrel M. Berg, 'C. P. E. Bach's Character Pieces and his Friendship Circle' in Stephen L. Clarke (ed.), *C. P. E. Bach Studies*, (Oxford, 1988), pp. 1–32.

55 A. Peter Brown, *Joseph Haydn's Keyboard Music* (Bloomington, Indiana, 1986), pp. 214 ff., and table VII-2 (p. 210). For Bach's treatise (published in Berlin, vol. I: (1753); vol. II: (1762)), see William J. Mitchell, *C. P. E. Bach: Essay on the True Art of Playing Piano Instruments* (London, 1949).

56 Bach's first supplement, *Fortsetzung von sechs Sonaten* (1761) was not available in Vienna until 1769; Mozart could have bought this set on his next visit of 1773.

57 *Anderson*, no. 446, 10 April 1782. On 24 December 1783 (*Anderson*, no. 502), Mozart asked Leopold to send him copies of some fugues by C. P. E. Bach. As he also owned volumes of Haffner's *Oeuvres melées*, some of which contain sonatas by Bach, it seems clear that the Mozarts were relatively familiar with this composer's piano works.

58 *Anderson*, no. 204. The fact that Leopold knew the publisher's name suggests that he owned a copy of C. P. E. Bach's sonatas, which Wolfgang presumably used as models for the works described as being 'in the same style'.

59 Published in The Hague that year. These were in fact Mozart's most recently composed examples in 1775, unless Leopold was referring to some examples unknown to Mozart scholarship. K.301–6 were not written until 1778.

60 K.284, in D, was actually composed at Munich, for Baron Thaddeus von Dürnitz (1756–1807).

61 *Köchel*[6] gives full information on these pieces, about which Nannerl Mozart corresponded with Breitkopf in the early 1800s. See chapter 8.

62 An earlier letter from Leopold to Breitkopf (*Anderson*, no. 158), 7 February 1772, offering Wolfgang's compositions for publication, mentions clavier compositions – though not specifically sonatas – along with other marketable genres which Wolfgang would be free to compose between February and September that year. As a postscript Leopold asks if some (unspecified) sonatas had been sold yet – perhaps K.App. 199–202/ 33[d-g]?

63 12 February 1781 (*Anderson*, no. 392). These 'clavier sonatas' are presumably the four, K.App. 199–202/ 33[d-g] from Breitkopf's 1770 handwritten catalogue, rather than the piano-and-violin sonatas, K.26–31, since within this letter Leopold is careful to distinguish between [solo] 'clavier sonatas' and 'sonatas for clavier and violin' (K.301–6, which had been published by Sieber in Paris in 1778). No solo piano sonatas by Mozart were published by Breitkopf during the composer's lifetime. Nannerl Mozart was still in possession of copies of K.App. 199–201/ 33[d-f] in 1800, when she offered them to Breitkopf; see *Briefe* vol. I, (1787–1857), no.1280. Two further letters from Nannerl, of 30 April 1804 (*Briefe*, no.1365) and 30 April 1807 (*Briefe*, no.1377), reveal her increasing frustration with the publisher and again mention these three sonatas.

64 Unless Leopold was *speculating*, announcing sonatas by Wolfgang that were not in fact complete at the time of writing, but which – given his son's ability to produce material in a hurry if required – he knew could be delivered should Breitkopf accept the offer. I am grateful to Cliff Eisen for this suggestion.

65 C. P. E. Bach, *Sechs Sonaten fürs Clavier mit veränderten Reprisen* (Berlin, 1760), ed. E. Darbellay (Courlay, 1986), no.5.

66 Translation from Philip Downs, *Classical Music: the Era of Haydn, Mozart and Beethoven* (New York and London, 1992), p. 139.

67 Carl Philip Emanuel Bach, *Zweyte Fortzetsung von Sechs Sonaten fürs Clavier ([Winter];* *Berlin, 1763)* ed. E. Hashimoto (Tokyo, 1984). The E flat sonata may date from as early as 1747.

68 However, for a later exception, see K.333/i.

69 Heina; Paris, *c.* 1782.

70 *Anderson*, no. 139. Giovanni Marco Rutini (1723–97) was a Florentine composer, noted especially for his piano music and operas; after working for a while in Austria and Germany he became *maestro di cappella* at Modena, while continuing to reside at the Florentine court. Several of his sets of sonatas were printed in Nuremberg, others in Bologna; see below.

71 This view is also held by Giorgio Pestelli in his article 'Rutini' in *The New Grove,* echoing F. Torrefranca's 'Il primo maestro di W. A. Mozart (Giovanni Marco Rutini)', *Rivista Musicale Italiana,* 40 (1936), 239–53. Pestelli's article contains a couple of errors: Leopold's letter of 18 August 1771 was not to his son, but his wife; and Rutini's Op.7 was published in Bologna, not Nuremberg. For the complicated publication history of Rutini's piano sonatas see W. S. Newman, *The Sonata in the Classic Era,* 3rd rev. edn (New York and London, 1983), pp. 205–6.

72 Copy in London, British Library, e.777. a.; the finale is reproduced in Archibold T. Davison and Willi Apel, *Historical Anthology of Music,* vol. 2 (Cambridge, Mass. and London, 1950; rep. 1973), no. 302.

73 *Sei sonate per cimbalo. Opera settimo* (Lelio della Volpe; Bologna, 1770). Copy consulted: Salzburg, Museum Carolino Augusteum 20494, which, though evidently in Salzburg from quite an early date, bears no markings to suggest it was ever owned by the Mozarts.

74 Alfred Einstein, *Mozart: his Character, his Work,* trans. Arthur Mendel and Nathan Broder (London, Toronto, Melbourne, Sydney, 1946), pp. 240–1.

75 However, Mozart begins the developments of K.309 (1777) and K.310 (1778) with a statement of the opening theme in the dominant minor (G minor) and relative major key (C) respectively, and those of K.333, K.457 and K.494 begin with modified dominant statements of the first subject, immediately reworked in new harmonic or contrapuntal combinations.

76 *Anderson*, no. 311.

77 Hüllmandel's London publications include the influential *Principles of Music,* Op.12 (1796; rev. edn 1815), containing important discussions of a number of aspects of piano performance practice.

78 Choron and Fayolle, *Dictionnaire Historique des Musiciens* (Paris, 1801; facsimile reprint New York, 1971). For further information on Hüllmandel, see *The New Grove* and G. de Saint-Foix, 'Les premiers pianistes parisiens: Nicholas-Joseph Hüllmandel',1751–1823 *La Revue Musicale,* 4 (1923), 193–205.

79 Grétry, *Essais sur la Musique,* vol. III (1797), p. 356; translation from 'Hüllmandel' in J. S. Sainsbury, *A Dictionary of Musicians from the Earliest Times* (London, 1825; facsimile reprint New York, 1966).

80 Hüllmandel, *Six sonates pour le clavecin ou forte piano avec accompagnement de violon . . . oeuvre* *I* (Oger; Paris, [1773–4]); *Trois sonates pour le clavecin ou piano forte avec un accompagnement de violon ad libitum . . . oeuvre IIIe* (Oger; Paris, [1777]); *Trois sonates pour le clavecin ou le piano forte . . . oeuvre IVe* (Oger; Paris, [1778]).

81 Copy consulted, London, British Library h. 1671 (2). An edition of the whole sonata is included as a supplement to G. de Saint-Foix's article, cited in note 78; regrettably, it

contains several wrong notes and bars 41–4 of the first movement are accidentally omitted. Another intriguing resemblance, this time to the opening of K.310, is found in a D major sonatina by Josef Mysliveček (1737–81), in which the second subject begins with a virtual quotation of bars 1–4 of Mozart's sonata. See *České Sonatiny: Sonatinen Alter Tschechischer Meister* selected by K. Emingerova (Supraphon; Prague, 1988), no.19, bars 19 ff. I am grateful to Gwen Hersee for drawing my attention to this piece. The dates of the sonatina and of Mysliveček's larger sonatas (of which nine survive in the Berlin Staatsbibliothek and the Bayerischer Staatsbibliothek, Munich) are uncertain. The 'Turkish' idiom of Mysliveček's second subject is rather sudden and betrays signs of having been transplanted by force; it is likely, therefore, that Mysliveček was copying Mozart here. The Mozart family owned sonatas by Mysliveček, with whom Mozart was on cordial terms; see *Anderson*, nos. 231, 241 and 219, relating a meeting between the two composers in a Munich sanatorium, where Mysliveček was being treated for venereal disease.

82 See, for instance, Marc Pincherle, 'Un oublié: Il divino Boemo', *Feuillets d'histoire de violon* (Paris, 1927), p. 57; George de Saint-Foix, 'Un ami de Mozart: Joseph Mysliweczek', *La Revue Musicale* 9/ 4–6 (1928), 124.

83 See *Anderson*, no. 219, 11 October 1777.

84 *Anderson*, no. 241, 13 November 1777.

85 *Six Easy Divertimentos* (London, 1777); *Six Easy Lessons* (Edinburgh, 1784). For Mysliveček bibliographies see J. Raček, 'Prispevek k otázce "mozartovského" stylu v české hudbe predklassiké', *Musikologie*, 5 (Brno, 1958), 90–120; German translation in *Kongressbericht: Wien Mozartjahr* (1956), pp. 493–524; R. Pecman, *Josef Mysliveček und sein Opernepilog* (Brno, 1970); 'Mysliveček, Josef', in *The New Grove*. For a recent study of possible influences of Mysliveček's sonatas on K.309 and K.311 (confined, however, to thematic and textural resemblances), see Daniel Freeman, 'Josef Mysliwecek and Mozart's Piano Sonatas K.309 and 311', *MJb* (1995), 95–109.

86 D-Bds, Ms. 14530; Mbs, Ms. 1712.; the sonatas in these manuscripts correspond to the 1784 print.

87 It bears a passing resemblance – in texture and melodic profile – to the opening of K.310: could Mozart have subconsciously 'reinterpreted' Mysliveček's theme here?

88 Alfred Einstein, *Mozart: his Character, his Work* (London, Toronto, Melbourne, Sydney, 1946), p. 241; also Jens Peter Larsen, 'Haydn and Mozart', in Ulrich Kramer (trans. and ed.), *Handel, Haydn and the Viennese Classical Style* (Ann Arbor and London, 1988), p. 21. On the general question of influence, see E. F. Schmid, 'Mozart and Haydn', in Paul Henry Lang (ed.), *The Creative World of Mozart* (New York and London, 1963), pp. 86–102 (originally published in *The Musical Quarterly*, 42 (1956), 145– 61).

89 See Marc Evan Bonds, 'The Sincerest Form of Flattery?: Mozart's "Haydn" Quartets and the Question of Influence', *Studi Musicali,* 22 (1993), 365–409.

90 Harold Bloom, *The Anxiety of Influence: A Theory of Poetry* (London, 1973). For a summary of these 'revisionary ratios' see pp. 14–16 of Bloom's book. For musical applications, see Kevin Korsyn, 'Towards a New Poetics of Musical Influence', *Music Analysis*, 10 (1991), 3–72; and Martin Scherzinger, 'The "New Poetics" of Musical Influence: a Response to Kevin Korsyn', *Music Analysis*, 13 (1994), 298–309.

91 '"Clinamen": [the] poet swerves away from his precursor . . . which implies that the precursor poem went accurately up to a certain point but should then have swerved, precisely in the direction that the new poem moves' (Bloom, *Anxiety*, p. 14).

92 For discussions of the supposed influence of Haydn's Op.20 quartets on Mozart's see Schmid, 'Mozart and Haydn', pp. 93–4; *The New Grove* 'Mozart'; and Stanley Sadie, *Mozart* (London, 1965), p. 84. A recent attempt to sort out this problem is A. Peter Brown's 'Haydn and Mozart's 1773 Stay in Vienna: Weeding a Musicological Garden', *The Journal of Musicology*, 10 (1992), 192–230.

93 Review of Bettina Wackernagel's, *Joseph Haydns frühe Klaviersonaten*, *Notes*, 30 (1976), 69–71. (One such example is the second movement of Honauer's Sonata, Op.1 no.5.)

94 Possibly Hob. V:2 (1766–7), for two violins and cello.

95 The same letter in which Rutini's sonatas are praised; Leopold also refers to works by Wagenseil and Adlgasser.

96 Peter Clive, *Mozart and his Circle* (London, 1993), p. 71; Schmid, 'Mozart and Haydn', p. 99. It is conceivable that Mozart may have come across the 'Esterházy' sonatas in manuscript through Michael Haydn (1737–1806), Mozart's colleague and friend in Salzburg. Michael Haydn was Konzertmeister there from 1763 and later (1777) organist at the Dreifältigkirche and the Domkirche (1781). However, there is little evidence that Michael had frequent contact with his elder brother, though on the rare occasions that they met they acknowledged each other's compositional acumen, particularly in fugal writing; see 'Michael Haydn', in *The New Grove*.

97 The exceptions are K.282, in E flat, and K.331, in A.

98 Its second-placed Minuet is based on the same theme (now recast in 3/4) as the opening of K.309.

99 For instance, Hob. XVI: 21 extends the second subject figure (bar 18) in new sequential ways from bar 23, while Hob. XVI: 26 announces at least four new ideas following the second subject at bars 8–9.

100 Thematic reordering is found in Mozart's K.279, but in the recapitulation, not the development (bars 82–5 transplant first subject material – from bar 9 – into the second-subject group). This is perhaps the movement that comes closest in idiom to Haydn's 'Esterházy' set.

101 The only exception being the transition of Hob. XVI: 21 in C, which ends with an imperfect cadence in bar 18.

102 However, the original, discarded, text of K.284 develops the exposition's closing tag of three upbeat crotchets and a feminine cadence; *Mozart Sonatas I*, p. 142, bars 51–2; 53 ff.

103 While the development of K.280 quotes the first subject, most of it is free-composed. In the finale of K.281 the development of a single theme is especially marked.

104 František Xaver Dušek, *Sonate per il Clavicembalo*, ed. J. Raček. Musica Antiqua Bohemica no. 8 (Supraphon; Prague, 1977). Mozart owned some of Dušek's sonatas; see the estate documents transcribed in Deutsch, *Doc. Biog.*, p. 590 (item 64).

105 Kozeluch's F major Sonata, Op.35 no. 1 (publ. 1791), has an extended first movement, notable for its quotation of the main subject in flat keys (E flat, A flat) in its development; it never subsequently appears in the tonic, though. See Milan Postolka's article, 'Kozeluch' in *The New Grove*; for an edition, see *České Sonatiny: Sonatinen Alter Tschechischer Meister*, selected by K. Emingerova (Supraphon; Prague, 1988), no. 21. This is all quite unlike Mozart's normal practice. The first movement of Mozart's K.570 in B flat (of February 1789) is, like Kozeluch's, an extended piece; its development opens in a remarkably flat key (D flat), not, however, with the main subject but the secondary idea first heard in bar 23. Mozart's is a more tautly structured movement, including a

tonic recapitulation of the first subject (though the second subject remains – as at bar 23 – in the unusual subdominant).

3 Six sonatas, K.279–84

1 *Anderson*, no. 192. Nannerl arrived at Munich on 4 January 1775; for Mozart's own report of the success of *La finta giardiniera*, see *Anderson*, no. 197, 14 January 1775.

2 Dürnitz, incidentally, never paid Mozart for the piece. Leopold was still reminding his son of this fact in 1777; see *Anderson*, nos. 213 and 222.

3 In the Uniwersytet Jagiellonska, Biblioteka Jagiellonska, Kraków, Poland, callmark V,5 (inw. no. 5995).

4 The crucial study of Mozart's developing handwriting is by Wolfgang Plath, 'Beiträge zur Mozart-Autographie II–Schriftchronologie 1770–1780', *Mozart-Jahrbuch (1976–7)*, 131–73. See also Plath, 'Zur Datierung der Klaviersonaten K.279–84', *Acta Mozartiana*, 21/ii (1974), 26–30.

5 See Alan Tyson (ed.), *Dokumentation der Autographen Überlieferung: Wasserzeichen-Katalog* (*NMA* Serie X Supplement Wg.33/ Abt.2); the mark is Tyson's number 34.

6 The same paper is found in parts of Mozart's *Litaniae de venerabili altaris sacramento*, K.243 (composed in Salzburg in 1772). Other works in which it occurs include Act I of *Il Rè pastore*, K.208 (Salzburg, April 1775) and the Church Sonata in B flat, K.212 (Salzburg, July 1775). It was used as late as *c*.1778 in Michael Haydn's serenata, *Endimione*. (I am grateful to Cliff Eisen for drawing this to my attention.)

7 For the discarded text, see *Mozart Sonatas I*, appendix, pp. 140–2. The two versions are discussed compositionally below; see also László Somfai, 'Mozart's first thoughts: the two versions of Mozart's Sonata in D major, K.284', *Early Music*, 19 (1991), 601–13. It is impossible to tell from the facsimile page reproduced in this article that the crossing-out of the exposition is in pencil, not ink (the abandoned development section, following the double-bar, on the other hand, is cancelled in ink). This distinction may perhaps mean that, although Mozart considered the development as 'beyond repair', the exposition contained useful structural ideas (that is, excluding thematic ones, reworked in the revision of K.284) to be reserved for a future occasion. Might that occasion have been the first movement of the D major sonata, K.311 (1777?), which begins similarly, includes an almost immediate repetition of the opening phrase (sacrificed in the revision of K.284) and begins its development (organised along not dissimilar tonal lines to the discarded original text of K.284) by taking up the closing exposition figure?

8 At least in so far as they are complete: the pages containing the first movement of K.279 are lost.

9 Some other examples: Schobert, Op.17 – C, F, D, F ; Eckard, Op.1 – B flat, G minor, F minor, A, C, E flat; Honauer, Op.1 – G, A, F, E flat, D, B flat; Op.2 – D, B minor, F, D minor, C minor, G minor; Op.3 – D, B flat, G, F minor, A, C; Raupach, Op.1 – B flat, C, A, E flat, F, D.

10 The published sonata sets were selected for their demonstrable or circumstantial connection to Mozart's own rather than for their key-preferences; the frequency of E flat was purely coincidence.

11 *Anderson*, no. 244

12 Although there is a note (*Anderson,* no. 225, of 17 October 1777) to the effect that Mozart 'played all . . . six sonatas by heart several times' he must have had copies with him, since

on 17 January 1778 (*Anderson*, no. 273a) Mozart had to send (to his lodgings) for the manuscript to show Abbé Vogler (for whom see note 16). Excluding the very early (and now lost) sonatas, K. App.199–202 (*Köchel*[6] 33[d–g]), K.279–83 were the only solo piano sonatas Mozart had available when he set out on his tour of 1777–8 and were therefore highly significant for him in making an impact as a piano composer-virtuoso at this stage in his career; K.309 and 311 were composed in November–December 1777 in Mannheim.

13 For references see Deutsch, *Doc. Biog.*, pp. 166–8 *passim*.

14 *Anderson*, no. 281.

15 *Anderson*, nos. 251, 253, 256, for instance.

16 In his letter of 4 February he continues immediately: 'On my honour I would rather hear my sonatas played by her than by Vogler!' The only possible reason for this continuation is some association in Mozart's mind with Vogler's awful mangling of some of his music the previous month, reported in a letter of 17 January that year. The piece in question in that amusing account is the C major Concerto, K.246, but earlier in the letter it is noted that, after dinner, some of Mozart's sonatas – probably K.279–84 – were played also. Johann Georg Vogler (1749–1814) was a composer and theorist who became Vice-*Kapellmeister* to Elector Karl Theodore, Elector Palatine in Munich in 1775 (and subsequently *Kapellmeister* at Mannheim in 1784). Mozart cared little for Vogler's music or his theories which he described as mere 'arithmetic' (*Anderson*, no. 241, of 13 November 1777).

17 *Anderson*, no. 204 of 6 October 1775, alluded to in chapter 2 above.

18 Full title: *Trois Sonates / pour / le Clavecin ou Piano Forte. / La Troisieme est Accomp: / d'un Violon Oblig: / Composées par / W.A. Mozart / Oeuvre VII* (Torricella; Vienna, 1784). Copy consulted Royal College of Music Library, London (LX II. D. 20).

19 *Mozart Sonatas I*, pp. 78–82.

20 See the letter of 17 October 1777, *Anderson*, no. 225, praising the Augsburg maker.

21 Coincidentally this begins with an almost identical falling scale-figure to variation 11 of K.284.

22 For instance, *Anderson*, nos. 243a, of 14 November 1777; 265, of 21–2 December 1777; and 276, of 25 January 1778.

23 In respect of the role of dynamic shading and subtle articulation slurs in achieving the *cantabile* nature of this variation it is puzzling that Beethoven allegedly described Mozart's playing as 'too choppy'. There are no printed fingerings in Torricella's 'Op.VII' print, although extensive manuscript fingerings are found in a copy of a Longman and Broderip reprint (*c*.1780) now in the Royal College of Music Library, London (LX II. D. 20); these lead to an unashamed *legato* (though the date at which they were added is a matter of debate; for the right hand + = thumb; 1= index finger; 2 = middle finger, and so on).

24 It is just possible that Mozart *may* have known this or a similar instrument, of course. See Kurt Birsak, 'Klaviere in Salzburger Museum Carolino Augusteum', *Salzburger Museum Carolino Augusteum Jahresschrift*, 34 (1988), 57.

25 See Richard Maunder, 'Mozart's keyboard instruments', *Early Music*, 20 (1992), 215. Wolfgang's portion of a letter of 23 October 1777 from Augsburg (*Anderson*, no. 228b) strongly suggests that he had played one of these sonatas on a clavichord there, followed by the 'Fischer' variations, K.179, while *Anderson*, no. 241 of 13 November 1777, we learn that he had played K.281 in B flat, and K.284 on a 'very good' clavichord in the

company of the piano virtuoso Ignaz von Beecke at Mannheim (for Beecke, see next footnote).

26 Deutsch, *Doc. Biog.* p. 153; Ignaz von Beecke (1733–1803) was in the employ of Count Oettigen-Wallerstein, and is mentioned occasionally in Mozart's correspondence – see *Anderson*, nos. 225, 228b, for instance.

27 See *Anderson*, no. 225 for details.

28 *Augsburgische Staats- und Gelehrten-Zeitung* (28 October 1777), cited in Deutsch, *Doc. Biog.*, p. 167–8.

29 *Anderson*, no. 276a, 28 December, 1777. This letter is also referred to in Katalin Komlós, '"Ich praeludirte und spielte Variazionen"': Mozart the Fortepianist', in Peter Williams and R. Larry Todd (eds.), *Perspectives on Mozart Performance* (Cambridge, 1991), pp. 27–54, especially pp. 51–2, which lists some of Mozart's observations on the fortepiano playing of others, as noted in his letters of this period. The qualities he most admired evidently included the following: a natural posture (*Anderson*, nos. 224, 16 October, 1777 and (288–288b), 23/5 January, 1778); a light touch (*Anderson*, no. 288b, 23/5 January, 1778]; precision of execution (*Anderson*, nos. 249a, 26 November, 1777 and 273a, 17 January, 1778); a thoroughly trained left hand (*Anderson*, no. 243a, 14 November, 1777); general abstention from rushed tempos (*Anderson*, no. 249a, 26 November, 1777); keeping strict time (*Anderson*, no. 288b, 23/5 January, 1778); and, above all, good taste and expression in general, as opposed to the insensitive and mechanical playing of which he sometimes accused others, including Clementi (*Anderson*, no. 441, 16 January, 1782] and Richter (*Anderson*, no. 511, 28 April, 1784).

30 This method of writing-out is already familiar to Mozart scholars; it is found in, for example, the autograph score of the D major String Quartet, K.575, the opening of which shows that the first violin melody was written first, since it is barred separately from the lower strings (it has its own individual barlines, added to just a single stave as the melody was written down, whereas the second violin, viola and cello – added next – have barlines extending straight through their three staves). A facsimile of this page is given in Marius Flothuis, 'A Close Reading of the Autographs of Mozart's Ten Quartets', in Christoph Wolff and Robert Riggs (eds.), *The String Quartets of Haydn, Mozart and Beethoven – Studies of the Autograph Manuscripts*, Isham Library Papers, Harvard University Department of Music (Cambridge, Mass., 1980), pp. 154–73 (facsimile 13). The same procedure of writing-out large tracts of the leading melody part can be traced from shorthand indications in the autograph of the Piano Concerto in C, K.467 (Pierpoint Morgan Library, New York; published in facsimile, ed. Jan La Rue (Dover; New York, 1985)).

4 Three sonatas, K.309–11

1 Wolfgang wrote to his father from Paris on 20 July (*Anderson*, no.315a) that 'My [violin] sonatas [K.301–6] will soon be engraved [by Sieber, though, not Heina, and at 15 louis d'or – a price below Mozart's original expectations] . . . As soon as they are ready I shall send them to you . . . together with . . . *a few of my clavier sonatas* [my italics].' He lists other works then ready for publication (the 'Paris' Symphony, K.297; a Sinfonia Concertante, K. App.9 (K. Anh. C.14.01 (297b), for the 'authenticity' of which, see the sixth edition of the *Köchel* Catalogue, p. 309, Wolfgang Plath, 'Zur Echtheitsfrage bei Mozart', *MJb* (1971–2), 56, and D. N. Leeson and R. D. Levin, 'On the Authenticity of

K. Anh. C.14.01 (297b), a Symphonia Concertante for Four Winds and Orchestra', *MJb*
(1976–7), 70–96; the two Flute Quartets, K.285 and 285a; and the Concerto for Flute
and Harp, K.299). The reference to 'a few of my clavier sonatas' is tantalising: were these
perhaps the three sonatas, K.309–11 in a finished form, or was Mozart intending to complete such a set at the end of July? It is apparent from his later letter of 11 September
(*Anderson*, no. 331) that he was hoping at that stage that Sieber ('the man who engraved
my sonatas [i.e. the clavier and violin sonatas, K.301–6, not, however, issued until
November that year]') might also publish the 'difficult' sonatas, K.279–84, so these may
be the clavier sonatas to which he was referring in July, rather than K.309–11. The matter
is complicated by calculated imprecision on Mozart's part in the letters of this time; he
was, after all, trying to convey to his father the impression that he had been productive
during the months spent in Paris and that he had good prospects for publication (and
therefore financial reward). The throwaway reference to 'a few of my clavier sonatas'
should be viewed with caution then; nevertheless, the possibility that K.309–11 were
being assembled for publication as a set between July and September 1778 cannot be
ruled out.

2   New York, Pierpoint Morgan Library, Robert Lehman deposit.

3   See *Anderson*, nos. 236, 5 November, 1777, and 254, 3 December, 1777. Saint-Foix first
suggested that the piece referred to in these letters might have been K.311; *Wolfgang
Amédée Mozart: sa Vie Musicale et son Oeuvre*, vol. III, p. 18. If so, then it would seem possible, at least that this D major sonata may have been the first of the group to be begun
(at some point between 24 September and 11 October), though it was evidently still
unfinished by 3 December, for Mozart thinks (hopes?) that Josepha Freysinger may have
forgotten all about it but nonetheless promises to Maria Anna Thekla Mozart that he will
complete it as soon as possible and send it to her in Augsburg for forward dispatch to
Munich. At any rate, no further mention is made of the sonata or its recipient.

4   See *Anderson*, no. 256, 6 December, 1777. It is conceivable that the sonata had its origin
in an improvisation during a concert of Mozart's music at Augsburg on 22 October
(Deutsch, *Doc.Biog.*, pp. 167–9); this item is mentioned in *Anderson*, no. 228b, 23
October, 1777: 'I then played another solo, quite in the style of the organ, a fugue in C
minor and then all of a sudden a magnificent sonata in C major out of my head.'

5   See *Anderson*, no. 235, 4 November, 1777, in which Mozart states that the sonata 'is
almost finished save for the Rondo'.

6   See *Anderson*, no. 238a, 8 November, 1777, a postscript to a letter from Maria Anna
Thekla Mozart to Leopold, in which Wolfgang writes: 'I wrote out . . . this morning the
Rondo.'

7   The first two movements were dispatched with the letter of 29 November (*Anderson*, no.
251), the Rondo followed on 3 December (*Anderson*, no. 253). Mozart discloses in the
first of these letters that music copying in Salzburg cost six kreuzer per sheet, one quarter
the price charged in Mannheim. In the event, Leopold copied the sonata himself, returning the autograph in instalments along with his next few letters to Mannheim.
Regrettably, the autograph of K.309 is now lost but Leopold's copy survives (in private
Swiss ownership); a facsimile of one page is reproduced in the first volume of *NMA*
IX/25 and in vol. XX of the *NMA Taschenpartitur-Ausgabe*.

8   *Anderson*, no. 256.

9   *Anderson*, no. 243a.

10 Described in detail in *Anderson*, no. 225, 17 October, 1777. The *pianissimo* marking found in the last two bars derives not from Leopold's copy but from the first edition.

11 *Anderson*, no. 259. Correct realisation of dynamic shadings naturally requires a touch-sensitive instrument. How Nannerl Mozart could have achieved 'great [dynamic] expression' in her playing of the Andante at home in Salzburg is problematic because of the apparent unavailability of a fortepiano in the Mozart household before 1780; see chapter 1, note 31, to which may be added the observation that in the letter cited in note 12 below Nannerl remarks only that 'The Andante requires indeed great concentration and exactness in playing' – characteristics which need not refer to dynamics at all, but instead to rhythm (for example, the many dotted rhythms, and especially the distinction between dotted semiquavers and dotted quavers in the opening bar) or to articulation (for example the numerous slurs).

12 *Anderson*, no. 257a.

13 The unison opening was a fingerprint of the Mannheimers that Wolfgang pointed out in a letter to his father on 20 November 1777 (*Anderson*, no. 245).

14 While the Rondo finale of K.309 undoubtedly contains 'orchestral' features similar to its first movement it should be remembered that Mozart had only posted it to Salzburg on 3 December, so that, even if it had reached its destination by the time Leopold mentioned the sonata's Mannheim features on 11 December, he would have had little time to absorb it stylistically. He evidently associated its 'Mannheim' characteristics principally with the first movement. Nannerl apparently was still awaiting the Rondo on 8 December; Leopold referred again to the whole sonata on 21–2 December (*Anderson*, no. 265) and had returned it to Wolfgang (after making a copy) by 5 February (*Anderson*, no. 282a).

15 Symphony no.57 (E flat 10). Edited in Eugene K. Wolf and Jean K. Wolf (eds.), *The Symphony at Mannheim*, The Symphony, 1720–1840 (Garland; New York, 1984), pp. 285–318.

16 Perhaps Leopold found the internal subdivision of K.309's seven-bar opening phrase a little puzzling from the theoretical point of view: Joseph Riepel's *Anfangsgründe zur musikalischen Setzkunst* (Regensburg and Vienna, 1752), which Leopold owned, notes that irregular phrase-lengths (such as seven-bar phrases) are departures from the (four-bar) norm, should not be used to excess and ought to be constituted, for instance, 3 + 4 bars (p. 23). Mozart's 2 + 3 + 2 division of the first seven bars hardly fits such a theoretical scheme. Riepel's theoretical work on periodicity and melodic construction will be referred to again in part III of the present study (chapter 12). For other theoretical musical texts owned by Leopold Mozart, see *Briefe*, vol . V: *Kommentar I/II* to no. 12 of 6 November 1755, *Briefe*, no.297 of 15 September 1773 (which refers to the Riepel and also to Johann Joseph Fux's *Gradus ad Parnassum* (Vienna, 1725)); and *Anderson*, no. 308, of 11 June 1778, in which Leopold notes the appearance of Abbé Georg Vogler's *Kurpfälzische Tonschule* (Mannheim, 1778) and lists several other theoretical texts: C. P. E. Bach, *Versuch über die wahre Art das Clavier zu spielen* (Berlin, 1753–62); Pier Francesco Tosi, *Opinioni de' cantori antichi o moderni, o sieno osservazioni sopra il canto figurato* (Bologna, 1723), translated by Johann Friedrich Agricola as *Anleitung zur Singkunst* (Berlin, 1757); Friedrich Wilhelm Marpurg, *Historisch-Kritische Beyträge zur Aufnahme der Musik* (Berlin, 1754–78); Meinrad Spiess, *Tractatus Musicus Compositorio-Practicus* (Augsburg, 1746); Johann Adolphe Scheibe, *Der critische Musicus* (Leipzig, 1738–40, repr. 1745), or possibly his *Über die musikalische Composition. Erster Theil: Die Theorie der Melodie und Harmonie*

(Leipzig, 1773); Jean le Rond D'Alembert, *Eléments de musique théorique et practique, suivant les principes de M. Rameau* (Paris, 1752), presumably in the German translation by Marpurg, *Herrn d'Alembert's . . . systematische Einleitung in die musikalische Setzkunst, nach den Lehrsätzen des Herrn Rameau.* (Leipzig, 1757); Jean-Philippe Rameau, *Traité de l'Harmonie reduits à ses principes naturels* (Paris, 1722). Leopold cites 'numerous others' without naming them. He clearly tried to keep abreast of contemporary theoretical musical debate.

17 K.311: Kraków, Biblioteka Jagiellonska VI,1 (inw. no.6425); K.310: New York, Pierpoint Morgan Library, Lehman deposit. Facsimiles: a page of the finale of K.311 is reproduced in the first volume of *NMA* IX/25 and in vol. XX of the *NMA Taschenpartitur-Ausgabe*; a facsimile of the whole of K.310 is published by Universal Edition; the first page of the first movement of K.310 and the first page of its finale are likewise reproduced in the first volume of *NMA* IX/25 and in vol. XX of the *NMA Taschenpartitur-Ausgabe*; an extract from the slow movement is in C. A. Banks and J. Rigby Turner (eds.), *Mozart: Prodigy of Nature* (London and New York, 1991), pp. 48–9; the first page of the first movement is also reproduced in *Early Music*, 20 (1992), 251.

18 That known as 'type III' in Alan Tyson's classification of *Klein-Querformat* paper; see A. Tyson, *Mozart: Studies of the Autograph Scores* (Harvard and London, 1987), pp. 166–7 and 172. The watermark is no. 42 in Alan Tyson's *Wasserzeichen-Katalog*.

19 Tyson, *Autograph Scores*, pp. 110–12.

20 *Anderson*, no. 312, 3 July, 1778, to Abbé Bullinger in Salzburg.

21 Referred to in Leopold's letter to Breitkopf and Son, of 10 August 1781 (*Anderson*, no. 420).

22 See Devriès and Lesure, *Dictionnaire*, vol.I, p. 79; vol.I 'Catalogues' contains a facsimile catalogue-page from 1782, advertising K.254 ('Divertissement') at 3 [livres] 12 [sous], and 'Trois Sonates par Amades Volfgange Mozart' (presumably K.309–11) at 6 [livres].

23 See *Anderson*, no. 331, 11 September, 1778.

24 *Anderson*, no. 338. In the same letter he remarks of the six clavier and violin sonatas, K.301–6, that he had left with Sieber that they should have appeared by the end of the previous month; these duly appeared in November that year, as 'Opus I', and Mozart presented them personally to their dedicatee, Electress Palatine Marie Elisabeth on 7 January 1779 (*Anderson*, no. 351, 8 January, 1779).

25 She engraved several others of Heina's publications, including Carl Stamitz's *6 Duos pour un violon et un alto* advertised in Heina's catalogues for the period 1777–82 (see Devriès and Lesure, *Dictionnaire*, vol. I, nos.93–5), and Mozart's Trio, K.254, which Heina issued in *c.*1782 as *Divertimento pour le clavecin ou forte piano a compagnement* [*sic*] *oeuvre IIIeme* (also in Devriès and Lesure, *Dictionnaire*, vol. I, no.95 as 'Divertissement').

26 It is by no means certain that the sonatas were engraved straight away. Heina's surviving catalogues do not record any sonatas by Mozart before 1782. This delay might, however, be accounted for by a failed attempt to publish the sonatas by subscription in late 1778. Writing to his father from Mannheim on 3 December 1777 (*Anderson*, no. 253) he states, optimistically, that in Paris 'you can get sonatas, trios and quartets engraved *par souscription*'. If Heina had not found a market for the sonatas in 1778 he may have been forced to wait a year or two – during which time Mozart's variations might have become popular – before issuing them. One further point, this time from K.311, is suggestive of a hastily prepared copytext. At bar 24 of the Rondeau finale Mozart forgot to insert a bass clef on the lower stave of the autograph (before the chordal figure commencing half-way through

the bar – shown editorially within square brackets in the *NMA* text); this is likewise
omitted in the Heina print.

5 Four sonatas, K.330–2; K.333

1 K.330–2 as *Trois sonates pour le clavecin ou pianoforte composées par W.A. Mozart Oeuvre VI*
  (Artaria; Vienna, 1784); K.333 included (along with K.284 and K.454) in *Trois sonates
  pour le clavecin ou pianoforte . . . composées par W.A. Mozart, dédiées à son excellence Madame la
  Comtesse Thérèse de Koblenz . . . Oeuvre VII* (Torricella; Vienna, 1784).

2 The 'new' Associated Board edition of the Mozart Sonatas, edited by Stanley Sadie and
  Denis Matthews, 2 vols. (London, 1970–81) was the first to take account of the revised
  dating.

3 Wyzewa and Saint-Foix, *Wolfgang Amédée Mozart*, vol. II, pp. 405–6. Associated with these
  works, which fall into Wyzewa and Saint-Foix's 'twenty-sixth and twenty-seventh style
  periods', are greater precision and the development of an expressive, narrative style
  ('L'expression devient plus précise, plus "parlant" et volontiers, plus "pathétique"'; p. 405).
  In adapting his style to the French taste, Mozart abandoned the virtuosity of his recent
  Mannheim works in favour of longer works displaying a more 'learned' idiom, incorporating rigorous thematic development ('Ses morceaux redeviennent à la fois plus longs et
  plus savants, avec une sérieuse élaboration thématique se substituant au goût de virtuosité
  rapporté naguère de Mannheim'; p. 406). In the third volume of this study, authored by
  Saint-Foix alone, the date of K.333 was revised by a few months (January–March 1779,
  in Salzburg). In *Köchel³*, Alfred Einstein reverted to the earlier (1778) date.

4 Wolfgang Plath, 'Beiträge zur Mozart-Autographie II – Schriftchronologie 1770–1780',
  MJb (1976/7), 131–73; see particularly p. 171.

5 Alan Tyson, 'The Date of Mozart's Piano Sonata in B flat, K.333/315c: the "Linz"
  Sonata?', in M. Bente (ed.), *Musik – Edition – Interpretation: Gedenkschrift Günther Henle*
  (Munich, 1980), pp. 447–54; reprinted in Tyson, *Autograph Scores*, pp. 73–81. The mark
  is no. 69 in Tyson (ed.), *Wasserzeichen-Katalog*.

6 This is the view taken by Tyson, *Autograph Scores*, pp. 20 and 30.

7 The watermarks for K.330 and 332 are identical (no. 53 in Tyson's *Wasserzeichen-Katalog);*
  that of K.331 is different, however (*Wasserzeichen-Katalog*, no. 67). Possibly, then, K.330
  and 332 were written as a pair, separately from K.331, the three sonatas only being collected together for publication in 1784.

8 Mozart notated some of the left-hand part of the slow movement of K.310 in the alto
  clef. In the first movement of K.332 (soprano clef), Mozart notated the second beat of
  bar 36 (right hand) at the wrong pitch (a third too low, as it if were in treble clef).

9 Fux, *Gradus ad Parnassum* (Vienna, 1725); Mozart's father bought a copy of Fux's treatise
  in 1746.

10 A further symbolism suggests itself: K.330 is in C major, a simple key, and perhaps, therefore, intended for beginners in composition, in the way that K.545 (in the same key) was
  later subtitled by the composer as 'für Anfänger'.

11 See *NMA* Serie X Supplement Wg.30/ Abt.1: *Thomas Attwoods Kompositionsstudien bei
  Mozart*, ed. E. Hertzmann, C. B. Oldman, D. Heartz, A. Mann (Kassel, 1965), I/8 ff.
  (pp. 13 ff.) and Abt. 2: *Barbara Ployers und Jakob Freystädtlers Theorie-und Kompositionsstudien
  bei Mozart*, ed. H. Federhofer, A. Mann (Kassel, 1989), A: Blatt 11a (p. 43), 11b (p. 45),
  12a (p. 47); B: I/3v ff. (pp. 62 ff.).

12 V,5 (inw. no.5995), bound together with the autographs of K.279–84. It measures *c*.30.2 (occasionally 31.2) × 23.8 cm. and covers four folios. Facsimile (second movement, entire): *NMA* Serie IX Wg.25/ Bd.2, pl. XXIII.

13 Containing bars 90 to the end of the 'Alla Turca' finale. Facsimile: *NMA* Serie IX Wg.25/ Bd.2, pl. XXIV.

14 Bars 107 to the end of the finale are lost. Facsimile (opening of first movement): *NMA* Serie IX Wg.25/ Bd.2, pl. XXV.

15 The origins of this manuscript, consisting of three very small leaves, and its relationship to others written by Mozart, are brilliantly pieced-together by Alan Tyson in the article cited in note 5 above. Facsimile (second movement, entire): *NMA* Serie IX Wg.25/ Bd.2, pl. XXVI. A good quality facsimile of the whole sonata (which, however, does not capture the intricate deportment of the original) is published by Ichthys Verlag (Stuttgart, 1966).

16 It is, naturally, probable that revisions were also made to the original, autograph, text of K.331, but this is impossible to determine as the manuscript is lost (excepting its last page).

17 As may be seen in the facsimile of this movement cited in note 12: following the F minor cadence in bar 40, Mozart simply indicates a 'Da Capo' of the first section.

18 Sadly, the print does not help the performer to resolve a query over Mozart's intended dynamic level for the opening theme of the first movement of K.330 and its reprise (bar 88). The first four bars have no mark in either autograph or print, though the implication is *f*, given the appearance of a (contrasting) *p* at bar 5. At bar 88 (the reprise) there is no mark, but two bars later (bar 90) there is a *f* marking, which might plausibly belong to bar 88. Such ambiguities reside in all copies of the Artaria print, including the (rare) first impression, subsequently re-engraved (with some errors).

19 In *Mozart Sonatas II* (and related *NMA* texts) the reprise is aligned with the original (unembellished) version for comparison.

20 See note 5 above.

21 See *Anderson*, no. 499 of 31 October 1783.

22 These stages of composition may relate to the rhetorical *dispositio* of the movement (the sequence of its ideas), a concept examined in part III.

23 They are not always straight – the left-hand barline between bars 47 and 48, for instance, continues downwards at a different angle from the right-hand barline for the stave above.

6 Fantasia and Sonata in C minor, K.475 and 457

1 For this occasion Sotheby's produced a handsome catalogue, *Fine Music Manuscripts: The Property of the Eastern Baptist Theological Seminary, Philadelphia* (Sotheby; London, 1990). The Mozart autograph was Lot 90.

2 Thérèse von Trattern (1758–93) was the wife of Mozart's landlord, the music publisher, Johann von Trattern, in Vienna when the Sonata was composed. For a time she was Mozart's pupil, and if the piece was written for her to play then she must have possessed considerable technical ability. The 'dedication copy' is currently in the Jewish National and University Library, Jerusalem. The date mentioned on the title-page accords with that of Mozart's handwritten thematic catalogue of his compositions, in which K.457 is entered as 'Eine Sonate für das Klavier allein'.

3 Advertised for sale in the *Wiener Zeitung* on 5 December 1785; in Mozart's thematic catalogue the Fantasia is dated 20 May 1785, and is again 'für das Klavier allein'.

4 This is investigated in detail in Eugene K. Wolf's article 'The Rediscovered Autograph
   of Mozart's Fantasy and Sonata in C Minor, K.475/457', *The Journal of Musicology*, 10
   (1992), 3–47. Wolf was the first musicologist to examine the manuscript in recent times,
   while it was still in the possession of Eastern Baptist Theological Seminary. His study,
   which includes several monochrome reproductions of the autograph, probes the issues of
   watermarks, rastrology and text in great depth. The following account is necessarily more
   of a summary and covers some of the same ground; however, all of my comments on the
   original text of the Fantasia and Sonata derive from work undertaken independently on
   the autograph itself in the spring of 1994 in the Mozarteum, Salzburg.

5 As may be seen in the colour facsimile edition of the autograph which has now been
   published: *Wolfgang Amadeus Mozart Fantasie und Sonate c-Moll für Klavier K.475 + 457.
   Faksimile nach dem Autograph in der Bibliotheca Mozartiana Salzburg*, intro. Wolfgang Plath
   and Wolfgang Rehm (Internationale Stiftung Mozarteum Salzburg, 1991) [henceforth
   Faksimile].

6 Including André's edition, *La Fantaisie & Sonate pour le pianoforté* (Offenbach, 1802) and
   that of the *[Alte] Mozart-Ausgabe*, Series XX (Leipzig, 1878), both of which cite their
   indebtedness to the autograph. (These claims could not be checked in detail before the
   re-appearance of the autograph in 1990, of course.)

7 The Breitkopf & Härtel *Œuvres Complettes*, Cahier VI (Leipzig, 1799).

8 Other solo piano sonatas which Mozart seemingly revised for publication at about this
   time are K.284 (Torricella, 1784) and K.330 and 332 (Artaria, 1784). Variation 11 of the
   finale of K.284 contains additional dynamics, slurrings and embellishments, noted above
   in chapter 3; The slow movement of K.330 contains a coda not present in the autograph;
   K.332 has a highly embellished reprise of the slow movement theme, indicated as a simple
   Da Capo in the autograph, as, originally, was the case in the Adagio of K.457.

9 A translation of the contract is given in Deutsch, *Doc.Biog.*, pp. 490–2; for the original
   see Otto Erich Deutsch, *Mozart: die Dokumente seines Lebens* (Kassel, Basel, Tours, 1961),
   pp. 528–31.

10 The appendix to the contract amounts to only a fraction of the available material: during
   the ensuing thirty years André published over fifty works by Mozart.

11 See Wolf, 'The Rediscovered Autograph of Mozart's Fantasy and Sonata in C minor,
   K. 475/457', p. 7 and his note 15. Further details on manuscripts owned by Stumpff are
   given in Alec Hyatt King, 'A Census of Mozart's Autographs in Great Britain', in *Mozart
   in Retrospect* (London, 1950; rev. edn 1970), pp. 82–5.

12 There are several systems of pagination and foliation in the autograph – none is wholly
   consistent and all have been ignored here (for discussion of the numberings see Wolf,
   'Mozart Autograph', pp. 8–10 and *Faksimile*, pp. 3,4 (German); 8,9 (English)). In the
   given diagrams the five rows indicate (starting from the top): number of bifolium; a,b,c,d,
   denoting *recto/ verso* sides of the bifolium represented on the row below by |___| (*=
   blank staves); [portion of Fantasia or Sonata on each bifolium (movements of the Sonata
   being represented by K.457 /1, /2 or /3)]; paper-type, according to watermark (for a
   detailed discussion of these, see Wolf, 'Mozart Autograph', pp. 9–26 *passim*, especially
   table 1 and figures 1–4).

13 Wolf, 'Mozart Autograph', p. 22.

14 There is some evidence that the Adagio was composed last. The paper on which it is written (Tyson's no.56) occurs more rarely than that on which the outer movements are written (Tyson's nos. 53 and 61) and, moreover, in predominantly *later* compositions than those containing papers 53 and 61. I am grateful to Cliff Eisen for this suggestion.

15 The slow movements of his piano concertos, for instance. Occasionally surviving copies do provide some examples of embellishment, such as that of a pupil reproduced in the *Kritische Berichte* to the A major Concerto, K.488, slow movement (*NMA*,Serie V; Wg.15/ Bd.2].

16 Virtually all the embellishment in the reprises is in the right-hand part; slight decoration is occasionally applied to the left-hand part, in bar 43 broken octaves are added (see bar 19) and in bar 46 the right-hand chromatic figure is imitated canonically at a quaver's distance. Substantially, though, these reprises comprise *melodic* variation over an unchanging harmonic foundation.

17 These are printed in *NMA*, Serie X Supplement Wg.30/ Abt.2: *Barbara Ployers und Franz Jakob Freystädtlers Theorie- und Compositionsstudien bei Mozart,* ed. Helmut Federhofer and Alfred Mann (Kassel, 1989). Freystädtler studied with Mozart sometime after 1786; Ployer two years earlier in 1784, the same year as K.457 was composed. In her exercises, Ployer was evidently asked to provide variants of her fundamental basses (Mozart sometimes obliged with further variants) while retaining the given melody, but never the other way round. Her studies with Mozart are mentioned in Joel Lester, *Compositional Theory in the Eighteenth Century* (Cambridge, Mass., 1992), pp. 182–7. See also Helmut Federhofer, 'Mozart als Schüler und Lehrer in der Musiktheorie', *MJb* (1971–2), 89–106; 'Mozart und die Musiktheorie seiner Zeit', *MJb* (1978–9), 172–5.

18 *NMA* Serie X Supplement Wg.30/ Abt.1: *Thomas Attwoods Theorie- und Compositionsstudien bei Mozart,* ed. Erich Hertzmann, Cecil B. Oldman, Daniel Heartz and Alfred Mann (Kassel, 1965). See also Erich Hertzmann, 'Mozart and Attwood', *JAMS,* 12 (1959), 178–84; Daniel Heartz, 'Thomas Attwood's Lessons in Composition with Mozart', *PRMA,* 100 (1973–4), 175–85.

19 Specifically pp. 243–5 and 253–4 of *Thomas Attwoods Theorie-und Compositionsstudien* .

20 *Thomas Attwoods Theorie- und Compositionsstudien,* pp. 244 and 253 respectively. In example 6.1 the four parts are condensed into short score.

21 The bar numbers correspond to those of the embellished (stage 2) text printed in the *NMA* text (*Mozart Sonatas II*), allowing for easy comparison between the two versions. For these bars (17–23 and 41–47) Mozart originally intended a simple 'Da Capo', which he indicated on bifolium 4, side a of the autograph.

7 Later Viennese sonatas, K.533 and 494; K.545; K.570; K.576

1 London, British Library, Add. MS. 47861. According to Mozart's *Verzeichnüss* the sonata was composed in February 1789.

2 *Sonate per il clavicembalo o piano-forte con l'accompagnamento d'un violino composta del Sigr. W.A.Mozart . . . opera 40* (Vienna; Artaria, 1796).

3 This is shown in *Mozart Sonatas II,* p. 132. There are some difficulties in interpreting the notation of incipits in the *Verzeichnüss*. Sometimes details are recorded differently from their appearance in the autographs, and the inconsistencies extend even to basis matters such as scoring (the Concerto, K.459, for instance).

4 *Sonate facile pour le pianoforte composée par W.A. Mozart . . . Oeuvre posthume* (Vienna; Bureau des Arts et d'Industrie, 1805).

5 The case is strengthened by the fact that the crotchet b in bar 7 is given not only in the 1805 edition but also in a reissue by André later that same year, *Sonate facile pour le pianoforté composée par W.A. Mozart ...A Vienne au mois de juin 1788* ... (Offenbach, 1805), and in a version printed by Johann Cappi, *Sonate (facile) pour le clavecin ou pianoforte par W.A. Mozart ... Oeuvre 112* (Vienna, 1809).

6 *Sonate pour le pianoforte composée par W.A. Mozart ... Oeuvre posthume* (Vienna; Bureau des Arts et d'Industrie, 1805).

7 *Sonate pour le forte-piano, ou clavecin composée par M' W.A. Mozart* (Vienna; Hoffmeister, 1788).

8 Two editions are known to exist from that year. The earlier is probably the text in *Storace's Collection of Original Harpsichord Music* (London; Birchall, 1788); the other was published by Bossler in Speyer; see also Hans Schneider, *Der Musikverleger Heinrich Philipp Bossler, 1744–1812* (Tutzing, 1985), p. 147. The autograph of the original Rondo does, in fact, survive in the collection of the late Felix Salzer, New York; a facsimile is given in H. Neumann and C. Schachter, 'The two versions of Mozart's Rondo, K.494', W. J. Mitchell and F. Salzer (eds.), *The Music Forum I* (1967) 1–34. Comparison of printed and manuscript texts confirms that the Storace and Bossler versions, while interdependent, are unrelated to the autograph. Such a discrepancy may be explicable by the remoteness of the publication from the Austrian capital: Mozart may simply have had no opportunity to check the plates. K.494 may originally have been intended as a set of three rondos, along with K.485 and K.511; the three pieces were ultimately published separately, though.

9 Salzburg, Internationale Stiftung Mozarteum copy Rara 533/3.

10 The printed texts of K.545, 570 and 576 are likewise, relatively sparse in their application of dynamics.

11 For example, bars 27 ff., 49 ff. (exhibiting stretto), most of the development section and significant portions of the recapitulation (such as the retransition at bars 153 ff.).

12 By Christoph Wolff, 'Musikalische "Gedankenfolge" und "Einheit des Stoffes." Zu Mozarts Klaviersonate in F-Dur (K.533 + 494)' in H. Danuser, H. de la Motte-Haber, S. Leopold and N. Miller (eds.), *Das musikalische Kunstwerk: Geschichte, Ästhetik, Theorie: Festschrift Carl Dahlhaus zum 60. Geburtstag* (Laaber, 1988), pp. 241–55. Wolff attempts, in his paper, to establish detailed thematic and textural links between the revised Rondo, K.494 and the first movement of K.533 to which it was attached. In this way, he argues, Mozart succeeded in creating an over-arching unity of material ('Einheit des Stoffes') in the sonata as a whole. While Wolff's closing table of similarities ('Gedankenfolge') may be taking resemblances too far for some, there can be no doubt of a general kinship between the work's outer movements.

13 We know from *Anderson*, no. 243a, of 14 November 1777, in which Mozart criticises Rosa Cannabich's playing, that his teaching method included the acquisition of secure keyboard geography in passages such as the Andante of K.545 by placing a handkerchief over the player's fingers, forcing a tactile, rather than visual approach.

14 Barbara Ployer, who was probably Mozart's student from 1784, was taught fundamental bass as well as three-part counterpoint (see chapter 6).

15 The corresponding phrase in the recapitulation is indicated by a 'Da Capo' so that this phrase is also unavailable in the composer's hand. In any case, at this point in the movement the retransition would have been largely a copying exercise, and therefore of limited use in revealing Mozart's actual thought process.

16 Particularly at bars 87 (implied 6-4) and 92–3 (unresolved 4-2 followed by implied 6-4).

17 London, British Library Add. MS. 47861.

18 Sonata, bars 13–16; Concerto, bars 20–3.

19 H. Eppstein, 'Warum wurde Mozarts K.570 zur Violinsonate?' *Die Musikforschung*, 16 (1963), 379–81; see also H. Redlich, 'Mozart's C minor Piano Concerto (K.491)', *The Music Review*, 9 (1948), 87–96, especially p. 93.

20 *Anderson*, no. 567. 'I am writing six easy sonatas for the Princess Friederika . . . which I will have published through Kozeluch at my own expense.' Leopold Kozeluch (1747–1818) was one of Mozart's most talented Viennese rivals, active in the imperial capital from 1778 as pianist, teacher, composer and publisher. His publishing house was founded in 1785. In June 1789 (the month before the composition of K.576) Kozeluch had published Mozart's variations on *Je suis Lindor*, K.354. In 1792 he succeeded Mozart as imperial 'Kammermusicus'.

21 *Mozart Sonatas II*, pp. x–xi.

22 On the other hand, this movement is richly polythematic, unlike the finale of K.576, which spends much of its length elaborating the opening theme. The finales of the A major Concerto, K.488, and the D major Concerto, K.537, provide further examples of the procedure.

23 *Anderson*, no. 567, 14 July 1789.

8 Fragments

1 *Anderson*, no. 392. The works referred to may, however, be the piano and violin sonatas, K.6–7; K.8–9.

2 In each of these, curiously, three, not four sonatas are mentioned.

3 *NMA* I:4/iv, p. 4. The ten-stave Salzburg paper of the added vocal items on which the Sonata fragment occurs is no. 21 in Alan Tyson (ed.), *Dokumentation der Autographen Überlieferung: Wasserzeichen-Katalog*, 2 vols. (Kassel, Basel, Tours, London, 1992).

4 André: 'Rondo. Allegro' (Offenbach, 1826), Nachgelassenen Werke, vol. V, no.1; Cipriani Potter: 'Les Chefs d'Oeuvre, (London, *c.* 1838), no.11. It was included by the editors of Breitkopf & Härtel's *Gesamtausgabe* (*W.A. Mozarts Werke* vol. XXIV, p. 26). In this century the piece has appeared in an edition by Bowen and Raymar (London, 1931) and in the Henle Urtext: *W.A. Mozart Klavierstücke*, ed. B. A. Wallner (Munich, 1955), no.13. *NMA* Serie IX Wg.25/Bd.2; Anh. no.2.

5 Otto Jahn, *W.A. Mozart* (Leipzig, 1856); English translation by Pauline D. Townsend, *Life of Mozart* (London, 1882), vol.II, pp. 250–1.

6 *Anderson*, no. 417.

7 Tyson, *Mozart: Studies of the Autograph Scores*, p. 142. The watermark is no. 95 in Alan Tyson (ed.), *Wasserzeichen-Katalog*, found also in the autographs of thirty-eight other pieces, including the symphonies, K.543, 550 and 551 and the Sonata in B flat, K.570.

8 The articulation of the *thesis – antithesis* is subtly altered: the *legato/* staccato opposition of K.590a is replaced by uniform cross-beat slurring in K.590b. In this sense K.590b moves a step closer to the eventual articulation of K.533.

9 Supertonic repetition *is* a feature of Mozart's eventual second subject, though, beginning at bar 41 of K.533. Perhaps the concept was retained, and transferred to this part of the movement for the sake of tonal variety.

10 See above, chapter 7, and C. Wolff, 'Musikalische "Gedankenfolge" und "Einheit des Stoffes". Zu Mozarts Klaviersonate in F-Dur (K.533+494)' in H. Danuser, H. de la

Motte-Haber, S. Leopold and N. Miller (eds.), *Das musikalische Kunstwerk. Geschichte, Ästhetik, Theorie: Festschrift Carl Dahlhaus zum 60. Geburtstag* (Laaber, 1988), pp. 441–53.

11 As 'Allegro morceau détaché. Oeuvre posthume'. Imprimerie Chymique, Vienna.

12 *Wolfgang Amadeus Mozarts Werke* (Breitkopf & Härtel; Leipzig, 1878), vol. XXII, p. 39.

13 For instance, the Henle Urtext: *W.A. Mozart: Klavierstücke*, ed. B.A. Wallner (Munich, 1955). In *NMA* it appears in Serie IX Wg.25/Bd.2; Anh. no.7.

14 Ms. M. Deneke Mendelssohn c.21; fol.8–9v. A good quality facsimile of the first page (f.8) is reproduced in A. Rosenthal and P. Ward Jones (eds.), *Mozart: a Bicentennial Loan Exhibition* (Oxford, 1991), p. 49. The manuscript is discussed in detail in M. Crum (comp.), *Catalogue of the Mendelssohn Papers in the Bodleian Library, Oxford Vol. II: Music and Papers* (Tutzing, 1983), pp. 78–85. On K.312, see John Irving, 'A Fresh Look at Mozart's "Sonatensatz", K.312 (590d)', *MJb*, 1995, 79–94.

15 This date is also suggested by Wyzewa and Saint Foix, *Wolfgang Amédée Mozart*, vol.II, pp. 192–3, who claimed both a resemblance with K.279, 282 and 283, and the influence of Haydn.

16 Tyson, *Autograph Scores*, p. 20. The watermark is no.100 in Tyson (ed.), *Wasserzeichen-Katalog*. This paper was also used in *Così fan Tutte, La Clemenza di Tito, Die Zauberflöte,* and in several chamber pieces, both complete (K. 589, 590 and 593) and fragmentary (Quartets, *Köchel*[6] 417d, 458a, 458b and 589b [=Anh.84, 75, 71, and 73]; Fugue for quartet, *Köchel*[6] 405a [=Anh. 77]; Clarinet Quintets, *Köchel*[6] 516c and 581a [=Anh. 91 and 88]; Sonata for Clavier and Violin, *Köchel*[6] 546a [=Anh. 47]; and String trio, *Köchel*[6] 562 e [=Anh. 66].

17 Tyson, *Autograph Scores*, p. 33–5.

9 Eighteenth-century views of sonata form

1 For example, Ebenezer Prout, *Musical Form* (London, 1893); Stewart MacPherson, *Form in Music with special reference to the designs of instrumental music* (London, 1908; 2nd edn 1912); William Cole, *The Form of Music* (London, 1969).

2 Adolph Bernhard Marx, *Die Lehre von der musikalischen Komposition*, 4 vols. (Leipzig, 1841–51), vol. III, p. 282.

3 Marx's work is anticipated to some degree in the theoretical writings of, for instance, Czerny, whose *School of Practical Composition*, though not published in its definitive English translation by John Bishop until 1848, was available in French from 1834. For a comprehensive survey of nineteenth-century writings on musical form see Ian Bent, *Analysis*, The New Grove Handboooks in Music (London, 1987), chapter 2; Bent, 'Analytical Thinking in the First Half of the Nineteenth Century', in Edward Olleson (ed.), *Modern Musical Scholarship* (London, 1980), pp. 151–66 and Ian Bent (ed.), *Music Analysis in the Nineteenth Century*, vol. I: *Fugue, Form and Style*; vol. II: *Hermeneutic Approaches* (Cambridge, 1994).

4 Koch, *Versuch einer Anleitung zur Composition*, vol. II (Leipzig, 1787), § 101,102. This is Koch's description of the form of a 'Symphony', but is applicable also to the solo sonata, as he notes in his §108. The translation of this, and other passages from Koch, is taken from *Heinrich Christoph Koch: Introductory Essay on Composition – The Mechanical Rules of melody, Sections 3 and 4*, translated, with an introduction by Nancy Kovaleff Baker (New Haven and London, 1983). Koch's remarks on the melodic definition within a sonata exposition are on pp. 199–200 of Baker's translation. Notice that Koch does not describe

the plan as 'sonata form;, but as the plan of the 'first allegro'. A similar description of the plan, from August Kollmann's *An Essay on Practical Musical Composition* (London, 1799), p. 5, is quoted in Leonard G. Ratner, *Classic Music*, pp. 217–18.

5 Notwithstanding differences of detail this is an adequate working summary of the sonata form as described in the following treatises: Heinrich Christoph Koch, *Versuch einer Anleitung zur Composition*, vol. II (Leipzig, 1787), p. 223; vol. III (Leipzig, 1793), pp. 301 ff. and 341 ff.; Johann Georg Portmann, *Leichtes Lehrbuch der Harmonie, Composition, und des General-Basses* (Darmstadt, 1789), p. 50; Georg Löhlein, *Clavierschüle*, 5th edn (Leipzig and Züllichau, 1791), pp. 182 ff.; Francesco Galeazzi, *Elementi teorico-practici di Musica*, vol.II (Rome, 1796), pp. 251 ff.; August Kollmann, *An Essay on Practical Musical Composition* (London, 1799), p. 5; Jerome de Momigny, *Cours complet d'Harmonie et de Composition* (Paris, 1806), pp. 332 ff.; Anton Reicha, *Traité de Mélodie* (Paris, 1814), pp. 46 ff.

6 Some treatises dealing with melody: Joseph Riepel, *Anfangsgründe zur musikalischen Setzkunst*, vol. I (Regensburg and Vienna, 1752); Christoph Nichelmann, *Die Melodie nach ihrem Wesen* (Danzig, 1755); Heinrich Christoph Koch, *Versuch einer Anleitung zur Composition*, 3 vols. (Leipzig, 1782, 1787, 1793); Johann Georg Portmann, *Leichtes Lehrbuch der Harmonie, Composition, und des General-Basses* (Darmstadt, 1789); Johann Friedrich Daube, *Anleitung zur Erfindung der Melodie* (Vienna, 1797–8); Jerome de Momigny, *Cours complet d'Harmonie et de Composition* (Paris, 1806); Anton Reicha, *Traité de Mélodie* (Paris, 1814). In teaching composition to Barbara Ployer, Mozart began by setting her melodies to harmonise in different ways – an approach suggestive of the primacy of melody in his own philosophy. See *Neue Mozart-Ausgabe* Serie X Supplement Wg.30/Abt.2 *Barbara Ployers und Franz Jakob Freystädtlers Theorie- und Compositionsstudien bei Mozart*, ed. Helmut Federhofer and Alfred Mann (Kassel, Basel, Tours, London, 1989). Among earlier eighteenth-century treatises dealing with melody – and especially with its possible rhetorical applications – two are outstanding: Johann David Heinichen, *Der General-Bass in der Composition* (Dresden, 1728) and Johann Mattheson, *Der vollkommene Kapellmeister* (Hamburg, 1739).

7 Later in the movement, as noted above (note 4), Koch draws attention to the coincidence of the return of the main key (at the beginning of the 'recapitulation') and the restatement of the opening theme.

8 Francesco Galeazzi, *Elementi teorico-practici di Musica*, 2 vols. (Rome, 1791, 1796), pp. 253–60. Translation taken from Bathia Churgin, 'Francesco Galeazzi's Description (1796) of Sonata Form', *JAMS*, 21 (1968), 181–99.

9 Churgin, 'Francesco Galeazzi's Description', pp. 195–6.

10 A simpler situation obtains in the first movement of the C major Sonata, K.545, in which the recapitulation begins in the *subdominant* at bar 42, this time with the main opening theme and continuing with the remaining exposition themes presented in their original order, but within the tonic, C.

11 Portmann, *Leichtes Lehrbuch*, pp. 50–3. A version of this diagram is reproduced in Beth Shamgar, 'On Locating the Retransition in Classic Sonata Form', *The Music Review*, 42 (1981), 130–43, at p. 132. Portmann notes: 'Reading or performing a work by Mozart, however, should make one forget my sonata, the basic harmonic plan of which, with careful forethought, I borrowed from him, in order, by comparison, to bring his work – which like all of his compositions should be in everyone's hands – to my reader's attention.' Translation from Cliff Eisen, *New Mozart Documents* (London, 1991), no.165.

12 Shamgar, 'On Locating the Retransition', note 8.

13 The line numbers do not appear in the original diagram but have been added here for ease of reference.

14 As implied by the very title of his treatise, *Die Lehre von der musikalischen Komposition*. In fact, Marx devotes more space to detailing the exceptions than to the outline of sonata form itself.

15 G.F. Meier, *Anfangsgründe aller schönen Wissenschaften*, 3 vols. (Halle, 1748–50); J. C. Gottsched, *Ausführliche Redekunst* (Augsburg, 1736, and many subsequent editions).

16 Pp. 5–6.

17 See Forkel's *Musikalischer Almanach für Deutschland auf das Jahr 1784*, pp. 31–2. The translation is from Bonds, *Haydn's False Recapitulations*, pp. 139–40.

18 'Die Aesthetische Ordnung', in *Allgemeine Geschichte der Musik* (Leipzig, 1788), vol. I, pp. 66–8; translation from Bonds, p. 136.

19 Mattheson, *Kern melodischer Wissenschaft* (Hamburg, 1737), p. 128; see the quotation given above in chapter 1, p. 5

20 Meier, *Anfangsgründe*, vol. III, p. 314; translation from Bonds, *Haydn's False Recapitulations*, p. 101.

21 Johann Friedrich Daube, *Der musikalische Dilettant* (Vienna, 1773), p. 162; quoted in Bonds, *Haydn's False Recapitulations*, p. 128–9. For an English translation of Daube, see Susan P. Snook-Luther, *The Musical Dilettante: A Treatise on Composition by J. F. Daube* (Cambridge, 1992).

22 Of course, *Zergliederungen* need not be confined to the development, but is a technique most most frequently associated with this section of the movement.

23 The most detailed survey of variations according to rhetorical principles yet published is Elaine R. Sisman, *Haydn and The Classical Variation* (Cambridge, Mass., 1993).

24 By far the most extensive study of the whole area of music and rhetoric (one which has influenced the following account to no small extent) is that of Marc Evan Bonds, *Wordless Rhetoric: Musical Form and the Metaphor of the Oration* (Cambridge, Mass. 1991); music as a language is discussed on pp. 61–8. Other studies: Elaine R. Sisman, *Haydn and the Classical Variation* (Cambridge, Mass., 1993), especially chapter 2; George Buelow, 'Rhetoric and Music', in *The New Grove* (which gives an extensive Bibliography); Buelow, 'The Loci Topici and Affect in Late Baroque Music: Heinichen's Practical Demonstration', *The Music Review*, 27 (1966), 161–76; Buelow, 'Music, Rhetoric and the Concept of the Affections: A Selective Bibliography', *Notes*, 30 (1973–4), 250–9; Warren Kirkendale, 'Ciceronians versus Aristotelians: The Ricercare as Exordium from Bembo to Bach', *JAMS*, 32 (1979), 1–44; Ursula Kirkendale, 'The Source for Bach's Musical Offering: The *Institutio oratoria* of Quintilian', *JAMS*, 33 (1980), 88–141; Alan Street, 'The Rhetorico-Musical Structure of the "Goldberg" Variations: Bach's *Clavier-Übung IV* and the *Institutio oratoria* of Quintilian', *Music Analysis*, 6 (1987), 89–131; Brian Vickers, *In Defence of Rhetoric* (Oxford,1988); Vickers, 'Figures of Rhetoric/ Figures of Music?', *Rhetorica*, 2 (1984), 1–44; Hans-Heinrich Unger, *Die Beziehung zwischen Rhetorik und Musik im 16.–18. Jahrhundert* (Würzburg, 1941). For a cautionary tale or two, see Peter Williams, 'The Snares and Delusions of Musical Rhetoric: Some Examples from Recent Writings on J. S. Bach', in P. Reidemeister und V. Gutmann (eds.), *Alte Musik: Praxis und Reflexion* (Winterthur, 1983), pp. 230–40. Most studies of 'Musical Rhetori' so far have been devoted to renaissance and baroque repertoires.

25 Mattheson, *Der vollkommene Capellmeister* (Hamburg, 1739), p. 180; Quantz, *Versuch einer Anweisung die Flöte Traversière zu Spielen* (Berlin, 1752), p. 102.

26 Forkel, *Allgemeine Geschichte*, vol. I, p. 24 (translation adapted from Bonds, *Wordless Rhetoric*, p. 49).

27 Quantz, *Versuch*, p. 100; quoted in Bonds, *Haydn's False Recapitulations*, p. 123. It is significant that Forkel's sequence of rhetorical devices, noted above, note 18, occurs in a section entitled 'Die Aesthetische Ordnung'.

28 According to Haydn's biographer, Griesinger, Haydn's education in the choir-school at St Stephen's, Vienna, included 'the scant instruction usual at the time in Latin, in religion, in arithmetic and writing'. Georg August Griesinger, *Biographische Notizen über Joseph Haydn* (Leipzig, 1810); quoted in Jens Peter Larsen, 'Haydn', in *The New Grove*. Leopold Mozart's education is described in Adolf Layer, *Eine Jugend in Augsburg – Leopold Mozart, 1719–1737* (Augsburg, n.d.). A more general study of education in Germany and Austria in this period is given in Fritz Keller, 'Rhetorik in der Ordenschule', in Herbert Zeman (ed.), *Die österreichischer Literatur: ihr Profil an der Wende vom 18. zum 19. Jahrhundert (1750–1830),* Jahrbuch für österreichischer Kulturgeschichte nos. 7–9 (1977–9), p. 57. The study of rhetoric was preceded by grammar. The principal classical texts were Aristotle, *The 'Art' of Rhetoric*, trans. J. H. Freese, Loeb Classical Library no. 193 (Cambridge, Mass. and London, 1926, repr. 1991); [pseudo-Cicero], *Ad Herennium*, trans. H. Caplan, Loeb Classical Library no. 403 (Cambridge Mass. and London, 1954, repr. 1989); Cicero, *De Inventione*, trans. H. M. Hubbell, Loeb Classical Library no. 386 (Cambridge Mass. and London, 1949, repr. 1976); Cicero, *De Oratore*, trans. E. W. Sutton and H. Rackham, Loeb Classical Library no. 348 (Cambridge Mass. and London, 1942, repr. 1988); Quintilian, *Institutio Oratoria*, trans. H. E. Butler, Loeb Classical Library nos. 124–7 (Cambridge Mass. and London, 1920, repr. 1989). It is now generally agreed that *Ad Herennium* is not the work of Cicero (though it shares some similarities with his *De Inventione*); see *Ad Herennium*, Introduction, pp. ix–xiv. *Ad Herennium*, Quintilian's *Institutio* and Cicero's *De Oratore* were all published for the first time in Italy during the later fifteenth century, and remained essential (and oft-reprinted) educational aids in Europe until the first half of the nineteenth century.

29 Leopold Mozart, *A Treatise on the Fundamental Principles of Violin Playing*. English translation by Edith Knocker (London, 1948; 2nd edn 1951).

30 *Briefe*, vol. I, nos. 2 and 8. See also vol. V (*Kommentar*) to these letters. Gottsched's works were enormously important in mid-eighteenth-century German letters and were widely reprinted. Leopold owned the *Ausführliche Redekunst* (Augsburg, 1736) and *Grundlegung einer Deutschen Sprachkunst* (Augsburg, 1748).

31 Leopold's bibliography includes works by Boethius, Ptolemy, Jehan des Murs, Glareanus, Zarlino, Gaffurius, Kircher, Artusi, Fux, Mattheson, Marpurg, Quantz and Riepel. His acquaintance with these theoretical writings will be discussed presently.

32 Quintilian, *Institutio*, vol. I, viii.

33 Leopold Mozart, *A Treatise on the Fundamental Principles of Violin Playing*, p. 22.

34 Gaffurius's *Practica* is reprinted in facsimile in 'Monuments of Music and Musical Literature in Facsimile' [MMMLF] vol. LXXV (New York, 1979); for the *Theorica*, see MMMLF vol. XXI (New York, 1967); for Glareanus's *Dodecacordon* see MMMLF vol. LXV (New York, 1967); for Zarlino's *Institutione* see MMMLF vol.I (1965); for the *Dimonstratione* see MMMLF vol. II (New York, 1965).

35 Facsimile in MMMLF vol. LX (New York, 1977), based on an Oxford imprint of 1682.

36 Aristoxenus, *Harmonica* trans. Henry S. Macan (Oxford, 1902); *Elementa* ed., intro. and trans. by Lionel Pearson (Oxford, 1990).

37 See MMMLF vol. LI (New York, 1977).

38 And several later editions, for instance, 2nd edn 1737; 3rd edn 1742; 4th edn 1751.

39 He knew Fux's treatise in the original Latin: his copy, dated 1746, still survives, and is owned by the Internationale Stiftung Mozarteum, Salzburg. In a letter to his wife of 15 September 1773 Leopold notes that a Herr Klieburstein had recently borrowed it: 'nämlich den *Fux* lateinisch und den *Riepl* deutsch' (*Briefe*, no. 297). Mizler had translated Fux's *Gradus* into German: *Gradus ad Parnassum, oder Anführung zur regelmässigen musikalischen Composition* (Leipzig, 1742). The 'Riepl' to which Leopold refers was presumably either the *Anfangsgründe* or else the *Grundregeln*. Further information on Leopold's theoretical knowledge is given above, chapter 4, note 16.

40 Cicero's *De Inventione*, II. ii, for instance, addresses its relationship to Aristotle's *Rhetoric*.

41 For instance, Aristotle's initial discussion of the arrangement of an oration (*Rhetoric*, III. xiii.1) claims that there are only two parts, statement and proof. However, his discussion of the arrangement analyses all the traditional six parts of introduction, statement, division, proof, refutation, conclusion (*Rhetoric*, III, xiv-xix).

42 Quintilian, *Institutio*, III, iii–vi has a detailed discussion of terminology.

43 Aristotle, *Rhetoric*, I.iii; [Cicero], *Ad Herennium*, I.ii; Cicero, *De Inventione*, I.ix-x; *De Oratore*, I.xxxi, 141; Quintilian, *Institutio*, III.iii–iv.

44 Aristotle, *Rhetoric*, I.ii; [Cicero], *Ad Herennium*, I.ii–iii; Cicero, *De Inventione*, I.vii; *De Oratore*, I.xxxi, 142; Quintilian, *Institutio*, III.iii.

45 This is the term preferred by Quintilian (*Institutio*, IV.iv) for that section of an oration following the *narratio* in which a summary is given of the accusation. Quintilian distinguishes between this, in which there is a single charge (*propositio*), and *partitio*, in which there is a listing of the variety of points at issue (*Institutio*, IV.v). Cicero describes simply the *partitio* (*De Inventione*,I.xxi–xxii); in [Cicero] *Ad Herennium* (I.x.17), the term is *divisio*, and is shown to be itself sub-divided into *enumeratio* (how many points are to be discussed) and *expositio* (what these are). As it applied in legal cases, the need for such a section is clear; in a musical piece, it is not.

46 Aristotle, *Rhetoric*, III.xiii.1 and III.xiv–xix; [Cicero], *Ad Herennium*, I.iii; Cicero, *De Inventione*, I.xiv; *De Oratore*, I.xxxi, 143; Quintilian, *Institutio*, IV–V. It will be noticed that the traditional ordering of proof and refutation was reversed in Mattheson and Forkel's musical applications. Possibly this was to do with the equation of 'proof/confirmation' with the return of the tonic key (either with or without the restatement of the main thematic material), and 'refutation' with a subsidiary key (in which contrasting thematic material might be heard). Within the tonal system, and especially that system as it developed during the eighteenth century, the return of the tonic key in the course of a piece or movement suggested *resolution* of its tonal and/or thematic conflicts, a condition analogous to the 'proof' in an oration, which therefore had to *follow*, rather than precede, the 'refutation'.

47 Cicero, *De Oratore*, I.xxxi.141.

48 Quintilian, *Institutio*, III.iii.14.

49 That is, the piece will end in the tonic key, all other contrary keys having been circumscribed within its orbit.

50 Aristotle defines rhetoric as 'the faculty of discovering the possible means of persuasion in reference to any subject whatever' (*Rhetoric*, I.2).

51 Aristotle, *Rhetoric*, III.xii.6. By 'style' here, Aristotle means the general characteristics of epideictic, as opposed to forensic or deliberative oratory, rather than the third of the *Partes*.

52 Cicero, *De Inventione*, I. vii.

53 Mattheson, *Kern melodischer Wissenschaft*; Koch, *Versuch*; Fux, *Gradus ad Parnassum*; Johann Georg Albrechtsberger, *Gründliche Anweisung zur Composition* (Leipzig, 1790).

10 Pre-compositional choices – the rhetorical *inventio*

1 Quintilian, *Institutio*, III.iii.
2 [Cicero] *Ad Herennium* I.ii.3, I.iii.1; Cicero, *De Inventione* I.vii, I.xiv.19.
3 Cicero, *De Inventione*, I.xiv.19.
4 Syllogism: a form of reasoning in which, from two propositions, a third is deduced. Induction: inferring of general from specific principles.
5 Aristotle, *Rhetoric*, I.ii.11.
6 On the level of *inventio*, this process of generating a theme from an *Urlinie* may be compared to the generation of successive variations (within the first movement of K.331, for instance) from the opening theme – a type of compositional planning that exists on the level of *dispositio*.
7 Alfred Mann (trans. and ed.), *The Study of Counterpoint from Johann Joseph Fux's Gradus ad Parnassum* (New York, 1965). Fig. 55 (p. 53) in third species, and fig. 82 (p. 64) in fifth species, may be regarded as figured melodies in relation to the first species original of fig.5 (p. 29). Mozart perhaps studied Fux's treatise – his father purchased a copy in 1746. Haydn learned counterpoint from this text.
8 Koch, *Versuch*, vol. III, p. 226, reproduced in L. Ratner, *Classic Music – Expression, Form, and Style* (Stanford, 1980), p. 95.
9 Portmann, *Leichtes Lehrbuch*, p. 22; reproduced in Ratner, *Classic Music*, p. 86.
10 The two versions of the opening of K.284 in D – in the second of which Mozart abandoned his original device of immediate repetition – also impinge on the border between *inventio* and *dispositio*. In each version the melodic invention is the same in bar 1; the subsequent differences in the revised text result from a change in arrangement.
11 Similar cases are the slow movements of K.332 and 457.

11 *Dispositio*: rhetoric and design

1 Mizler, *Neu-eröffnete musikalische Bibliothek*, vol. I (Leipzig, 1738), pp. 38–9. Quoted in Bonds, *Wordless Rhetoric*, p. 87.
2 Mattheson, *Der vollkommene Capellmeister*, pp. 25–6. For a complete English translation, see Ernest C. Harriss, *Johann Mattheson's 'Der vollkommene Capellmeister': A Revised Translation* (Ann Arbor, 1981); the passage in question is at pp. 62–3.
3 Aristotle, *Rhetoric*, III.xiv.4.
4 Cicero, *De Inventione*, I.lii. The *peroratio* is discussed in similar terms by Aristotle, *Rhetoric*, III.xix and [Cicero] *Ad Herennium*, II.xxx.
5 Bonds, *Wordless Rhetoric*, pp. 124–5. The translation quoted here is that of Bonds.
6 Aristotle, *Rhetoric*, III.xiii.
7 For example, [Cicero], *Ad Herennium*, II.xxx.
8 Quintilian, *Institutio*, VI.i.4.
9 [Cicero], *Ad Herennium*, I.iii.4.
10 Though this is not, rhetorically, an ideal solution: see pp. 147–50.
11 Aristotle believed there to be only four (not six) divisions, for he groups partition, confirmation and refutation together as different types of 'proof'.

12 Cicero, *De Inventione*, I.xv.

13 Quintilian, *Institutio*, IV.i.58–60.

14 Cicero, *De Inventione*, I.xv; Quintilian, *Institutio*, IV.i.42.

15 Warren Kirkendale, 'Ciceronians versus Aristotelians: The Ricercare as *Exordium* from Bembo to Bach', *JAMS* 32 (1979), pp. 1–44.

16 Cicero, *De Inventione*, I.xv.

17 Aristotle, *Rhetoric*, III.xiii.1–4. On epideictic narrative see also [Cicero], *Ad Herennium*, III.vi–x.

18 Cicero, *De Oratore*, II.lxxvii.

19 Aristotle, *Rhetoric*, III.xiv; Cicero, *De Inventione*, I.xix; [Cicero], *Ad Herennium*, I.ix; Quintilian, *Institutio*, IV.ii.

20 In his most considered rhetorical text, *De Oratore*, Cicero remarks that 'the narrative gains liveliness when it brings in several characters and is broken up with speeches' (II.lxxx). In this treatise Cicero makes it plain that the technique of *narratio* is different from that of other portions of an oration (in which, for example, arguments are developed or refuted). In musical terms, too, the nature of an exposition (in which the 'statement' of the main thematic material is made) is different to that of a development section (in which the thematic material is developed) or an episode (in which alternative or opposing material is introduced).

21 Aristotle, *Rhetoric*, I.ix.

22 [Cicero], *Ad Herennium*, III.vi–ix.

23 Cicero, *De Inventione*, I.xix; see also *Ad Herennium*, I.viii.13.

24 The only 'monothematic' expositions in Mozart's sonatas are found in the first movements of K.570 and K.576, and the slow movement of K.533, in all of which the secondary key-area is introduced by a restatement of the opening theme in the dominant. In each case, however, these sections continue polythematically.

25 There is no actual modulation into the dominant here, simply an imperfect cadence ending on a G major chord at bar 18; Mozart's recapitulation is a (decorated) repetition of the opening exposition, leading once again to an imperfect cadence on G in bar 105, after which, however, there follows a restatement of the theme of bar 19 still in the dominant (an unusual tonal strategy at this point in the movement); at bar 109, just before the repetition of this theme occurs, Mozart effects a memorable shift into the tonic, C major, a graceful move that reinforces the main tonality from this point onwards. Another example of an opening paragraph ending with an imperfect cadence on the dominant is found in the first movement of the F major Sonata, K.280. Normally, Mozart modulates within his expositions, either to the dominant, or else to the dominant-of-the-dominant. The finale of K.330, for example has a modulation to the dominant (bar 32) before introducing a new theme in the secondary key area in the following bar. The same process may be seen in the earlier G major Sonata, K.283: both its first movement and finale modulate to the dominant just before introducing the secondary area. Other examples include the first movements of K.281, K.284, K.311, K.545/i and K.576/i. Normally where Mozart does this, he repeats the exposition material exactly (or almost so) in the recapitulation, where the arrival of the dominant key sounds like a dominant preparation for the reprise of the secondary area in the main tonic. In the special case of K.545 the whole of the opening paragraph is transposed into the subdominant. Elsewhere, Mozart modulates one further degree sharpwards in the exposition (dominant-of-the-dominant), and modifies the recapitulation transition so as to reach only the dominant key at this

later stage in the movement. Among the numerous examples in the sonatas, may be cited K.279/iii, K.280/iii, K.309/i, K.310/i (where the modulation is to the dominant of the relative major, C), K.332/i, K.333/i and K.533/i.

26 Another instance (albeit on a smaller scale) of a counterbalancing coda is found in the slow movement of K.330, bars 60–4 (cf. bars 36–40).

27 Aristotle, *Rhetoric*, I.ix.40; see also II.xviii.5.

28 Cicero, *De Inventione*, I.xxxiv–vi; II.xxxii–iv. In his *De Partitione Oratoria*, Cicero remarks that amplification was best reserved for the *Peroratio*, though it could be employed elsewhere in the speech. He describes amplification as 'a more impressive affirmation . . . which by moving the mind wins belief in speaking' (*De Partitione*, VIII.xxvii).

29 [Cicero], *Ad Herennium*, II.xxx.48–9.

30 Quintilian, *Institutio*, VIII.iv.

31 Whereas the detailed use of rhetorical–musical *figures* to create continuity within a section of a movement belongs to the level of *elocutio* (style) and will be discussed at that stage (chapter 12). Techniques of amplification are discussed here purely in so far as they influence the *structure* of a development section.

32 Quintilian, *Institutio*, VIII.iv.3. Quintilian's example, quoting an actual speech by Cicero, illustrates the progression to a climax by increasingly emotive language: 'It is a *sin* to bind a Roman citizen, a *crime* to scourge him, little short of the *most unnatural murder* to put him to death; what then shall I call his *crucifixion*? [my italics indicate the stages in the exaggeration].'

33 Quintilian, *Institutio*, VIII.iv.26–7.

34 Quoted above, chapter 9, pp. 100–2 For an interesting approach to the retransition, in which the tonic key is gradually resumed, see Beth Shamgar, *The Retransition in the Piano Sonatas of Haydn, Mozart and Beethoven*, Ph.D dissertation, University of New York (1978). Shamgar investigates the emphasis or deliberate blurring of sub-divisions within these sonata developments, and has some interesting comments on the co-ordination of different textural elements in achieving either type.

35 As in K.332/i, bars 225–6, K.333/i, bar 81 or K.533 in F, bars 116–25. In K.284/i, bars 58–9 and K.330/i, bars 69–70 this tonal degree is unemphasised, progressing directly into the relative minor.

36 As in K.279/iii, bar 76; K.280/i, bar 66; /iii, bar 106; K.281/i, bar 54 (enhanced by a diminished-seventh chord).

37 Bars 82 and 55, respectively.

38 And also in the Adagio first movement of K.282.

39 Bar 85 of the finale might be related to the opening of that movement, though the reference is coincidental rather than significant.

40 A strategy similar to that followed in the original (cancelled) version of the first movement of K.284, whose development begins with the exposition codetta before continuing freely. This approach is also found in the first movement of the C major Sonata, K.545.

41 Summing-up, amplification and 'appeal to pity' (or 'emotion'). [Cicero], *Ad Herennium*, II.xxx.

42 Aristotle, *Rhetoric*, III.xix; Cicero, *De Inventione*, I.lii.98; Quintilian, *Institutio*, VI.i.1. *Ad Herennium* gives considerable emphasis to amplification. Cicero, in his treatise on 'topics', *Topica* (trans. H. M. Hubbell [Loeb Classical Library, vol.386], Cambridge Mass., 1949; rep.1976), records that 'the peroration . . . makes especial use of amplification' (XXVI.98). This treatise, written as an explanation of Aristotle's treatise, *Topica* (trans. H.

Tredinnick [Loeb Classical Library, vol.391], Cambridge Mass., 1960; rep.1989), was on argumentation, though it exceeds its original brief and includes mention of the three species of oratory, among other subjects. Though preserved in manuscripts dating from the 10th century onwards Cicero's *Topica* was not as widely read as his other work on rhetorical matters. Many of its arguments, however, are developed at greater length in the widely-known *De Inventione* and *De Oratore*. Quintilian specifically divides the peroration into two classes: that which deals with facts; and that which deals with emotional aspects.

43 On the recapitulation retransition, see Nicholas Marston, 'The Recapitulation Transitions in Mozart's Music', *Bericht über den Internationalen Mozart-Kongreß Salzburg 1991* (=MJb, 1991), 793–809.

44 A much simpler kind of amplification in the recapitulation transition is found in K.332/i, bars 155–76, in which the descending sequence of bars 23–40 of the exposition is extended one step further, to B flat minor (bar 167), from which point the bass line (D flat – C – B natural – C) progressively reinforces the dominant (C) by chromatic neighbour-note motion. In K.570/i, bars 155–70, the reverse happens: Mozart cuts out the last stage of the original sequence (bars 23–40), so that harmonically it extends only as far as F, the dominant.

45 [Cicero], *Ad Herennium*, II.xxx.47.

46 A similar strategy is found in the first movement of the Clavier and Violin Sonata in D, K.306 (written in Paris the following year).

47 Reordering within a slow-movement sonata form occurs only in the Andante of K.279, in which the reprise of bar 62 is withheld until bar 68 (and in the Adagio that opens K.282).

48 [Cicero], *Ad Herennium*, II.xxx.47. This comment applies principally to forensic rhetoric, of course. As stated above, p. 118, in musical discourse there is no separate *divisio*, outlining in advance the points to be addressed in the *confirmatio* and *refutatio*; the development section (the 'proof') simply happens.

49 Sixteen authentic sets survive, scattered across the whole of his creative career. For a Schenkerian study of Mozart's variations see Esther Cavett-Dunsby, *Mozart's Variations Reconsidered* (New York, 1990), which includes a consideration of K.613 (on 'Ein Weib ist das herrlichste Ding') and the finale of the C minor Concerto, K.491. Elaine Sisman includes mention of K.455 (on Gluck's 'Unser dummer Pöbel meint') in *Haydn and the Classical Variation* (Cambridge, Mass. and London, 1993), pp. 199–201.

50 Dual references to particular bars in this movement are given, reflecting two editorial traditions of numbering from 1–17 within each variation (eg. the *NMA*), or else 1–260 in a continuous sequence through to the end of var.12 (eg. Sadie and Matthews's Associated Board edition). The first bar of var.1 is therefore expressed as bar I:1/17.

51 The reprise of the first half begins at bar XI:8/195; the second half begins at bar XI:16/203, reprised at bar XI:22/209, reflecting the A A'\ B B' structure of the theme. Judging from revisions to his autograph, Mozart's original structure was AB\A'B'. See chapter 3, p. 52.

52 In the published version of this sonata, issued by Torricella in 1784, the right-hand embellishment is somewhat fuller than in the 1775 autograph and additional dynamics are applied. See chapter 3, p. 54.

53 The reprise of the first half begins at bar XII:9/195; the second half begins at bar XII:16/203, reprised at bar XI:25/212, reflecting the A A'\ B B' structure of the theme.

54 Dual bar-references are again given.

55 Sisman, *Haydn and the Classical Variation*, chapter 2.

56 Erasmus, *De duplici copia rerum ac verborum commentarii duo* (Paris, 1512–34); trans. B. Knott as *Copia: Foundations of the Abundant Style*, in C. R. Thompson (ed.), *The Collected Works of Erasmus, Literary and Educational Writings, 2* (Toronto, 1978).

57 A figure of speech in which 'a saying is drawn from life . . . for example: "Every beginning is difficult" ' (*Ad Herennium*, IV.xvii.24).

58 A figure of speech which 'of two opposite statements uses one so as neatly and directly to prove the other, as follows: "Now how should you expect one who has ever been hostile to his own interests to be friendly to another's?" ' (*Ad Herennium*, IV.xviii.25).

59 Self-evident; discussed in *Ad Herennium*, IV.xlv.59 – xlvi 62.

60 Discussed in *Ad Herennium*, IV.xlv.58 and in Quintilian, *Institutio*, IX.i.27.

61 Quintilian, *Institutio*, IX.i.26–8. The original is in Cicero, *De Oratore*, III.liii.202.

62 That is, Book IV of *Ad Herennium*; Book VIII of Quintilian's *Institutio*.

63 Erasmus, *De Copia*, p. 302 (the relevant passage is quoted in Sisman, *Haydn and the Classical Variation*, p. 28); Quintilian, *Institutio*, VIII.iii.87.

64 Noted, and in part quoted, in Sisman, *Haydn and the Classical Variation*, p. 27.

65 Quintilian, *Institutio*, IX.i.26–8.

66 In that it 'may employ digressions and then . . . make a neat and elegant return to our main theme', though 'dwelling upon the point' may prove a suitable rhetorical model for episodic forms (this will be explored presently).

67 Sisman applies it – in a highly novel and illuminating way – to the special case of the rondo finale of the Concerto, K.382, which is not a straightforward variation set, but a combination of an episodic structure with variation.

68 Which is how the author of *Ad Herennium* actually describes *expolitio* (IV.xliv.58).

69 *Ad Herennium*, IV.xxxii.43; also Quintilian, *Institutio*, VIII.vi.59. Leonard Ratner, with characteristic economy, expressed *periphrasis* as 'many notes where one will do' *Classic Music*, p. 91. Sisman, *Haydn and the Classic Variation*, pp. 38–9 and 43–7.

70 Sisman, *Haydn and the Classic Variation*, p. 38. *Pleonasm* was regarded with derision by orators, though.

71 *Ad Herennium*, IV.xxxi – xxxiv.

72 Quintilian, *Institutio*, VIII.vi.

73 Quintilian, *Institutio*, VIII.vi.1–3.

74 Quintilian, *Institutio*, VIII.vi.4–9 *passim*.

75 In all the variations except var.3 Mozart fills-in the silence halfway through the second section by an extension of the dominant degree, A – a harmonic *metaphor* of 'sound' for 'silence'.

76 Quintilian, *Institutio*, VIII.vi.16.

77 Quintilian, *Institutio*, VIII.vi.50–1.

78 Allowing for the different phraseology, the theme of K.284's variations exhibit the same structure.

79 Quintilian, *Institutio*, VIII.vi.51.

80 Quintilian, *Institutio*, VIII.vi.67–76.

81 Quintilian, *Institutio*, VIII.vi.67–8. In *Ad Herennium*, *hyperbole* is described as 'a manner of speech exaggerating the truth, whether for the sake of magnifying or minifying something' (IV.xxxiii.1).

82 Quintilian, *Institutio*, VIII.vi.70; the original is from Cicero's *Philippics*, II.xxvii.67, a speech in which he condemns Antony.

83 Quintilian, *Institutio*, VIII.vi.73.

84 A further 'quotation' – this time in the tonic reprise of the episode – occurs at bar 61.

85 Among other such 'quotations' in the sonatas may be cited K.311/iii, bars 154–6 (cf. bars 19 ff.); K.533/iii, bars 55–6 (cf. bars 2–3 of the opening theme); K.570/ii, bars 41–2 (cf. bars 15–19); /iii, bars 71 and 75 ff. (cf. bars 23 ff. and 49 ff.).

86 *Ad Herennium*, IV.xxxiii.44–5, where it is named as *intellectio*; Quintilian, *Institutio*, VIII.vi.19–22.

87 Quintilian, *Institutio*, VIII.vi.19.

88 See chapter 6.

89 *Ad Herennium*, I.iv.6.

90 *Ad Herennium*, I.iv.6 and I.vi.9. This was noted previously, in relation to the *exordium*; see pp. 119–21.

91 Cicero, *De Inventione*, I.xv.

92 Quintilian, *Institutio*, VIII.vi.54. Irony is also discussed in *Ad Herennium*, IV.xxxiv.46. In both texts irony is considered as a trope of embellishment, rather than a trope of meaning, that is, an 'adornment' to the structure rather than a generator of structure in itself.

12 The rhetorical *elocutio*

1 Cicero, *De Oratore*, III.xliii.172.

2 His discussion of style begins at III.i, that of arrangement at III.xiii.

3 *Ad Herennium*, IV.xix–xlvi and xlvii–lxix; Quintilian, *Institutio*, VIII–IX, especially IX.i.

4 Cicero, *De Oratore*, III.lii.200.

5 Cicero, *De Oratore*, III.liv.206.

6 Cicero, *De Oratore*, III.xliv.173–94.

7 Cicero, *De Oratore*, III.xliv.174, 175.

8 Kirnberger, *Die Kunst des reinen Satzes in der Musik*, Pt. II, § 1, p. 105. Quoted in Bonds, *Wordless Rhetoric*, p. 75. For Kirnberger's treatise, see David Beach and Jürgen Thym (trans. and ed.), *Johann Philipp Kirnberger: The Art of Strict Musical Composition* (New Haven, and London 1982).

9 Most probably, this was either Riepel's *De rhythmopoeïa, oder von der Taktordnung* (Frankfurt and Leipzig, 1752) or *Grundregln zur Tonordnung insgemein* (Frankfurt and Leipzig, 1755), although by 11 June 1778 (*Anderson*, no. 308), when Leopold refers to unspecified theoretical writings by Riepel, all five of his books were available in print. Riepel's other published writings were *Gründliche Erklärung der Tonordnung insbesondere* (Frankfurt and Leipzig, 1757), *Erläuterung der betrüglichen Tonordnung* (Augsburg, 1765), and *Unentbehrliche Anmerkungen zum Contrapunct* (Augsburg, 1768).

10 Riepel, *Grundregln*, pp. 36–71 *passim*.

11 A dual system of bar-reference is again employed in order to conform to the different systems found in different editions.

12 Another twelve-bar opening, this time divided as 4 + 8 bars, occurs at the opening of the B flat Sonata, K.570 (whose dance 'topic' is the Minuet). The consequent, eight-bar, segment is itself sub-divided as 4 + 4, built from repetition of bars 5–8.

13 Internal motive-repetition is taken to extreme in the Trio, in which, following the first bar, each successive pair of bars is immediately repeated an octave higher, ending with three cadential bars (13–16/ 62–4), comprising repetition at the lower octave.

14 Another fourteen-bar phrase, this time involving elision of the successive seven-bar segments, occurs at the beginning of the Andante cantabile of K.310.

15 Mattheson, *Der vollkommene Capellmeister*, Pt.II, ch.14, ¶ 40. See also Sisman, *Haydn and the Classical Variation*, pp. 30–5 and Ratner, *Classic Music*, pp. 91–8.

16 For further discussion of the subsequent development of these ideas during the baroque, era along with a selective catalogue (with musical examples) of 'figures', see George Buelow, 'Rhetoric and Music' in *The New Grove*.

17 Forkel, *Allgemeine Geschichte*, vol. I, pp. 53 ff.

18 Compare, for instance, bars 1, 17, 45, 65; 9, 25; and 33, 53.

19 Quintilian, *Institutio*, IX.i.13.

20 Quintilian, *Institutio*, VIII.vi.65; also described in *Ad Herennium*, IV.44.

21 In bar 21 the syncopation, highlighting the second quaver, is less obvious because of the repeated semiquaver Es.

22 See Quintilian, *Institutio*, VIII.iv.44–53. Allegory was described by Cicero (Quintilian's model in his discussion of tropes, as in so much else in the *Institutio*) as 'consisting of a series of several metaphorical terms strung together . . . a matter not of word but of sentence': that is, a structural figure (*De Oratore*, III.xliii.169).

23 Translated by T. S. Dorsch in *Classical Literary Criticism* (Harmondsworth, 1965; repr.1977), pp. 97–158. The true authorship of the treatise is, like that of *Ad Herennium*, in question. It probably dates from the first century AD. It was widely read during the eighteenth century. See also Elaine Sisman, *Mozart: 'Jupiter' Symphony* (Cambridge, 1993), pp. 13–20.

24 Dorsch, *Classical Literary Criticism*, p. 141.

25 Possibly Mozart intended the reprise to be ornamented in performance, as, for instance, with the successive reprises in the Adagio of K.457.

26 The keyboard writing here is reminiscent of the declamatory intensity found in parts of the slow movements of the piano concertos, K.466 and K.488, and is perhaps to be regarded as another instance in Mozart's late sonatas of the importation of more 'public' rhetorical elements of display, associated with the concerto, into the 'domestic' solo repertoire.

27 For a review of these, see Quintilian, *Institutio*, II. xv. He acknowledges that none of the definitions he quotes is wholly satisfactory.

28 Quoted in Cliff Eisen, *New Mozart Documents* (Stanford, 1991), no.211. The date of Götz's edition, *Trois sonates pour le clavecin ou le forte piano . . . oeuvre V* (*RISM* M6754) is unknown.

29 *Anderson*, no. 476, 28 December 1782.

Select bibliography

Albrechtsberger, Johann Georg, *Gründliche Anweisung zur Composition* (Leipzig, 1790)

Anderson, Emily (trans. and ed.), *The Letters of Mozart and his Family*, 3rd edn rev. Stanley Sadie and Fiona Smart (London, 1985)

Angermüller, Rudolph and Schneider, Otto, *Mozart-Bibliographie (bis 1970)* (Kassel, Basel, Tours, London, 1976) [= *Mozart-Jahrbuch* 1975]

Angermüller, Rudolph and Senigl, Johanna, *Mozart-Bibliographie 1986–91 mit Nachträgen zur Mozart-Bibliographie bis 1985* (Kassel, Basel, Tours, London, 1992)

[Anon.], 'Fantasia and Sonata in C minor', *Dwight's Journal of Music*, 22 (1863), no. 12, p. 91

Aristotle, *The 'Art' of Rhetoric*, trans. John Henry Freese. Loeb Classical Library no. 193 (Cambridge, Mass. and London, 1926, repr. 1991)

Arne, Thomas Augustine, *VIII Sonatas or Lessons for the Harpsichord* (Walsh; London, 1756)

Bach, C. P. E., *Sechs Sonaten fürs Clavier mit veränderten Reprisen* (Winter; Berlin,1760)
Zweyte Fortsetzung von Sechs Sonaten fürs Clavier (Winter; Berlin, 1763)
Six Sonatas for Clavier, Wq 51, ed. J. M. Rose (Bryn Mawr, 1973)

Bach, J. C., *Twelve Keyboard Sonatas*, facsimile edition, intro. Christopher Hogwood, 2 vols. (Oxford, 1973)

Bach, J. C., *Keyboard Music: Thirty-five Works from Eighteenth-Century Manuscript and Printed Sources*, intro. and in part ed. Stephen Roe (New York and London, 1989)
Joh. Chr. Bach: Klaviersonaten, ed. Ernst-Günther Heinemann, 2 vols. (Munich, 1981)

Badura-Skoda, Eva, 'Haydn, Mozart and their contemporaries', trans. Margaret Bent, in Denis Matthews (ed.), *Keyboard Music* (Harmondsworth, 1972), pp. 108–65

Baker, Nancy K., 'Heinrich Koch and the Theory of Melody', *Journal of Music Theory*, 20 (1976), 1–48
'"Der Urstoff der Musik": Implications for harmony and melody in the theory of Heinrich Koch', *Music Analysis*, 7 (1988), 3–30

Bent, Ian, 'Analytical thinking in the first half of the nineteenth century', in Edward Olleson (ed.), *Modern Musical Scholarship* (London, Stocksfield, Boston, Henley, 1980), pp. 151–66
Analysis, The New Grove Handboooks in Music (London, 1987)

Bent, Ian, (ed.), *Music Analysis in the Nineteenth Century*, vol. I: *Fugue, Form and Style*; vol. II: *Hermeneutic Approaches* (Cambridge, 1994)

Benton, Rita, 'Hüllmandel's article on the clavecin in the Encyclopédie Méthodique', *The Galpin Society Journal*, 15 (1962), 34–44

Benton, Rita, 'Hüllmandel', *The New Grove Dictionary of Music and Musicians*, 6th edn (London, 1980), ed. Stanley Sadie

Berg, Darrel M. 'C. P. E. Bach's character pieces and his friendship circle', in *C. P. E. Bach Studies*, ed. Stephen L. Clarke (Oxford, 1988), pp. 1–32

Bilson, Malcolm, 'Interpreting Mozart', *Early Music*, 12 (1984), 519–22

'Execution and expression in the Sonata in E flat, K.282', *Early Music*, 20 (1992), 237–43

Bonds, Marc Evan, *Haydn's False Recapitulations and the Perception of Sonata Form in the Eighteenth Century*, Ph.D dissertation, Harvard University, 1988

Wordless Rhetoric: Musical Form and the Metaphor of the Oration (Cambridge, Mass., 1991)

Braunbehrens, Volkmar, *Mozart in Vienna*, trans. Timothy Bell (Oxford, 1991)

Broder, Nathan, 'Mozart and the Clavier', in *The Creative World of Mozart* (New York and London, 1963), pp. 76–85

Brook, Barry S. (ed.), *The Breitkopf Thematic Catalogue: the Six Parts and Sixteen Supplements, 1762–1787* (New York, 1966)

Brown, A. Peter, 'The structure of the exposition in Haydn's keyboard sonatas', *The Music Review*, 361 (1975), 101–29

[review of] Bettina Wackernagel, *Joseph Haydns frühe Klaviersonaten*, *Notes*, 30 iii/i (1976), 69

Joseph Haydn's Keyboard Music (Bloomington, Indiana, 1986)

'Haydn and Mozart's 1773 stay in Vienna: weeding a musicological garden', *The Journal of Musicology*, 10 (1992), 192–230

Brown, Clive, 'Dots and strokes in late 18th- and 19th-century music', *Early Music*, 21 (1993), 593–609

Broyles, Michael, 'The two instrumental styles of classicism', *Journal of the American Musicological Society*, 36 (1983), 210–42

Buelow, George J. 'The Loci Topici and Affect in late baroque music: Heinichen's practical demonstration', *The Music Review*, 27 (1966), 161–76

'Music, Rhetoric and the Concept of the Affections: A Selective Bibliography', *Notes*, 30 (1973–4), 250–9

'The concept of "Melodielehre": a key to classic style', *Mozart-Jahrbuch* (1978–9), 182–94

'Rhetoric and Music' in *The New Grove*

Burney, Charles, *Music, Men and Manners in France and Italy, 1770* ed. H. E. Poole (London, 1969)

The Present State of Music in Germany, the Netherlands and United Provinces, facsimile of the 1775 London Edition, 2 vols. (New York, 1969)

Cherbuliez, Antoine E. 'Sequenztechnik in Mozarts Klaviersonaten', *Mozart Jahrbuch*, (1952), 77–94

Choron A. and Fayolle F. *Dictionnaire Historique des Musiciens* (Paris, 1801; facsimile reprint New York, 1971)

Churgin, Bathia, 'Francesco Galeazzi's description (1797) of sonata form', *Journal of the American Musicological Society*, 21 (1968), 181–99

Cicero, *De Inventione*, trans. H. M. Hubbell, Loeb Classical Library no. 386 (Cambridge Mass. and London, 1949, repr. 1976)

De Oratore, trans. E. W. Sutton and H. Rackham, Loeb Classical Library no. 348 (Cambridge Mass. and London, 1942, repr. 1988

[pseudo-Cicero], *Ad Herennium* trans. H. Caplan, Loeb Classical Library no. 403 (Cambridge Mass. and London, 1954, repr. 1989)

Clive, Peter, *Mozart and his Circle* (London, 1993)

Cole, William, *The Form of Music* (London, 1969)

Czerny, Carl, *School of Practical Composition* (Paris, 1834; repr. London, 1848)

Dahlhaus, Carl, *Esthetics of Music*, trans. William Austin (Cambridge, 1982; repr. 1995)

D'Alembert, Jean le Rond and Diderot, Denis (eds.), *Encyclopédie ou dictionnaire raisonné des sciences, des arts et des métiers*, 17 vols. (Paris, 1751–65)

Darbellay, Eugene (ed.), *C. P. E. Bach Sechs Sonaten mit veränderten Reprisen (Berlin, 1760)* (Courlay, 1986)

Daube, Johann Friedrich, *Der musikalische Dilettant* (Vienna, 1773)

Anleitung zur Erfindung der Melodie (Vienna, 1797–8)

Dennerlein, Hanns, *Der unbekannte Mozart – die Welt seiner Klavierwerke* (Leipzig, 1951)

'Der unbekannte Mozart – die Welt seiner Klavierwerke' *Mozart-Jahrbuch* (1951), 87–8

Deutsch, Otto Erich, *Mozart: a Documentary Biography*, trans. Eric Blom, Peter Branscombe and Jeremy Noble (London, 1990). Original German version, Otto Erich Deutsch, *Mozart: Die Dokumente seines Lebens* (Kassel, Basel, Tours, 1961).

Devriès, A. and Lesure, F. *Dictionnaire des Editeurs de Musique français*, vol. I, *Des Origines à environ 1820* (Geneva, 1979)

Downs, Philip, *Classical Music: the Era of Haydn, Mozart and Beethoven* (New York and London, 1992)

Dušek, František Xaver, *Sonate per il Clavicembalo,* ed. Jan Raček. Musica Antiqua Bohemica, no. 8 (Prague, 1977)

Eckard, Johann Gottfried, *Six Sonates pour le Clavecin . . . 1er oeuvre* (Paris [1763])

Einstein, Alfred, *Mozart: his Character, his Work*, trans. Arthur Mendel and Nathan Broder (London, Toronto, Melbourne, Sydney, 1946)

Eiseman, David, 'Mozart's maturity: harmonic goal, structure and expression', *Bericht über den Internationalen Mozart-Kongreß Salzburg 1991* [=*Mozart-Jahrbuch* (1991)], 63–70

Eisen, Cliff, 'The symphonies of Leopold Mozart: their chronology, style, and importance for the study of Mozart's early symphonies', *Mozart-Jahrbuch* (1987–8), 181–93

New Mozart Documents (Stanford, 1991)

Eitner, Robert, *Biographisch-Bibliographisches Quellen-Lexicon der Musiker und Musikgelehrten* (Leipzig, 1900–4; repr. New York, n.d.)

Eppstein, Hans, 'Warum wurde Mozarts K.570 zur Violinsonate', *Die Musikforschung,* 16 (1963), 379–81

Federhofer, Hellmut, 'Ein Salzburger Theoretikerkreis', *Acta Musicologia*, 36 (1964), 50–79

'Mozart als Schüler und Lehrer in der Musiktheorie', *Mozart-Jahrbuch* (1971–2), 89–106

'Mozart und die Musiktheorie seiner Zeit', *Mozart-Jahrbuch* (1978–9), 172–5

'Zur Einheit von Stimmführung und Harmonik in Instrumentalenmusik Mozarts', *Mozart-Jahrbuch* (1956), 75–87

Fenlon, Iain, *Catalogue of the Printed Music and Music Manuscripts before 1801 in the Music Library of the University of Birmingham, Barber Institute of Fine Arts* (London, 1976)

Finscher, Ludwig, 'Aspects of Mozart's compositional process in the quartet autographs: I. The early quartets, II. The genesis of K.387', in Christoph Wolff and Robert Riggs (eds.), *The String Quartets of Haydn, Mozart and Beethoven – Studies of the Autograph Manuscripts*, Isham Library Papers, Harvard University Department of Music (Cambridge, Mass., 1980), pp. 121–53

Flothuis, Marius, 'A close reading of the autographs of Mozart's ten late quartets', in

Christoph Wolff and Robert Riggs (eds.), *The String Quartets of Haydn, Mozart and Beethoven – Studies of the Autograph Manuscripts*, Isham Library Papers, Harvard University Department of Music (Cambridge, Mass., 1980), pp. 154–73

'Mozarts Fantasie und Sonate in c-Moll – ein Wendepunkt?, in Rudolf Bockholdt (ed.), *Über das Klassische* (Frankfurt, 1987), pp. 276–87

Forkel, Johann Nikolaus, *Über die Theorie der Musik* (Göttingen, 1777)

Musikalischer Almanach für Deutschland auf das Jahr 1784 (Leipzig, 1784)

Allgemeine Geschichte der Musik (Leipzig, 1788)

Freeman, Daniel, 'Josef Mysliwecek and Mozart's Piano Sonatas, K.309 and 311' *Mozart-Jahrbuch* (1995), 95–109

Frey, Martin (ed.), *Sonatenbuch der Vorklassik* (Mainz, 1949)

Fubini, Enrico, *Music and Culture in Eighteenth-Century Europe*, trans. and ed. Bonnie J. Blackburn (Chicago and London, 1994)

Fux, Johann Joseph, *Gradus ad Parnassum* (Vienna, 1725)

Galeazzi, Francesco, *Elementi teorico-practici di Musica*, 2 vols. (Rome, 1791, 1796)

Gassner, Josef, *Die Musikalien-Sammlungen im Salzburger Museum Carolino Augusteum* (Salzburg, 1962)

Gottsched, Johann Christoph, *Ausführliche Redekunst* (Augsburg, 1736)

Grundlegung einer Deutschen Sprachkunst (Augsburg, 1748).

Grave, Floyd K. '"Rhythmic Harmony" in Mozart', *Music Review* (1980), 87–102

Griesinger, Georg August, *Biographische Notizen über Joseph Haydn* (Leipzig, 1810); quoted in Jens Peter Larsen, 'Haydn' in *The New Grove*

Haberkamp, Gertraut, *Die Erstdrucke der Werke von Wolfgang Amadeus Mozart*, 2 vols. (Tutzing, 1986)

Haffner, Johann Ulrich, *Oeuvres melées, contenant vi sonates pour le clavessin de tant de plus célèbres compositeurs*, 12 vols. (Nuremberg, 1755–66)

Hager, Nancy, 'The first movements of Mozart's Sonata K.457 and Beethoven's *opus* 10 no.1: a C minor connection?', *Music Review* (1986–7), 89–100

Hashimoto, E. (ed.), *Carl Philip Emmanuel Bach: Zweyte Fortsetzung von Sechs Sonaten fürs Clavier (Winter; Berlin, 1763)* (Tokyo, 1984)

Haydn, Joseph Gesammelte Briefe und Aufzeichnungen, ed. Denés Bartha (Kassel, Basel, Tours, London, 1965)

Sämtliche Klaviersonaten, Band I-III, ed. Georg Feder (Munich, 1972)

Heartz, Daniel, 'Thomas Attwood's lessons in composition with Mozart', *Proceedings of the Royal Musical Association*, 100 (1973–4), 175–85

Heinichen, Johann David, *Der General-Bass in der Composition* (Dresden, 1728)

Hertzmann, Erich, 'Mozart and Attwood', *Journal of the American Musicological Society*, 12 (1959), 178–84

Hiller, Johann Adam, *Wochentliche Nachrichten und Anmerkungen, die Musik betreffend* (Leipzig, 1766–70). Facsimile reprint by G. Olms Verlag (Hildesheim, 1970)

Hoboken, Anthony van, *Joseph Haydn: Thematisch-bibliographisches Werkverzeichnis*, Band I (Mainz, 1957)

Honauer, Leontzi, *Six sonates pour le clavecin, livre premier* (Paris, *c.*1765)

Six sonates pour le clavecin, livre second (Paris, *c.*1765)

Six sonates pour le clavecin, avec accompagnement de violon ad libitum . . . oeuvre 3 (Paris, *c.*1770)

Hosler, Bellamy, *Changing Aesthetic Views of Instrumental Music in Eighteenth-Century Germany* (Ann Arbor, 1981)

Humphries, Charles and Smith, William C., *Music Publishing in the British Isles*, 2nd edn (Oxford, 1970)

Irving, John, 'A fresh look at Mozart's "Sonatensatz", K.312 (590d)', *Mozart-Jahrbuch* (1995), 79–94

'Johann Schobert and Mozart's early sonatas', in Harry White and Patrick Devine (eds.), *Proceedings of the Maynooth International Conference 1995*, Irish Musical Studies, vol. 5 (1996), pp. 82–95

Jahn, Otto, *Life of Mozart*, trans. Pauline D. Townsend, 3 vols. (London, 1882). Original German edition *W. A. Mozart* (Leipzig, 1856)

Jenkins, John, 'Mozart's good friend Dr Laugier,' *Music and Letters*, 77 (1996), 97–100

Jones, Peter, 'The aesthetics of Adam Smith', in *Adam Smith: International Perspectives*, ed. H. Mizuta and C. Sugiyama (London, 1993), pp. 43–62

Just, Martin, 'Zur Klaviersonate F-Dur KV 332', *Mozart-Jahrbuch* (1973–4), 211–16

Kamien, Roger, 'Style change in the mid-18th-century keyboard sonata' *Journal of the American Musicological Society*, 19 (1966), 37–58

Keller, Fritz, 'Rhetorik in der Ordenschule', in Herbert Zeman (ed.), *Die österreichischer Literatur: ihr Profil an der Wende vom 18. zum 19. Jahrhundert (1750–1830)*, Jahrbuch für österreichischer Kulturgeschichte, nos. 7–9 (1977–9), p. 57

Kimball, G. Cook, 'The second theme in sonata form as insertion', *Music Review*, 52 (1991), 279–93

Kirkendale, Ursula, 'The source for Bach's Musical Offering: The *institutio oratoria* of Quintilian', *Journal of the American Musicological Society*, 33 (1980), 88–141

Kirkendale, Warren, 'Ciceronians versus Aristotelians: The Ricercare as *Exordium* from Bembo to Bach', *Journal of the American Musicological Society*, 32 (1979), 1–44

Kirnberger, Johann Philipp, *Die allezeit fertige Menuetten-und Polonoisenkomponist* (Berlin, 1757)

Die Kunst des reinen Satzes in der Musik, 3 vols. (Berlin and Königsberg, 1774–79)

Methode Sonaten aus'm Ermel zu Schüddeln (Berlin, 1783)

Johann Philipp Kirnberger: The Art of Strict Musical Composition, trans. and ed. David Beach and Jürgen Thym (New Haven and London, 1982)

Koch, Heinrich Christoph, *Versuch einer Anleitung zur Composition,* 3 vols. (Leipzig, 1782, 1787, 1793)

Heinrich Christoph Koch: Introductory Essay on Composition – the Mechanical Rules of Melody, Sections 3 and 4, trans. Nancy Kovaleff Baker (New Haven and London, 1983)

Köchel, Ludwig Ritter von, *Chronologisch-thematisches Verzeichnis sämtlicher Tonwerke Wolfgang Amadé Mozarts,* ed. Franz Giegling, Alexander Weinmann and Gerd Sievers, 6th edn (Leipzig, 1964) [also consulted: 3rd edn ed. Alfred Einstein (Ann Arbor, 1947)]

Kollmann, August, *An Essay on Practical Musical Composition* (London, 1799)

Komlós, Katalin, 'Mozart and Clementi: a piano competition and its interpretation', *Historical Performance* (1989), 3–9

'Fantasia and Sonata K.475/457 in contemporary context', *Bericht über den Internationalen Mozart-Kongreß Salzburg 1991 [=Mozart-Jahrbuch* (1991)], 816–23

'"Ich praeludirte und spielte Variazionen": Mozart the Fortepianist', in Peter Williams and R. Larry Todd (eds.), *Perspectives on Mozart Performance* (Cambridge, 1991), pp. 27–54

Fortepianos and their Music: Germany, Austria and England, 1760–1800 (Oxford, 1995)

Krikkay, Eva, 'Zur Funktion der Ornamentik in den Klaviersonaten Mozarts', *Bericht über den Internationalen Mozart-Kongreß Salzburg 1991 [=Mozart-Jahrbuch* (1991)], 686–92

La Rue, Jan, 'Significant and coincidental resemblances between classical themes', *Journal of the American Musicological Society*, 14 (1961), 224–34

Lach, Robert, *W. A. Mozart als Theoretiker* (Vienna, 1918)

Larsen, Jens Peter, 'Sonata form problems', in Ulrich Kramer (trans. and ed.), *Handel, Haydn and the Viennese Classical Style* (Ann Arbor and London, 1988), pp. 269–79

Laufer, Edward, 'Motivic continuity and transformations in the piano sonatas', *Bericht über den Internationalen Mozart-Kongreß Salzburg 1991* [=*Mozart-Jahrbuch* (1991)], 1029–38

Layer, Adolf, *Eine Jugend in Augsburg – Leopold Mozart, 1719–1737* (Augsburg, n.d.)

Le Huray, Peter and Day, James, *Music and Aesthetics in the Eighteenth and Early Nineteenth Centuries* (Cambridge, 1981)

Leeson, Daniel N. and Levin, Robert, 'On the authenticity of K.Anh. C.14.01 (279b), a Symphonia Concertante for Four Winds and Orchestra' *Mozart-Jahrbuch* (1976–7), 70–96

Lester, Joel, *Compositional Theory in the Eighteenth Century* (Cambridge, Mass. 1992)

Lesure, François, *Catalogue de la Musique Imprimée Avant 1800 Conservée dans les Bibliothèques Publiques de Paris* (Paris, 1981)

Levin, Robert D. 'Improvised embellishments in Mozart's piano music', *Early Music*, 20 (1992), 221–33

Löhlein, Georg, *Clavierschüle*, 5th ed (Leipzig and Züllichau, 1791)

Longyear, Rey M. 'The minor mode in 18th-century sonata form', *Journal of Music Theory*, 15 (1971), 182–229

    'Parallel universes: Mozart's minor-mode reprises', *Bericht über den Internationalen Mozart-Kongreß Salzburg 1991* [= *Mozart-Jahrbuch* (1991)], 810–15

Lowinsky, Edward, 'On Mozart's rhythm', in *The Creative World of Mozart*, ed. Paul H. Lang (New York and London, 1963), pp. 31–55

MacPherson, Stewart, *Form in Music with special reference to the designs of instrumental music* (London, 1908; 2nd edn 1912)

Mann, Alfred (trans. and ed.), *The Study of Counterpoint from Johann Joseph Fux's Gradus ad Parnassum* (New York, 1965)

    'Zur Kontrapunktlehre Haydns und Mozarts', *Mozart-Jahrbuch* (1978–9), 195–9

Marguerre, Karl, 'Die Violinsonate K.547 und ihre Bearbeitung für Klavier allein', *Mozart-Jahrbuch* (1959), 228–33

    'Mozarts B-Dur-Sonate KV 570 "auf das Klavier allein"', *Musica*, 15 (1971), 361–3

Marpurg, Friedrich Wilhelm, *Historisch-Kritische Beyträge zur Aufnahme der Musik* (Berlin, 1754–78). Facsimile reprint by G. Olms Verlag (Hildesheim, 1970)

Marshall, Robert L. (ed.), *Mozart Speaks: views on Music, Musicians and the World* (New York, 1991)

    Eighteenth-Century Keyboard Music (New York, 1994)

Marston, Nicholas, 'The recapitulation transitions in Mozart's music', *Bericht über den Internationalen Mozart-Kongreß Salzburg 1991* [=*Mozart-Jahrbuch* (1991)], 793–809

Mason, Walter, 'Melodic unity in Mozart's piano sonata K.332', *Music Review*, 22 (1961), 28–33

Mattheson, Johann, *Kern melodischer Wissenschaft* (Hamburg, 1737)

    Der vollkommene Capellmeister (Hamburg, 1739)

Maunder, Richard, 'J. C. Bach and the early piano in London', *Journal of the Royal Musical Association*, 116 (1991), 201–10

    'Mozart's keyboard instruments', *Early Music*, 20 (1992), 207–19

Maunder, Richard and Rowland, David, 'Mozart's pedal piano', *Early Music*, 23 (1995), 287–96

Meier, G. F. *Anfangsgründe aller schönen Wissenschaften*, 3 vols. (Halle, 1748–50)

Mercado, Mario, *The Evolution of Mozart's Pianistic Style* (Carbondale, 1992)

Mizler, Lorenz, *Neu-eröffnete musikalische Bibliothek* (Leipzig, 1739–43)

Moldenhauer, Hans, 'Übersicht der Musikmanuskripte W. A. Mozarts in den Vereinigten Staaten von Amerika (1956)', *Mozart-Jahrbuch* (1956), 88–99

Momigny, Jerome de, *Cours complet d'Harmonie et de Composition* (Paris, 1806)

Morrow, Mary Sue, 'Mozart and Viennese Concert Life', *The Musical Times*, 126 (1985), 453–4

    Concert Life in Haydn's Vienna: Aspects of a Developing Musical and Social Tradition (New York, 1989)

Mozart, Leopold, *Leopold Mozart: Ausgewählte Werke,* intro. and ed. Max Seiffert, Denkmäler der Tonkunst in Bayern, Jg.9/Bd.2 (Leipzig, 1908)

    A Treatise on the Fundamental Principles of Violin Playing, trans. by Edith Knocker (London, 1948; 2nd edn 1951)

Mozart, Wolfgang Amadeus, *W. A. Mozart: Pianoforte Sonatas,* ed. Y. Bowen and A. Raymar (Associated Board of the Royal Schools of Music; London, 1931)

    Mozart: Briefe und Aufzeichnungen, Gesamtausgabe, ed. Wilhelm A. Bauer, Otto Erich Deutsch and Joseph Hans Eibl, 7 vols. (Kassel, Basel, Tours, London, 1962–75)

    Neue Mozart-Ausgabe, Serie X Supplement Wg.30/Abt.1, *Thomas Attwoods Theorie-und Kompositionsstudien bei Mozart,* ed. Erich Hertzmann, Cecil B. Oldman, Daniel Heartz and Alfred Mann (Kassel, Basel, Tours, London, 1965)

    Mozart: Sonatas for Pianoforte, ed. Stanley Sadie and Denis Matthews (Associated Board of the Royal Schools of Music; London, 1970–81)

    Wolfgang Amadeus Mozart: Verzeichnis von Erst- und Frühdrucken bis etwa 1800. Offprint from *Répertoire Internationale des Sources Musicales,* series A/I: *Einzeldrücke vor 1800,* ed. Karlheinz Schlager (Kassel, Basel, Tours, London, 1978)

    Wolfgang Amadeus Mozart: Piano Sonatas, ed. Wolfgang Plath and Wolfgang Rehm, 2 vols. (Kassel, 1986). Urtext taken from *W. A. Mozart Neue Ausgabe sämtlicher Werke,* issued by the Internationale Stiftung Mozarteum Salzburg, Serie IX, *Klaviermusik,* Werkgruppe 25

    W. A. Mozart Neue Ausgabe sämtlicher Werke: Taschenpartitur-Ausgabe, vol. XX, *Klaviermusik* [= *W. A. Mozart Neue Ausgabe sämtlicher Werke,* Internationale Stiftung Mozarteum Salzburg. Series IX, *Klaviermusik* Werkgruppe 25/Bd.1–2]

    Neue Mozart-Ausgabe, Serie X Supplement Wg.30/Abt.2, *Barbara Ployers und Franz Jacob Freystädtlers Theorie- und Compositionsstudien bei Mozart,* ed. Helmut Federhofer and Alfred Mann (Kassel, Basel, Tours, London, 1989)

    Mozart – Eigenhändiges Werkverzeichnis Faksimile, intro. and ed. Albi Rosenthal and Alan Tyson, British Library, Stefan Zweig MS 63 (Kassel, Basel, Tours, London, 1991)

    Wolfgang Amadeus Mozart: Fantasie und Sonate c-Moll für Klavier, KV 475 + 457. Faksimile nach dem Autograph in der Bibliotheca Mozartiana Salzburg, intro. Wolfgang Plath and Wolfgang Rehm (Salzburg, 1991)

Neumann, Frederick, 'Der Typus des Stufengangen der Mozartschen Sonaten-durchführung', *Mozart-Jahrbuch* (1959), 247–61

    'Zur formalen Anlage des Seitensatzes der Sonatenform bei Mozart', *Mozart-Jahrbuch* (1960–1), 219–32

Ornamentation and Improvisation in Mozart (Princeton, 1986)

'Dots and Strokes in Mozart', *Early Music*, 21 (1993), 429–35

Neumann Hans, and Schachter, Carl, 'The two versions of Mozart's Rondo, K.494', William J. Mitchell and Felix Salzer (eds.), *The Music Forum I* (New York, 1967), 1–34

The New Grove Dictionary of Music and Musicians, ed. Stanley Sadie, 20 vols., 6th edn (London, 1980)

Newman, William S. 'Kirnberger's *Method for Tossing off Sonatas'*, *The Musical Quarterly*, 47 (1961), 517–25

'K.457 and op.13: two related masterpieces in C minor', *Music Review*, 28 (1967), 38–44

The Sonata in the Classic Era, 3rd rev. edn (New York and London, 1983)

Nichelmann, Christoph, *Die Melodie nach ihrem Wesen* (Danzig, 1755)

Oldman, Cecil B. *Catalogue of Printed Music in the British Museum: Accessions Part III – Music in the Hirsch Library* (London, 1951)

Olleson, Edward, 'Gottfried van Swieten: Patron of Haydn and Mozart', *Proceedings of the Royal Musical Association*, 89 (1962–3), 63–74

Oppenheim, Walter, *Europe and the Enlightened Despots* (London, Sydney, Auckland, Toronto, 1990)

Paradies, P. D. *Sonate di Gravicembalo* (London, [1754])

Parish, George, 'Multi-level unification in Mozart's Piano Sonata, K.333 (315c)', *Bericht über den Internationalen Mozart-Kongreß Salzburg 1991* [= *Mozart-Jahrbuch* (1991)], 1039–49

Pauly, Reinhard G. 'Michael Haydn', in *The New Grove*

Plath, Wolfgang, 'Beiträge zur Mozart-Autographie I – die Handschrift Leopold Mozarts', *Mozart-Jahrbuch* (1960–1), 82–118

'Zur Echtheitsfrage bei Mozart', *Mozart-Jahrbuch* (1971–2), 19–67

'Zur Datierung der Klaviersonaten K.279–84', *Acta Mozartiana*, 21/ü (1974), 26–30

'Beiträge zur Mozart-Autographie II – Schriftchronologie 1770–1780' *Mozart-Jahrbuch* (1976–7), 131–73

Portmann, Johann Georg, *Leichtes Lehrbuch der Harmonie, Composition, und des General-Basses* (Darmstadt, 1789)

Postolka, Milan, *Leopold Kozeluch: zivit a dilo* [life and works] (Prague, 1964)

'Kozeluch', in *The New Grove*

Prout, Ebenezer, *Musical Form* (London, 1893)

Quantz, Johann Joachim, *Versuch einer Anweisung die Flöte traversière zu spielen* (Berlin, 1752)

Quintilian, *Institutio Oratoria*, trans. H. E. Butler, Loeb Classical Library nos. 124–7 (Cambridge Mass. and London, 1920, repr. 1989)

Radcliffe, Philip, 'Keyboard music' in *The New Oxford History of Music*, vol. VII: *The Age of Enlightenment*, ed. Egon Wellesz and Frederick Sternfeld (Oxford, 1973), pp. 574–610

Rainer, Werner, 'Verzeichnis der Werke A.C. Adlgassers', *Mozart-Jahrbuch* (1962–3), 280–91

Ratner, Leonard G. 'Harmonic aspects of classic form', *Journal of the American Musicological Society*, 2 (1949), 159–68

'Eighteenth-century theories of musical period structure', *The Musical Quarterly*, 42 (1956), 439–54

'*Ars combinatoria* – chance and choice in eighteenth-century music', in H. C. Robbins Landon and Roger Chapman (eds.), *Studies in Eighteenth-Century Music* (London, 1970), pp. 343–63

Classic Music – Expression, Form, and Style (Stanford, 1980)

'Topical content in Mozart's keyboard sonatas', *Early Music*, 19 (1991), 615–19

Reeser, Edwin (ed.), *J. G. Eckard: Oeuvres Complètes pour le Clavecin* (Kassel, 1956)

Reicha, Anton, *Traité de Mélodie* (Paris, 1814)

van Reijen, Paul, 'Weitere Berichtungen und Ergänzungen zur Sechsten Auflage des Köchel-Verzeichnis', *Mozart-Jahrbuch* (1971–2), 342–401

Répertoire Internationale des Sources Musicales Series A: *Einzeldrücke vor 1800* (Kassel, Basel, Tours, London, 1971–92)

Riepel, Joseph, *Anfangsgrunde zur musikalischen Setzkunst*, 2 vols.: vol. I *De rhythmopoeïa, oder von der Taktordnung* (Regensburg and Vienna, 1752); vol. II *Grundregln zur Tonordnung insgemein* (Frankfurt and Leipzig, 1755)

Robbins Landon, H. C. 'Haydn's piano sonatas', in *Essays on the Viennese Classical Style: Gluck, Haydn, Mozart, Beethoven* (London, 1970)

  Mozart: The Golden Years (London, 1989)

  1791: Mozart's Last Year (London, 1989)

Robbins Landon, H. C. (ed.), *The Mozart Compendium* (London, 1990)

Rosen, Charles, *The Classical Style: Haydn, Mozart, Beethoven* (New York and London, 1971)

  Sonata Forms, rev. edn (New York and London, 1988)

Rosenblum, Sandra P. *Performance Practices in Classic Music* (Bloomington, 1988)

Rowland, David, *A History of Pianoforte Pedalling* (Oxford, 1993)

Rumbold, Valerie and Fenlon, Iain, *A Short-Title Catalogue of Music Printed Before 1825 in the Fitzwilliam Museum, Cambridge* (Cambridge, 1992)

Rutini, G. M. *Sei Sonate per Cembalo* [Op.VII] (Bologna, 1770)

Sadie, Stanley, *Mozart* (London, 1965)

  'Mozart', in *The New Grove*

Saint-Foix, Georges de, 'Jean Schobert (vers 1740–1767)', *La Revue Musicale*, 3 (1922), 121–36

  'Les premiers pianistes parisiens: 'Nicholas-Joseph Hüllmandel, 1751–1823', *La Revue Musicale*, 4 (1923), 193–205

Schmid, Ernst Fritz, 'Mozart and Haydn', in Paul H. Lang (ed.), *The Creative World of Mozart* (New York and London, 1963), pp. 86–102

Schmid, Manfred Hermann, 'Klaviermusik in Salzburg um 1770', *Mozart-Jahrbuch* (1978–9), 102–11

Schobert, Johann, *Six Sonates pour le clavecin avec accompagnement de violon . . . op. 14. Les parties d'accompagnement sonts ad libitum* (Paris, 1766). Facsimile Jeanne Roudet, (ed.), *Six Sonates pour le clavecin Oeuvre XIV 1766* (Courlay, 1990)

  Deux Sonates pour le clavecin avec accompagnement de violon ad libitum . . . op.III (R. Bremner, London, c.1770)

  Deux Sonates pour le clavecin . . . op.IV ([R. Bremner] London, c.1770)

  Deux Sonates pour le clavecin avec accompagnement de violon . . . op.I (Longman and Broderip, London, c.1780)

Schroeder, David P. *Haydn and the Enlightenment: the Late Symphonies and their Audience* (Oxford, 1990)

Serwer, Howard, 'C. P. E. Bach, J. C. F. Rellstab, and the Sonatas with Varied Reprises', in *C. P. E. Bach Studies*, ed. Stephen L. Clarke (Oxford, 1988), pp. 233–44

Shamgar, Beth, *The Retransition in the Piano Sonatas of Haydn, Mozart and Beethoven* (Ph.D. dissertation, University of New York, 1978)

Siegmund-Schultze, Walther, 'Zur Datierung von Mozarts Klaviersonaten KV 330–333', in

Festschrift Wolfgang Rehm zum 60. Geburtstag, ed. D. Berke and H. Heckmann (Kassel, Basel, Tours, London, 1989), pp. 93–4

Simon, Edwin J. 'Sonata into concerto: a Study of Mozart's first seven concertos', *Acta Musicologia*, 31 (1959), 170–87

Sisman, Elaine R. 'Small and Expanded Forms: Koch's Model and Haydn's Minuet', *The Musical Quarterly*, 68 (1982), 444–75

Haydn and the Classical Variation (Cambridge, Mass., 1993)

Sliwinski, Zbigniew, 'Ein Beitrag zum Thema: Ausführung der Vorschläge in W.A. Mozarts Klavierwerken', *Mozart-Jahrbuch* (1965–6), 179–94

Snook-Luther, Susan P. *The Musical Dilettante: A Treatise on Composition by J. F. Daube* (Cambridge, 1992)

Somfai, László, 'Mozart's first thoughts: the two versions of Mozart's Sonata in D major, K.284', *Early Music*, 19 (1991), 601–13

Squire, William Barclay, *Catalogue of Printed Music in the Royal College of Music Library, London* (London and Leipzig, 1909)

Catalogue of the King's Music Library Part III: Printed Music and Musical Literature (London, 1929)

Steglich, Rudolf, 'Das Auszierungswesen in der Musik W. A. Mozarts', *Mozart-Jahrbuch* (1955), 181–237

'Tanzrhythmen in Mozarts Musik' *Mozart-Jahrbuch* (1958), 44–58

Štěpán, Josef Antonín, *Štěpán, Josef Antonín, Composizioni per piano*, vol. I ed. Jan Raček; vol. II, ed. Dana Setková (Prague, 1968)

Stevens, Jane R. 'Theme, harmony, and texture in classic-romantic descriptions of concerto first-movement form', *Journal of the American Musicological Society*, 27 (1974), 25–60

'Georg Joseph Vogler and the "second theme" in sonata form: some 18th-century perceptions of musical contrast', *Journal of Musicology*, 2 (1983), 278–304

Storace, Stephen (ed.), *Storace's Collection of Original Harpsichord Music* (London, 1788)

Street, Alan, 'The rhetorico-musical structure of the "Goldberg" variations: Bach's *Clavier-Übung IV* and the *Institutio oratoria* of Quintilian', *Music Analysis*, 6 (1987), 89–131

Sulzer, Johann Georg, *Allgemeine Theorie der schönen Künste* (Leipzig, 1771–5)

Till, Nicholas, *Mozart and the Enlightenment* (London and Boston, 1991)

Tovey, Donald F. *A Companion to Beethoven's Pianoforte Sonatas* (London,1948)

Beethoven, ed. Hubert J. Foss (London, 1944; repr.1975)

Essays in Musical Analysis, vol.I (London, 1935; 15th imp. 1976)

Tyson, Alan 'The date of Mozart's Piano Sonata in B flat, K.333/315c: the "Linz" Sonata?', in M. Bente (ed.), *Musik – Edition – Interpretation: Gedenkschrift Günther Henle* (Munich, 1980), pp. 447–54

Mozart: Studies of the Autograph Scores (Harvard and London, 1987)

Tyson, Alan (ed.), *Dokumentation der Autographen Überlieferung: Wasserzeichen-Katalog*, 2 vols. (Kassel, Basel, Tours, London, 1992)

Unger, Hans-Heinrich, *Die Beziehung zwischen Rhetorik und Musik im 16.-18. Jahrhundert* (Würzburg, 1941).

Verba, Cynthia, *Music and the French Enlightenment: Reconstruction of a Dialogue, 1750–1764* (Oxford, 1993)

Vickers, Brian, 'Figures of rhetoric/ figures of music?', *Rhetorica*, 2 (1984), 1–44

In Defence of Rhetoric (Oxford,1988)

Wagenseil, Georg Christoph, *6 Divertimenti für Cembalo I*, ed. H. Scholtz-Michelitsch (Munich, 1975)

Wagner, H. (trans., intro. and ed.), *Wien von Maria Theresia bis zur Franzosenszeit: Aus den Tagebüchen des Grafen Karl von Zinzendorf* (Vienna, 1972)

Weber, William, 'Learned and General Music Taste in Eighteenth-Century France', *Past and Present*, 1 (1980), 58–85

'Sonata Form § 6: Theory', in *The New Grove*

Weinmann, Alexander, *Vollständiges Verlagsverzeichnis Artaria and Comp.* (Vienna, 1952)

Beiträge zur Geschichte des Alt-Wiener Musikverlages. Kataloge Anton Huberty (Wien) und Christoph Torricella (Vienna, 1962)

Wightman, W. P. D. and Bryce, J. C. (eds.), *Adam Smith – Essays on Philosophical Subjects* (Oxford, 1980)

Williams, Peter, 'The snares and delusions of musical rhetoric: some examples from recent writings on J. S. Bach', in P. Reidemeister und V. Gutmann (eds.), *Alte Musik: Praxis und Reflexion* (Winterthur, 1983), pp. 230–40.

Williams, Peter, and Todd, R. Larry (eds.), *Perspectives on Mozart Performance* (Cambridge, 1991)

Wolf, Eugene K. 'The rediscovered autograph of Mozart's Fantasy and Sonata in C minor, K.475/457', *The Journal of Musicology*, 10 (1992), 3–47

Wolff, Christoph, 'Creative exuberance *vs.* critical choice: thoughts on Mozart's quartet fragments', in Christoph Wolff and Robert Riggs (eds.), *The String Quartets of Haydn, Mozart and Beethoven – Studies of the Autograph Manuscripts,* Isham Library Papers, Harvard University Deparment of Music (Cambridge, Mass., 1980), pp. 191–210

'Musikalische "Gedankenfolge" und "Einheit des Stoffes". Zu Mozarts Klaviersonate in F-Dur (KV 533+494)', in *Das Musikalische Kunstwerk. Geschichte, Ästhetik, Theorie: Festschrift Carl Dahlhaus zum 60. Geburtstag,* ed. H. Danuser, H. de la Motte-Haber, S. Leopold and N. Miller (Laaber, 1988), pp. 441–53

Wotquenne, A. *Catalogue de la Bibliothèque du Conservatoire Royale de Bruxelles,* vol.IV (Brussels, 1912)

Wyzewa, Théodore de and Saint-Foix, Georges de, *Wolfgang Amédée Mozart: sa Vie Musicale et son Oeuvre,* 5 vols. (Paris, 1912–46)

Zaslaw, Neal, *Mozart's Symphonies: Context, Performance Practice, Reception* (Oxford, 1989)

Zimmermann, Ewald, 'Eine neue Quelle zu Mozarts Klaviersonate KV 309 (284b)', *Die Musikforschung,* 11 (1958), 490–93

Index

(References in *italics* are to pages containing musical examples.)